SHOOTING GHOSTS

SHOOTING GHOSTS

A U.S. MARINE,
A COMBAT PHOTOGRAPHER,
AND THEIR JOURNEY
BACK FROM WAR

Thomas J. Brennan, USMC (Ret.),
and Finbarr O'Reilly

VIKING

VIKING

An imprint of Penguin Random House LLC
375 Hudson Street
New York, New York 10014
penguin.com

ISBN: 9780399562549 (hardcover)
ISBN: 9780399562563 (e-book)

Printed in the United States of America
1   3   5   7   9   10   8   6   4   2

Set in Photina MT Pro
Designed by Francesca Belanger

It makes no difference what men think of war, said the judge. War endures. As well ask men what they think of stone. War was always here. Before man was, war waited for him. The ultimate trade awaiting its ultimate practitioner. That is the way it was and will be. That way and not some other way.

—Cormac McCarthy, *Blood Meridian*

CONTENTS

SHOOTING GHOSTS

Prologue: An Odd Alliance

We can imagine that among those early hunters and warriors single individuals . . . saw what others did not. . . . It is when two such persons discover one another, when, whether with immense difficulties and semi-articulate fumblings or with what would seem to us amazing and elliptical speed, they share their vision—it is then that Friendship is born. And instantly they stand together in an immense solitude.

—C. S. Lewis, *The Four Loves*

Finbarr, Nabu Agha, Helmand Province, southern Afghanistan, November 1, 2010

An explosion. The shock wave kicks through my chest. Then silence, a moment of calm as the battle holds still in that instant before everything changes. Dust hangs in the air. Two Marines are down, motionless. Then another bolts toward them through the haze of confusion. There's shouting and shooting. The spell is broken. Time resumes, sprints forward. They move; I move. My shutter clicks, recording the aftermath of a blast that will weld my life to that of an injured Marine, Sergeant Thomas James Brennan, leader of Third Platoon, Fourth Squad, Able Company, First Battalion, Eighth Marines.

The emotional impact of the explosion reverberates across continents. A few hours later, Sergeant Brennan's mother, Karen, is at Boston Children's Hospital, where she works as a radiology assessment nurse. Karen's husband, Jim, sends her an e-mail with a Web link that automatically updates my photos as I file them from Afghanistan. He often does this so they can keep tabs on their twenty-four-year-old son, whom they both call TJ. Between the time Jim sends the message and the time Karen clicks on the refreshed link, photos of TJ lying limp in the dirt have been added to the news feed. Karen recoils from her desk when the images pop up on her screen. She can't read the captions. All she can see is her son's pale, blank face. She pitches forward and drops her head between her knees. Three coworkers rush over to ask what's wrong. Karen gestures at the screen while hyperventilating. "I don't know if he's alive or dead," she says. One of her coworkers, who is also from a military family, reads the photo caption and tells Karen that TJ has been injured by an explosion but that he's alive. Karen asks the nurse to close the computer. Then she weeps.

Finbarr, Boston, October 2012

Two years later, TJ and I sit side by side in a silver sedan, cruising down an open highway as strip malls and autumn scenery slide by. It's a Saturday afternoon in late October and we're in Massachusetts, on our way to his parents' house in Randolph, a suburban town with wide, curving roads and large houses set among trees. We are six and a half thousand miles from where we first met. The last time we sat together was nineteen months ago in Afghanistan. Much has changed. Over there, he was the leader of fourteen U.S. Marines (and one Navy Corpsman) deployed to Helmand Province. I was a photojournalist embedded with his unit. We were leaner back then, our bodies tapered by the demands of our jobs. No matter how many high-calorie ration packs we consumed, the weight still melted from our bodies on long foot patrols under the burden of heavy gear and brutal heat. Now we're both living in the United States, far from the conflicts that have marked our lives and within striking distance of countless fast-food joints. I'm no longer carrying my cameras everywhere and he's no longer armed with a rifle. Our individual journeys from Afghanistan to here have not been easy, but we've leaned on each other in unexpected ways. The skepticism and even hostility we first felt toward each other have grown into trust.

War tears people apart, but it also flings them together. Through the unpredictability of war and its aftermath, Sergeant Brennan and I became friends. Like most people who know him well, I call him TJ. He calls me Fin. We forged an unlikely bond patrolling together through the dusty alleyways of Helmand Province and camping side by side for weeks in the desert. That bond only deepened after TJ was injured during that Taliban ambush and then later, after we both returned from Afghanistan. When TJ began to suffer from the effects of his injury and from the painful memories of his tours in Iraq and Afghanistan, he told me about his struggles. They sounded familiar.

People rarely consider it, but war correspondents experience similar rates of post-traumatic stress as combat veterans. The causes can be different, but guilt plays a prominent role for both. For TJ it's the things he's done, or didn't do, that haunt him. My own conscience is nagged by the fact that I am paid to photograph people at their most vulnerable while I'm able to do little to help. I photographed TJ moments after he was injured and nearly killed. Now our friendship offers us both a shot at redemption. TJ sought my help as he confronted his altered reality. Collaborating with him restored something within me at a time when I was confronting my own struggles in the wake of war. It took getting to know each other for us to understand what trauma means, what it does to those who live with it, and how to cope. We are still learning.

Our perspectives on war differ—I'm a witness and TJ is a participant. But like TJ and many other young men, I was drawn to conflict zones. TJ had his own reasons (including the belief that his Marine dress blues would get him laid) whereas I saw the intensity of combat as an ancient rite of passage into manhood, a measure of my worth (and yes, sure, as a way to impress women). He may have known a little about what he was getting into, but I was ignorant of what that journey might cost. TJ and I now embody the stereotypes of the broken military veteran and the damaged war journalist, but such labels—while true—hardly tell the whole story, and serve little purpose. Neither of us is a victim. We both chose to go to war. We seek no sympathy or pity. What we're trying to figure out now is how we can lead purposeful lives after experiencing the sense of loss and meaninglessness wrought by war. The last thing we want to do is perpetuate the myth of the trauma hero.

"Every true war story is a story of trauma and recovery," author and

Iraq war veteran Roy Scranton wrote in a 2015 article for the *Los Angeles Review of Books*. "A boy goes to war, his head full of romantic visions of glory, courage, and sacrifice, his heart yearning to achieve heroic deeds, but on the field of battle he finds only death and horror. He sees, suffers, and causes brutal and brutalizing violence. Such violence wounds the soldier's very soul."

Afterward, upon returning home, Scranton writes, the boy, now a man and a veteran, is haunted and unable to make sense of his memory whereas most people don't want to know about the awful truths of war, the political powers want to sanitize its horrors, and anyone who wasn't there can't understand what it was like.

"The truth of war, the veteran comes to learn, is a truth beyond words, a truth that can be known only by having *been there*, an unspeakable truth he must bear for society. So goes the myth of the trauma hero."

Focusing solely on the psychological trauma American service members have endured allows us to forget the death and destruction they are responsible for, Scranton warns. Or, as the Scottish comedian Frankie Boyle puts it, "Not only will America go to your country and kill all your people, but they'll come back twenty years later and make a movie about how killing your people made their soldiers feel sad."

The joke cuts deep for the bitter truth it reflects. America's interventions in Iraq and Afghanistan have been disastrous, and costly, both in human and financial terms. Iraq and Afghanistan are even more divided than before, the region is in a state of chaos, and the resulting instability has spilled into Europe and caused a backlash at home. So why risk excusing the aggressors? Because this isn't a book about American foreign policy, or those who make the decision to go to war, or who is the true aggressor. It's about one low-ranking individual who carried out his nation's order to fight and is forced to live with the consequences of his government's actions.

And it's about how our stories became entangled and how, after years of striving to produce artfully composed photographs of violence and suffering, I grew wary of my role covering conflict and of the myth of the war photographer—the Hollywood archetype of the dashing, scarf-adorned loner flitting from one war zone to the next with girlfriends as expendable as bullets. That cliché ignores the doubts, fears, questions, loneliness, and pain that shadow those who do this kind of work—and all the things that create the other cliché of the war photographer as tragic, fallen hero. The reality, of course, is more nuanced.

As a culture, we romanticize war—through films, TV, video games, and the media—and, as younger men socialized to idolize heroes, both TJ and I were seduced by the idea of war as a proving ground. We dreamed of exploits we could be proud of—not of experiences that might kill, maim, or break us, although such risks were inherent in the appeal. We needed to know whether we could meet those challenges and rise to the occasion.

"We went to expose ourselves to fear and interrogate it," Elena Ferrante writes in *My Brilliant Friend*. So it was with us, and this book is the result of that reckoning.

People have been narrating their encounters with violence since the first cavemen etched stick figures into stone, depicting their hunting exploits. Like them, we have zeroed in on our individual experiences. Our stories are not those of Iraqis or Afghans, Congolese or Libyans, and we wouldn't presume to explore those stories here. We do not know their inner worlds, their hopes and fears, but we imagine their struggles are as real and complicated as our own. I've spent my career documenting other people's lives in turmoil. Most journalists are averse to becoming the story. Our profession expects us to be impartial chroniclers of unfolding events. Remaining objectively detached lies at the heart of what we do, especially for a newswire journalist. In keeping with this ethos, I was initially reluctant to offer myself up for public consumption, but I've drawn inspiration from TJ. He's shown me how writing about personal trauma can be cathartic, and how telling one's own story can help others, whether they are members of the military, the media, or fellow civilians facing their own personal struggles. We both grapple with our less-than-heroic—but very human—behavior in the face of fear, regret, and confusion. Our book is about the things we have seen and done, the ways we have been affected, and how we have navigated the psychological aftershocks of war. It's the latter part of that journey that matters most.

The forty-minute drive from Boston gives me time to think about what I'll say to Karen and Jim once we reach their house on Smith Road. I owe them an apology. My haste to file dramatic combat images of TJ crumpled in the dust means they saw my pictures before the military could send word of what had happened.

When TJ told me how it all unfolded, I felt awful. I not only capitalized on the suffering of others but made the situation worse. Every Marine or soldier I photographed, of course, had a family—but few were on my direct daily feed. Parents of deployed service members have enough to contend with without hearing through the media that their son or daughter has been hurt. War has always been violent, brutal, and traumatic, but the explosion of digital technology and the immediacy of news coverage from Iraq and Afghanistan have brought those wars closer to home than ever before. For friends and family this has the disorienting effect of allowing them to witness war from afar without being able to fully understand the depth of that experience or, sometimes, to have proper context or preparation for what they're seeing. For those who are deployed, access to Skype or Facebook and overseas calls allow them to feel both more connected to and more isolated from their lives back home. As it always did, family life continues without them, only now they can see pixelated versions of their children growing up online while marriages and relationships grow—or unravel—in real time, with pictures and a soundtrack. Technology has narrowed the gap created by being sent off to distant lands to fight, but it has not eased war's burden, nor the sense of dislocation it breeds upon returning home. It took Homer's Odysseus two decades to return from the Trojan wars, but today's service members can fly back to the United States in a matter of hours. The disorientation can be a shock to any system.

That sense of dislocation is something to which I can relate. By 2012 I was forty-one and had lived in Africa for more than a decade, covering conflicts across the continent, in the Middle East, and in Afghanistan. I was no stranger to violence and suffering. My career as a journalist is built on it. Bouncing from one trouble zone to the next, a willing witness with cameras, I've found myself in places where our primal urges play out in deadly confrontations. I've always sought the light in such places—while covering wars I've reported on Congolese music and hair-styles, Ivorian art, and graffiti in Libya and Afghanistan—but over time, my ability to find hope amid despair begins to fade. A constant shadow is cast by grim realities: violence, deprivation, and the suffering brought about by the nastier impulses of human nature. Working in such places has given my life a sense of purpose, meaning, and adventure. But it has also taken a toll. The emotional weight has grown heavy.

I'd been in touch with TJ's family before his injury, e-mailing them oc-casional photos from Afghanistan at his request. I've also been in contact with them online a number of times since, but this visit to their home in Randolph is the first time I'll meet them in person. We park the car in the driveway and I'm welcomed with a hug from Karen and a handshake from Jim. It's a week before Halloween and a small carved pumpkin sits on the front porch. Inside, a fake skeleton with a life-sized skull stares into the kitchen of the cozy and cluttered home. A rotary phone hangs at shoulder height on the wall, the curly cord dangling to the floor. A pit bull stands on its hind legs, looking in through the living room window. The house is dec-orated with family pictures perched on countertops and wedged into the glass panels of crockery cupboards. Stacks of baseball caps sit atop the shelving units. The walls are adorned with framed embroideries, including one that says HOME SWEET HOME and another, KAREN AND JAMES, with their wedding date, 4-3-82, and the words TRUE HEARTS UNITED.

A separate bit of framed embroidery includes the words of an old Irish blessing that my paternal grandfather once wrote for me in calligraphy. I kept a copy of it on my bedroom wall for many years and it feels strange yet familiar to see it here again:

> May the road rise to meet you.
> May the wind be always at your back,
> May the sun shine warm upon your face,
> The rains fall soft upon your fields.
> And until we meet again,
> May God hold you in the hollow of His hand.

A longer version of the blessing includes another line: May the hand of a friend always be near.

TJ's brother, Kevin, who at twenty-two is five years younger than TJ, sits on the couch watching TV while Taylor, their twenty-year-old sister, helps in the kitchen. It's late afternoon and TJ suggests we take a walk along his street and through the woods behind his house to the Rock, a granite mound rising above the treetops.

Our odd alliance is sometimes uncomfortable, and by 2012 our roles have grown even more disparate than they were in Afghanistan. I'm at Harvard, where I'm spending a year on a fellowship studying psychology and trauma. TJ is a high school graduate in the dying weeks of his Marine Corps career with no job prospects in sight. He's a self-described "dumb grunt," an infantryman whose "best before" date has passed. Physically broken and mentally scarred, he will be medically retired in two months and faces the difficult transition from military to civilian life. Yet we make fun of our differences and remain steadfast in a relationship anchored in shared experience.

"Just because you're some fancy Ivy Leaguer now, don't go thinking you're something special," he says.

"I'm obviously not that special if I'm still hanging out with the likes of you, Pawn," I say, using the nickname TJ has adopted in reference to his role as a disposable piece in America's war games.

As we scramble to the summit of the Rock, TJ says he used to hang out here as a kid, playing cops and robbers or cowboys and Indians with his cousins and friends. He would build piles of sticks and stones and pretend they were booby traps laden with dynamite. He would detonate them on his friends by calling out his own explosive sounds.

"Then we would argue about why they should be wounded or killed," he says. "It's easier to deny the effects of imaginary explosives."

TJ tells me the Rock is where he let his childhood imagination run wild, but aside from occasionally enacting skirmishes as G.I. Joes with his cousins, he rarely indulged in war games. He preferred the idea of rebelling against the law and, like many boys, including me, he had a destructive streak and enjoyed the idea of making things go boom. "I was a homegrown terrorist," he says with a laugh. When he got to high school, the Rock was where he came to smoke cigarettes and weed, get drunk, and fool around with girls. Sometimes he would steal his dad's beer to trade for smokes and pot.

"It's where I did things I didn't want my parents to catch me doing," he says.

The leafy suburban neighborhood in Randolph isn't so different from where I grew up in Vancouver, Canada, and where my younger brother, Donal, and I had a fascination with playing soldiers. With our friends we would read World War II comics and dress up in army fatigues and enact heroic battle scenes, our faces muddied as we scrambled over backyard obstacle courses and lobbed pinecones as grenades and opened fire at each other with cap guns. Sometimes my brother and I played these games while visiting our grandmother on the small dairy farm where my mother grew up in southern Wales. A German fighter plane had been shot down and crashed in one of the farm's back fields during World War II and, imaginations running wild, Donal and I would creep along the hedgerows pretending to hunt the downed pilot while trying to find any lingering trace of the doomed plane. On one of those summer visits to Wales when I was a teenager, my mother's father, Ivor Bradshaw, told me about his travels in India, North Africa, and Italy during World War II. It was the only time I ever heard him talk about those days, and the story has always stayed with me. He described the dry heat of the Libyan Desert ahead of the Allied amphibious landing on Sicily in July 1943, and how they came ashore on the Italian island amid strong winds. Then came the noise, the dust, and the thirst.

"They told us we would have air cover for the landing, and we did," he said. "But it was from the bloody Germans."

As Ivor told it, he scrambled forward through enemy fire. Artillery pounded the beach and the sea behind him, sending plumes of sand and water skyward. A piece of shrapnel tore the arm off the soldier next to him. Others nearby were killed. And the noise. Ivor thought he would go deaf. But by the end of the day, the Allies had moved off the beach and taken control of the port of Syracuse. Ivor didn't see much action after that—at least not of the combat variety—and spent the rest of the war enjoying the pleasures of Italian food, drink, and women. The only injury he sustained was a broken ankle from falling off a cliff while staggering home drunk late one night. His war stories became etched in my young mind. Ivor had been part of something historic, something important. But most of all, Ivor had seen combat and survived. To a young boy, nothing else compared.

"Bloody awful it was," he said, rolling a cigarette. "You're lucky you don't have to go to war."

In an effort to understand what he'd lived through, I read war comics and history books and watched war films and documentaries. The moral clarity of World War II and the heroic light in which its victors were portrayed only elevated Ivor's status in my youthful eyes. When I dressed up and played war games with Donal and our friends, I imagined reliving scenes Ivor had described. And while I never considered joining the military, I glorified war the way boys do. It's easy to understand why young men lust for war. Every soldier is imagined as a hero, never a broken victim.

Reflecting on my own path to Afghanistan, I wonder what inspired TJ to leave a place like Randolph to go and fight in foreign wars. He tells me that when he finished high school in 2003, he knew he wasn't ready for college. His mother was tough on him about his grades and he didn't want to disappoint her by screwing up. He was more afraid of telling her he would fail in school than he was about going to war. During high school he'd spent four years working as a breakfast cook and dishwasher in Sal's calzone restaurant, saving up enough money to buy himself a muscle car, a maroon 1973 Mercury Cougar XR-7, which he painted black. He learned the value of a dollar by paying for his own gas and insurance.

"I didn't want to fuck it up and wind up with debt and no degree," TJ says, adding that his dad told him he had to get a job if he wanted to live at home. "He wasn't gonna let me be a lazy dick just sitting around the house."

Cooking breakfast at Sal's wasn't going to cut it. Both TJ's grandfathers were Navy veterans of the Second World War, with his grandfather John having served in the Pacific. His father had also wanted to serve, but partial blindness in both eyes kept him from duty. After the 9/11 attacks, the United States was engaged in a major overseas conflict for the first time in a generation. An imagination honed on the Rock turned to the war in Iraq.

"I wanted to know if I had what it took," TJ says. "I thought I was ready to kill. Serial-killer shit always fascinated me. Not, like, doing it, but their minds. And I read about war and how you just flip a switch. I was curious whether I had the switch."

During his junior year of high school TJ had talked with his parents about joining the reserves so that the military would cover the cost of his college tuition. Two years later, when he came home nine days before the second anniversary of 9/11 and told his parents that he'd enlisted for active duty with the Marine Corps infantry, Karen went silent. Then she made him promise he would still go to college. Jim asked him if it was what he really wanted to do. With the certainty and invincibility of youth, TJ assured him that it was.

The stories fill in some of the outlines of TJ's life that he'd only sketched in Afghanistan. I'm curious to know more, but it's getting late and we're hungry. We scramble down from the Rock and wander back to the house, where Karen has prepared something special for dinner. TJ tells me not to expect too much. In Afghanistan we shared weeks of bland military rations, but he always teases me about my preference for what he calls "exotic menus"—sushi, calamari, pungent French cheeses, spicy Indian curries, gourmet coffee, and African dishes featuring crocodile, ostrich, or antelope. TJ loves his mother's cooking but thinks I need a heads-up.

"I know you have a refined palate, so just be ready for some good American home cooking."

The Brennan family clearly wants to impress me, so I'm curious when we're summoned to the dinner table. Out comes the main course, an entire chicken battered in—what the hell is that?

"It's Cap'n Crunch chicken," TJ announces, explaining that this dish is poultry rolled in egg and dipped in crushed-up Cap'n Crunch, a sweet corn and oat breakfast cereal, and then baked. "You've never heard of Cap'n Crunch chicken?"

It's a new one for me, that's for sure. We dig in.

Dinner conversation revolves around questions about the nature of my work, my family, and what I've been doing during my first two months at Harvard. I eventually pluck up the courage to make my long-planned apology. I had previously e-mailed Karen to express my regret about causing her and Jim grief and anxiety by sending those pictures on the day TJ was injured. I still feel the need to do so in person. Karen eases my guilt, echoing what she's already told me over e-mail.

"Yes, the way I found out about TJ's injury was not the best, but at least I knew, and knew that he was OK, so to speak. I work in a hospital, so my colleagues took great care of my emotional needs," she wrote in our exchanges. "We obviously were all very upset. I was not angry with you per se, but I'm not very computer or media savvy so was shocked that this happened in front of my eyes."

I learn that when she saw my pictures on the day of the ambush, it took Karen more than fifteen minutes before she could stand up to go and find somewhere private to call Jim. When he answered the phone, Karen yelled at him.

"Why would you send me that picture?"

"What picture?" Jim asked.

Unaware that the Web link had updated my photos, Jim thought he'd sent Karen images from the previous day showing TJ on a foot patrol and during a quiet day at the outpost where he was based. Jim was on the phone at the same time with TJ's wife, Melinda, who had called from Jacksonville, North Carolina, where the couple lives, to let them know about TJ's injury and my photos. But it was too late. The damage was done.

Much later I will learn that Karen and Jim had already buried one child, Caitlyn, who was born fourteen weeks prematurely in 1987. She was delivered by emergency C-section and lived for two days. Jim held her only once before she died. Karen never saw her alive. The couple spent years in therapy afterward. They rarely spoke about Caitlyn's death with their other children, but on Halloween the family painted pumpkins for her, and they visited Caitlyn's grave on her birthday. At the graveyard TJ and Kevin and would play hide-and-seek behind the headstones as their father cleared the overgrown grass from the edges of

Caitlyn's pink marble stone. Jim would brush the dirt and grass clippings from the engraved letters and the outline of a lamb. When the parents stood to leave, Jim always hugged Karen as she cried. The kids gave them their time but always watched to see whether Jim would cry. They never caught him. Caitlyn's death wasn't the first in Karen's family. Her brother was murdered when she was a teenager living in New Jersey. She and Jim have lived with violence and loss. Knowing that my photos added to their pain is unsettling.

Still, they tell me that having my regular updates and reports from Afghanistan actually put their minds at ease. At least they could see the dangers their son faced daily on deployment and felt closer to him as a result. With my images, and an audio slide show showing firefights, explosions, and foot patrols through hostile villages, it was impossible for TJ to pretend he'd been posted to some quiet location far from the fighting—as many service members tell their families to relieve worry back home. Their assurances don't eliminate my sense of guilt, but I believe the family doesn't hold anything against me. And as it turned out, neither TJ's parents nor his wife, Melinda, ever heard anything from the military about the incident or his injuries.

"I was surprised by that," Karen says.

She shouldn't have been. It's only an early hint of the looming disaster that will soon emerge as the monumental failure of the U.S. government to provide adequate care for those who have fought and served overseas.

After dinner TJ drives me home to my apartment near Harvard. On parting we wonder when we'll meet again. We agree to make it happen before too long. Seeing each other away from the battlefield has been strange but also reassuring. Things have been difficult for us both for a variety of reasons, but we've made progress together and individually. We have no idea that, for both of us, the hardest parts of our journeys still lie ahead.

PART ONE

Afghanistan

Chapter 1

Misfits Go to War

Be polite, be professional, but have a plan to kill everybody you meet.

—General James "Mad Dog" Mattis, U.S. Marine Corps

TJ, Kyrgyzstan and Afghanistan, July–October 2010

The base in Manas, Kyrgyzstan, is a clash between the airport terminal's bleak Soviet architecture and American military prefab buildings erected next to a tent city dubbed "Hotel Alaska," the transit point for thousands of U.S. service members heading to and from Afghanistan. Makeshift shops and kiosks line an array of repurposed shipping containers where local vendors sell Muslim prayer rugs and storefront windows offer us the small tokens of our "worldly travels"—as once promised to us by our recruiters back home. Offensive Velcro patches, including ones with the word "infidel," are sold despite regulations that forbid wearing such flair. The base's Internet cafés, the communal showers, and the bar where Marines are banned from drinking with airmen because of interservice fistfights will soon cease to be part of my daily routine. The overpriced postcards and Russian *matryoshka* dolls (made in China) mark the final threshold before we enter the war in Afghanistan.

Once there, our mission is to spend our seven-month tour dislodging the Taliban from villages around Musa Qala District in Helmand Province, helping the Afghan government extend security and services. This will involve daily foot patrols and the use of violence—gun battles, air strikes, and artillery—to weaken enemy forces, push them back, take territory, and secure control of the area: clear, hold, and build. This three-stage process forms the basis of the war's counterinsurgency doctrine, known as COIN, which has emerged as the military strategy of choice by the ninth year of the Afghan occupation.

My unit's transit week in Kyrgyzstan revolves around counting and re-counting and cleaning and recleaning our weapons, night-vision goggles, and thermal optics. I kill time eating single-serving packets of Kellogg's cereal at a chow hall inside a vinyl tent. I eat sandwiches with sliced deli meats, baked bread still warm from the oven, and local produce. It's one of the last chances I'll have to enjoy fresh food for the duration of our deployment. The snowcapped peaks of nearby mountains remind me of the Appalachian Trail. I wonder if I will ever ski those mountains again.

For three days our flight into Afghanistan is delayed due to weather. I call home as often as I can and I speak with my wife, Mel, for thirty minutes at a time. I try to hide my fears. I can't talk with Mel about the fact that I'm heading into one of the deadliest districts in Helmand Province. That will have to wait. But I'm disturbed by the thought of seeing fellow Marines killed or dismembered, as I saw in Iraq on my first deployment, six years earlier. And I think about the possibility of my own death. Mel knows I won't share my concerns with her, but I can tell she senses my trepidation. We don't want to stress each other out by talking about it. Our conversations become awkward. My mind plays tricks on me. Memories from home make me think I may not live to make new ones. Talking about our daughter, Madison, or Maddie, makes me worry that she might have to grow up without me. Mel doesn't probe. Instead we talk about buying a new house when I get home and about having another child. We focus on our future together—the idea of a life and of happiness after this war gives us hope, something to cling to during the lonely months ahead. As we talk, I can hear Maddie playing with her toys in the background and shouting, "Mommy, look!" Each time I hang up, I think it could be the last time I tell my girls I love them.

"It's not good-bye; it's 'see you later,'" I tell Mel at the end of each call. Then I hand my prepaid phone card to the next Marine waiting in line.

The last image I have of Mel and Maddie is of them in tears as our bus pulled out of the parking lot at Camp Lejeune, North Carolina, one week earlier. I can't stop thinking about that moment. I hold my emotions in check until I can get outside. I don't want anyone here to see me crying. Leaving this time isn't like my previous deployment to Iraq in 2004. That was easy. I wasn't yet a husband or a father. I was nineteen, fresh out of high school and in my first year of a four-year enlistment. I still didn't know what war was like. I got one last "mommy hug," as my mother and I call them, and strolled through Boston's airport security without any luggage. Everything I needed was in the barracks in North Carolina or locked inside the armory on base. On the day of our departure, I sat on the bus as other Marines and sailors said their good-byes. They had people to see them off. I didn't.

My second deployment, to Kuwait in June 2006 at the end of my first enlistment, was basically a seven-month booze cruise through the Mediterranean on the USS *Iwo Jima*, with short party stops in France and Italy, lots of time to kill on board with constant drills and training, and longer stopovers in Djibouti and Jordan. The start of that trip was also my last dry-eyed walk onto a deployment bus. I waited for Mel to leave before wiping away my tears. I was a "salty" lance corporal with combat experience, and while deploying had become part of my routine, I couldn't imagine what it must be like for her saying good-bye to someone going to war. We were both twenty-one. Being the one to deploy allowed me to feel in control—that I was smart enough and strong enough to keep myself from getting hurt or killed. But I figured I'd come back either in a wooden box or in one piece. There was no in-between. We'd met the year before, shortly after I returned from Fallujah, Iraq, and I knew if we made it through that deployment, I would propose. She said she knew what she was getting herself into, but neither of us really knew what to expect. When I returned from Kuwait in December 2006, I reenlisted for four more years. I still hadn't decided on making a career in the Marines, but I knew I could at least get some college credits while stationed at Parris Island, where I'd have a job that wouldn't involve going overseas. I set my sights on becoming a rifle and pistol marksmanship instructor at Marine Corps boot camp in South Carolina—training recruits how to kill. And in April 2007 Mel and I got married.

Now, four years later, I have a two-year-old daughter who stood on the pavement shouting, "Daddy, don't go! Just stay. Don't go. Please!" Mel was crying too. It nearly made me crumple. I was the cause of their sadness and I had no way to comfort them.

I stepped onto the white school bus alongside three dozen Marines leaving for Afghanistan and reached through the window to blow my girls a few last kisses and a flurry of "I love yous." When the tires rolled forward, my fingers grazed Mel's and I read her lips as we pulled away. *Be safe*. I couldn't answer.

A week later, in Kyrgyzstan, that bus ride is all I can think about as I smoke my Marlboros in the shade of a gazebo. I wipe the tears from my face as it sinks in that I won't see Maddie for seven long months. Smokes are my therapy. I can't go back inside until I regain my composure. A few minutes and several deep breaths later, I flick my butt into a repurposed ammo can overflowing with smoldering filters.

My rifle bounces against my body as I stroll back to my bunk bed. I lie on the bottom mattress and prop my head on the last clean pillow I'll see for months. The springs of the bed overhead bulge and creak each time the Marine above me shifts in his sleep. Beneath the wire mesh cradling his mattress, a single sentence in permanent marker spans the width of the bunk.

"One ticket to Allah coming your way!"

I hope it isn't meant for me.

Our company wakes at sunrise the next morning. Our flights to Afghanistan will leave in the afternoon and we hustle to finish prepping. We look over our gear one last time to make sure no pouches or straps are loose or inaccessible. My company commander, Captain Daniel F. O'Brien, who is in charge of our unit of some two hundred men, calls me over. O'Brien is a combat veteran of Iraq and is different from many of the leaders I've served under during my seven years as a Marine. He seems to care more about us than about earning his next promotion. He's blunt and brash, but he looks out for us. He isn't afraid to push back against senior commanders and he doesn't play "fuck-fuck games," the pointless tasks generated for no reason other than to keep us busy or to punish us for petty infractions.

During the months leading up to our deployment, O'Brien appointed me as the section leader for more than a dozen assaultmen—teams of three to four Marines who specialize in demolitions, rockets, and dynamic breaching, which basically means kicking down doors or blowing them open. It isn't my ideal role. It means my job in Afghanistan will be different from on my previous deployments. In Fallujah in 2004 I was a boot infantryman, and on my 2006 Mediterranean cruise I was an assaultman squad leader in charge of four Marines. My time in Afghanistan will be spent traveling from base to base as my individual teams go on patrols with other squads. I'll be tasked with supervising them, training alongside the riflemen, and interacting with other Marines, but I won't actually command men of my own on the battlefield. It means my role will be to follow rather than lead. As an infantryman I want to do both. My chances of seeing combat seem slim. It looks like I'll be a nomad of sorts, bouncing from place to place without the kind of group cohesion that makes the hardships of deployment and the distance from home more bearable. But in war things change quickly.

O'Brien tells me he needs an additional squad and that I'm being put in charge of fifteen men. It's exactly what I want, but it makes me more nervous, scared even. I hope I'll get men I know or have worked with during training. Instead I'm given a ragtag group of troublemakers and wiseasses culled from across our two-hundred-man unit. No platoon wants to give up its best Marines hours before we set foot in hostile territory. A few of the Marines I'm assigned have good track records and tactical know-how, but none have seen combat. Several of them have been demoted or denied promotions as punishment for offenses such as drugs, hazing, or drunk driving. They've signed up to kill and maybe to die for their country, but most are still too young to drink back home. They love drinking anyway, which is often what gets them into trouble. I've been tasked with leading a group of misfits and outcasts on the day we're due to fly into Afghanistan. They don't know me, and I don't know them. We haven't spent months building the kind of trust and cohesion essential to holding men together during the stress of combat. I look at my squad for the first time as they gather outside our tent. All I see are question marks when what I need is certainty.

I walk beside them toward the woods in a distant corner of the base. Some sit, others kneel, and a few stand as I introduce myself. As simply as I can, I lay out how our relationship will work during our deployment:

If I tell you to shoot, you will shoot. If you tell me to shoot, I will shoot. I don't care where you've been, what you've done, or the mistakes you made. Today you get a clean slate. You dictate your own tomorrow.

We've all trained for months, but never as a group. Without cohesion and practice, there is no trust. Without trust in one another, we are nothing. I need to be sure my men are good to go. During the next few hours, I test them on as many things as possible. Can they use a radio to call in for air support or a medical evacuation? Can they provide first aid? Do they know how to use their equipment properly? Have they cleaned their weapons? Are their pouches and first-aid kits in a place that makes sense for them? I doubt them, but I also doubt myself. Even with my previous combat experience, following orders as a young Marine in Iraq is different from leading men under fire in Afghanistan. Will I be able to get them—and myself—through our deployment alive? The only thing to do now is to make sure we are ready for whatever lies ahead. When we board the C-130 military cargo plane bound for Camp Leatherneck in Afghanistan, I have yet to see any of my squad fire their weapons. I have no idea whether they will follow my orders when it counts.

During our first two weeks together, I drill them hard. Those who make mistakes pay for them in sweat, as does everyone else, including me. If someone makes a mistake in combat, others suffer. I make sure it's the same in training. If they bitch or moan, I order them to chisel away at the hard ground with pickaxes to fill sandbags for hours on end. I'm not above playing fuck-fuck games.

When our machine gunner, Lance Corporal Benjamin Brickman, assembles our automatic grenade launcher incorrectly, we take turns practicing his job alongside him until our fingers bleed. While we practice, Brickman begins his journey of fortifying Afghanistan with sandbags—punishment for his frequent mistakes. After a while I lose count of how many hours he has spent filling them.

If my Marines miss a simulated explosive in the ground, I scatter hundreds of small shards of metal in the dirt around us. It takes hours to find them all, but we don't end the drill until every last shard is recovered. Our explosives-sniffing dog, Kate, is an adorable black Labrador that doesn't always listen to her handler, Lance Corporal James Palmer. It's difficult to remember that she's not a full-time pet we can treat like our dogs back home, and many of us scratch her belly behind Palmer's back. She makes me miss my dog, Damien—a skittish red-nosed pit bull and Maddie's loyal best friend, protector, and partner in crime. We joke with Palmer that not even Kate can understand him because of how fast he speaks and how his words seem to blur together. The sound of Palmer calling out his special catchphrase, "hip-toe," at Kate carries across the base. Kate is a unique member of our squad, but she still has a crucial job to do, and when she fails a task, I make her and Palmer repeat it until it becomes ingrained. Everyone struggles to understand Palmer—who is twenty but because of his thin, receding hair looks like an old man—but we laugh when he talks to Kate. Palmer is goofy but genuine, and his gentle compassion soon grows on each of us, no matter how annoying and repetitive his "hip-toe" refrain becomes. It's the sound of a lifeline against IEDs. The pair practices drills around our base, searching for dog toys containing the Taliban's weapon of choice, a deadly mixture of ammonium nitrate and aluminum, which we abbreviate to the acronym "ANAL." The mixture is stuffed into jugs and buried beneath the earth, and it is our biggest and most constant fear. None of us wants ANAL from the enemy, or so the joke goes.

Marines will not function on the battlefield without a trusted Corpsman, a Navy sailor with combat trauma training who can mean the difference between life and death. Navy Corpsmen are assigned to squads of Marine Corps infantrymen as attachments—they live, eat, sleep, and shit with their Marines. They're the first to hand us Motrin or tell us to change our socks and the last to comfort dying Marines on the battlefield. Marines may carry more weight on patrol, but Corpsmen have the unenviable responsibility of having to keep us alive when things go wrong. I love Corpsmen. I don't envy them. When our Corpsman, Donald Howard, bungles a lifesaving drill or screws up a test call for medical evacuation, I ride him the hardest. He's fine administering first aid on a docile, cooperative patient, but when one of us writhes, bucks, and screams the way a wounded Marine or sailor would, he struggles. It doesn't fill us with confidence. All Marines are trained in basic combat trauma, but the maxim for hierarchy of care is "self-aid, buddy aid, Corpsman aid"—do it yourself, find a buddy, grab the Corpsman. The Corpsman focuses on treating injured Marines so the others can focus on killing the enemy. I order Howard to do sprints until he can barely stand, then make him apply tourniquets to simulated amputations while still gasping for breath. Doing this simulates an adrenalized state and helps ready him—physically at least—to act under pressure in combat. He crawls on his hands and knees until he nearly pukes, and I make him explain treatments for potential injuries. He sticks us with more needles than he probably used during his entire three years at a naval hospital. We deprive him of sleep and force him to recite procedures for medical evacuations, our blood types, and our ZAP numbers, the series of letters and numbers representing our name, military unit, and partial Social Security number. These serve as our unique identifiers in case we are injured—an abbreviated dog tag for the digital age.

Through the tedium and misery of my drilling, we begin to bond. Nicknames are flung about with the unique humor of the infantry. Any political correctness we possessed as Marines has been left behind in North Carolina. I become "Sarge" while one of my Marines becomes "Needle Dick" despite being well endowed. Our Corpsman, Howard, is the only black member of our squad and, aside from being called "Doc," is also dubbed "Carlton Banks" for his resemblance to Will Smith's cousin on *The Fresh Prince of Bel-Air*, in both appearance and demeanor. Howard often jokes about the "slave strength" of my towering and muscle-bound assistant patrol leader, Shawn Clarkson, who becomes "Big Nig." Our machine gunner, Brickman, is "Das Boot," and Brian Scearse becomes "Scary Spice."

When I was in Fallujah, Iraq, in 2004, one of my leaders was personable and patient. I try to mold myself in his style. Sometimes he was lenient, but there were things we knew not to do: Never make fun of his sports teams, the Raiders and the Tar Heels, never stop running during PT, and under no circumstances ever leave pubes in the shower. On these counts, and on everything else, he demanded perfection.

Nearly six years after Fallujah, I arrive with my new squad at Patrol Base Habib. We are one of three squads based there. Within four hours of our arrival, I'm on my first patrol with three of my Marines. The Marine unit we're relieving guides us. We keep our eyes on the dirt paths, praying we don't get our legs blown off or get killed on our first outing. While we patrol through rustling cornfields on the outskirts of the village, the rest of my men stay behind to learn about Taliban tactics in our area. This mostly involves identifying and digging up mock explosives. Our enemy wears no uniform and their buried bombs come with no markers. It is my first patrol and I'm already ready for the fields to be harvested and the eerie rustling of the corn to be no more.

Two hours into our patrol, we're destroying our first improvised explosive device. This is for real; there are no second chances. It sets us straight and it gives me an even sharper focus. Out here it's hunt or be hunted. Kill or be killed.

My men have done everything right, but we've yet to patrol together in hostile terrain. We've worked as a team for less than one week. I fear we still aren't ready. I probe their weaknesses, demand perfection, and punish them even harder. It's brutal, but we have to rely on one another and be prepared to thrive under fire.

It will be a month before we actually see close combat, but during the sweltering heat of August, we start to learn what pure hatred looks like—distant muzzle flashes from a faceless enemy, the loose fabric of their clothing flapping behind them as they disappear along the winding dirt roads of rural Afghanistan. Men and boys we've never met want to kill us. The locals we pass on our patrols don't trust us. We don't trust them. But among us—and behind our barrage of munitions—a form of love grows. I see my men sacrificing their own well-being for one another while on patrol. They chip into the earth with pocketknives searching for IEDs meant to maim and kill. Soon they will sprint through machine-gun fire to help one another and risk their lives to aid our wounded. In war—the most gruesome human act possible—our unconditional love for one another is what will help us kill our enemy and keep us alive.

Of all the men in my squad, Lance Corporal James Roche has the best reputation, even though he has served for less than two years in the Corps. A highly opinionated twenty-year-old, "Jim" has a confusing twang that makes it sound like he's from below the Mason-Dixon, rather than his home in New Jersey. Jim and his team leader, Dustin Moon, consume more chewing tobacco than I thought was humanly possible. When Jim finds his first IED out on patrol, he looks up at me as I peer over his shoulder. "This is a real treat, Sarge," he says, his smile twisted from a wad of dip.

Jim has volunteered as my point man—the first Marine on patrol—and if he isn't being a wiseass, it means he's upset. He's one of the few Marines who never misses a patrol. He's the most experienced with the metal detector and wants to be the one to use it. Of the Marines in my squad, I trust him the most. He often jokes that if anyone is to lose their legs to an IED, it should be him, but I know he's not joking. With every step on patrol, he knows that if he makes a mistake, it will most likely be someone else who gets hurt, not him. Jim makes sure this doesn't happen. Throughout our deployment, the only things that will keep him from sweeping our patrol route are dysentery and being wounded. He discovers more than two dozen explosive devices during our tour. There are countless false alarms, but we know he's found the real thing when he calls out, "Oh, come on!" The only things Jim ever complains about are running low on Copenhagen chewing tobacco and waiting hours—sometimes overnight—for explosive-disposal technicians to show up and destroy the hidden roadside bombs he uncovers.

In his downtime Roche is usually found playing grab-ass with his childhood friend, Serge Huber, a Russian orphan who was more or less adopted by Jim's family during his teenage years, after Serge relocated to the United States. The baby-faced Serge lost weight so he could join the Marines with Jim. The two are virtually inseparable, and our only break from their childish banter is when they are asleep. The quickest way for any of us to win an argument with Serge is to remind him that he has been in fewer firefights than the rest of us, as though it were some sort of a competition, which of course it is. He is easily irritated—or "butt hurt," as we say—and pouts at our teasing. Serge's body resembles that of Ivan Drago from *Rocky IV*, but with the face of Baby Huey.

Our platoon sergeant, in charge of three other squads besides mine, was a drill instructor up until our deployment. He's a staff sergeant who loves fuck-fuck games. He's a "motard"—a Marine who has drunk the Kool-Aid and has lost the ability to think for himself. I don't question his love for his men or that he is more senior than me, but his methods are not to my liking. My staff sergeant wants his Marines to be prepared and demands the same perfection I do from mine, but his approach pisses me off.

One afternoon in July, he makes our entire platoon scale a twelve-foot wall with a flimsy aluminum ladder and drop onto the other side. We do it in full gear—flak jacket, four plates of armor, rifles, Kevlar helmet, boots, gloves, nearly two hundred bullets, machine gun, explosives, and more. Without gear I weigh just more than two hundred pounds. With all of my gear, radios, and equipment, I'm more than three hundred pounds. The training is supposed to be about avoiding explosives in doorways, but someone is going to get hurt.

I pull the staff sergeant aside and voice my concerns. We're already low on men and this exercise is senseless. He screams at me and belittles me in front of my Marines. I look him in the eye as he shouts inches from my face. When I don't respond with "Aye aye, Staff Sergeant!" his "frog voice"—the drill instructor rasp—gets even louder. In a calm voice, yet loud enough for my men to hear, I tell him to watch his tone.

"Staff Sergeant, I'm not a dumb-ass recruit on Parris Island. Don't talk to me like that in front of my Marines."

"Your Marines?" he says, veins pulsing in his neck and temples. "I'm the fucking platoon sergeant."

"I'm not a recruit, Staff Sergeant. Talk to me like a man."

I'm treading in dangerous territory. The staff sergeant outranks me, and it's a move that could cost me my rank, my role as squad leader, and money in my pocket for the next few months. But I think it's worth the risk. The staff sergeant finally backs off and cancels the drill. He occasionally joins us on patrols after that but mostly leaves my squad and me alone. I prefer it that way.

We're starting to learn about one another. We fill in the downtime with our stories, jokes from back home, and memories from our former squads. We share our gripes from our old platoons. More than anything we hate other Marines who can't admit when they are wrong. When we're relaxing, I'm not Sarge. I'm TJ, the twenty-five-year-old "Masshole" with a raw sense of humor and a distaste for ignorance, abuse of power, and entitlement. Getting too informal with junior Marines is something many commanders frown upon, but I think it helps us build our team more quickly. When the bullets start to fly, my men still know who's in charge.

By our second month on deployment, we've slipped into a routine. Patrol times vary, but we always patrol. We clean our weapons, read up on intelligence briefs, and find out the latest enemy tactics. Chow time breaks up the day, as does writing letters to friends and family. When I stand radio watch in the company headquarters, I make sure to send e-mails to my Marines' families to let them know their sons, husbands, and fathers are doing okay. Access to computers in the headquarters shack is a privilege of my rank, but if I can e-mail my family, I can do the same for my men.

Access to such luxuries is short-lived "inside the wire"—which means within the confines of a larger, fortified, and relatively safe base. It's time to move. My company commander, Captain O'Brien, tells our platoon that we are launching a sweep through a village more than five kilometers away. It is "an enemy stronghold" and we "should expect heavy casualties" during "a potential weeklong battle." That we should expect to see friends in body bags over the coming days isn't something we want to hear, but at least we're finally going to "get some."

Our mission brief lasts more than two hours. Commanders move pieces around a terrain model—an easily destroyed map made out of earth, scraps, food, and other random items. They tell us the size, activity, location, uniform, time of report, and equipment of our enemy. There are a shitload of them and they're ready to fight. They're everywhere and we can't tell them apart from the civilians. We're repeatedly told to ex-pect casualties. I have twenty pounds of C-4 and a variety of other explo-sives. I can't wait to use them. Demolitions are when I get to do my magic. I love how it feels when I make things disappear. Even people. Killing the enemy is what I'm trained for. It's what I've been sent here to do. I have no qualms about that—not yet, anyway.

Dozens of vehicles belonging to both coalition and Afghan forces are staged in full view of the enemy about a kilometer away. Fixed-wing and rotary aircraft are "on station" for immediate air strikes. Soldiers from the U.S. Army's psychological operations unit use a tactic that includes mounting speakers on a mine-resistant vehicle to blare Miley Cyrus's "Party in the USA" and the sounds of screaming women and children over the recorded noise of gunfire and explosions. Just as in Miley's lyrics, my butterflies begin to fly away.

The enemy knows something's up, and civilians and Taliban alike are speeding off on motorbikes—"squirters," we call them—with their dust trails leading to the opposite side of the village and over the ridgeline. Open-back delivery trucks holding twice their height in cargo follow them. The three-day operation is completed without a shot fired. To search many of the compounds housed inside each ten-foot mud wall and gate we use explosives to blast our way in. I joke with Jim that it's "a real treat." My squad doesn't find a single rifle, bullet, or Taliban fighter. In one compound we find what appear to be nonexplosive materials used to build roadside bombs, but none of what we find tests positive for explo-sive residue. We seize hundreds of dollars' worth of supplies from who-ever fled from the compound. During the sweep, I detonate dozens of explosive charges and easily destroy tens of thousands of dollars' worth of personal property. When our unit leaves Afghanistan five months later, only a small percentage of villagers in the area will have been able to return home. I don't care. I'm doing what the mission calls for.

As our three-day operation winds down and the music, the noise of the aircraft, and the whiff of explosives fade, I'm told that my squad will become responsible for Outpost Kunjak, a tiny combat outpost atop a hill. It's where we staged for the push and I know it's a mess. We're ordered to make our way straight there without returning to the main patrol base. I'm not thrilled. I wanted to live rough, but OP Kunjak is a shit hole.

We strap on our gear. Folding lawn chairs, extra boots, pots and pans, and a slew of odds and ends are zip-tied to our bulging rucksacks as we help one another heave them onto our backs. When we load our weapons and march beyond friendly lines, we look like a ragged band of gypsies.

The hike to Kunjak would normally be two hours. It takes us nearly three. The weight of my pack is so great that my arms start to go numb as the padded straps press through my armored plate carrier. The physical demands of the patrol make it difficult to remain alert and oriented and to keep scanning for IEDs, and we risk becoming oblivious to the threats around us as streams of sweat pour into our eyes. The crushing weight of our packs makes it easy to focus on our own agony and forget where we are. If there's ever an opportune time for the enemy to attack, this is it.

From a distance, the hill to OP Kunjak looks massive. The small base at the top is no larger than a high school gymnasium. On three sides a near-vertical cliff drops toward the wadi, or riverbed. Scaling the cliff would be impossible with all our gear. We trudge up a side slope, fine sand that resembles processed flour kicking up around our boots. The slope is about a sixteen-degree grade and two football fields in length, and just as terrible as I imagined.

"Kunjak, Kunjak, this is Able 3-4, requesting permission to enter friendly lines," I wheeze into my radio as we near the summit.

The radio crackles back our permission to enter the base. We weave through a maze of razor wire that slices our gear, utilities, and flesh. This damned thing has to go. We drag our feet as we stagger behind a wall of cardboard boxes and dump our gear on the ground. Before I even set my rifle down, I notice a gaunt, bearded man sitting atop a cot inside our sleeping area. He looks out of place. His strong handshake isn't enough to convince me he isn't some pussy. We exchange introductions and I'm less than pleased. Not only am I responsible for an outpost, two villages, millions of dollars in gear, and fifteen Marines, but now a journalist as well? Even worse, a photographer?

This is the last thing I need. I want to scream and throw him over the cliff. I feign friendliness, but all I can hope is that he'll leave soon. I don't want him to find whatever he's looking for here. War and journalism don't mix. I've seen Marines get in trouble thanks to reporters. During the operation we've just completed, one media outlet published photos of Marines in our platoon with the sleeves of their flame-resistant uniforms cuffed above their wrists—a violation of our strict uniform policy—and each squad leader, including me, was disciplined with a letter of caution. It wasn't serious, just a formality so my leaders could say they did something. Marine Corps bullshit. All part of the dog and pony show. There's no way in hell I'll let that happen again. My leaders won't be as forgiving the second time around. I start thinking of ways to get rid of him.

The next morning I'm ordered over the crackling radio to take the journalist out on patrol. I argue with my leaders back at the district HQ about having him with us on our first patrol into Nabu Agha, a notoriously hostile village. I have a tired squad that's still struggling tactically, a new village to patrol, and a host of safety concerns aboard our outpost. The journalist is one of them. He's told me he's been in conflict zones before, but people say that when they're stationed with the Air Force in a country adjacent to the one at war, hundreds of miles from a threat and more likely to catch cold than to be shot at. I've been on Navy ships where sailors said they were in hostile "conflict zones." The food was incredible. No luxurious base or sea vessel is as intense as being pinned down by enemy fire with only cinder blocks for protection. I figure the journalist is suffering a midlife crisis and seeking cool war stories to impress his friends back home. Mommy issues. Great. Every photographer I saw in Iraq had pristine body armor. In Fallujah the BBC journalists who joined us arrived with vests that looked practically unused. The word PRESS was written in large white block letters across the front and back. I guess you have to look good for the cameras during combat. At least this guy doesn't have a gleaming PRESS patch on his flak jacket. His gear is faded, worn, and splotched with tan spray paint. It looks like a hand-me-down purchased at a surplus store. He looks like a man with a hobby, not someone who does this for a living. Why would anyone need three cameras to take one photo? A rookie, I guess. But orders are orders and my leaders don't want a headline that says the Marine Corps prevented a journalist from doing his job. I figure if he "bitches out" he will accidentally get shot in the foot (by the enemy, of course). I'm not above finding a solution if he turns out to be a problem.

Chapter 2

Outpost Kunjak

I wanted to live deep and suck out all the marrow of life, to live so sturdily and Spartan-like as to put to rout all that was not life.

—Henry David Thoreau, *Walden*

Finbarr, Helmand Province, October 2010

I'm stretched out on a camp cot at OP Kunjak. Camouflage netting draped overhead filters the afternoon sun and shreds the sky into tiny blue fragments. I'm bored and watching videos on my laptop when a squad of about a dozen heavily laden Marines arrives and dumps their gear all around me, turning the cramped space into a jumble of packs, boots, weapons, ammunition, and camp cots. I snap my laptop shut. The last thing I want is for a bunch of sweaty and dust-covered Marines who have just staggered in exhausted from a four-day operation against the Taliban to see what I'm watching. When I'm in places like Afghanistan, TV series are my guilty pleasure—a silly respite from the stress, loneliness, and fear of being in a place like this—but I would rather my mother catch me watching porn than have U.S. Marines know I'm watching the campy high school drama *Glee* in the middle of a war zone. Marines don't much like the media to begin with, and the leader of the arriving squad, Sergeant Thomas James Brennan, a no-nonsense twenty-five-year-old from Randolph, Massachusetts, doesn't seem thrilled to find a stranger bunked in the tiny outdoor sleeping quarters allocated to him and his men.

"Who are you?" Brennan asks, eyeing my beard and civilian clothing.

"I work for Reuters," I say.

"What's that?"

"It's a global news agency. I'm a photographer."

"Okay," Brennan says, then positions himself between his men and me.

I ask him how I should address him.

"Call me TJ; everybody else does."

TJ orders his squad to organize their shit as they settle in. I'm always surprised at the youth of the U.S. military compared to the armed forces of other countries. Despite his age, TJ appears cocky and self-assured, which to a Canadian like me seems very American. Our countries share the world's longest land border and many cultural similarities, but there are clear distinctions when it comes to national character. Canadians take pride in our reputation for tolerance and politeness and we view Americans as brash and aggressive. We self-identify as the nation that created international peacekeeping. We tend to view the United States as the world's biggest superbully. With its overt patriotism, permissive gun laws, and hawkish politicians, our southern neighbor sometimes seems like a hypermilitarized nation on steroids. The invasion of Iraq and the war in Afghanistan, which I've been covering since 2007, have done little to dispel such a notion. TJ is polite enough, but I know he's wary of my presence and I can sense he'd rather not have me around. I imagine he's a bit of a redneck—the kind of guy who could spend hours picking off birds or rodents with an air rifle just out of boredom. I watch him unpack. He arranges a child's drawings and photographs of a woman and little girl at the head of his camp cot, creating a family shrine of sorts. It's the first personal touch I've seen since arriving a few days earlier at OP Kunjak, a tiny combat outpost perched atop a hill.

The base is named after an adjacent village and offers views stretching across the sun-bleached pebbles of a wide riverbed and over an undulating expanse of barren landscape. To the north a triangular mountain looms above the dark outline of more distant peaks. Warm desert winds blow gusts of fine moondust over the outpost and through sparsely populated villages below. Each village is a scattered maze of mud-mortared walls and compounds hunched thick and low to the ground—sturdy Afghan fortresses built to keep intruders out. OP Kunjak is designed to do the same, but apart from its elevated hilltop position, the lines of defense are bone thin. The outpost is about the size of three basketball courts ringed by a wall of HESCO barriers—squat blocks of thick cloth and steel wire filled with earth that stand shoulder high and just as wide and function as blast walls when stacked side by side. Coils of razor wire crown the HESCO walls while Marine sentries stand watch around the clock from behind .50-caliber machine guns mounted on three sandbagged lookout posts. For Sergeant Brennan and about two dozen men from the First Battalion, Eighth Marines, OP Kunjak will be home for most of their seven-month deployment to Helmand, Afghanistan's largest province and the war's deadliest, with nearly a thousand coalition troops killed since 2001.

By October 2010 the conflicts in Iraq and Afghanistan have been grinding along for nearly a decade. It will be another year before the United States withdraws the last of its forces from Iraq in December 2011, but attention has already shifted to Afghanistan. President Barack Obama launched his first major military push a little more than a year ago, in the summer of 2009, with Operation Khanjar, one of the largest offensives since Western forces invaded Afghanistan in 2001. Obama's surge strategy has seen 21,000 reinforcements deployed to the country with the aim of pushing the Taliban from their strongholds in the southern districts of Helmand Province. Spearheaded by 4,000 U.S. Marines and supported by more than 180 aircraft, Operation Khanjar was the Marine Corps' biggest offensive since Phantom Fury in November 2004. That operation ousted Iraqi insurgents during the battle of Fallujah but did little to suppress a broader insurgency that cost the lives of tens of thousands of Iraqis and thousands of Americans. It's clear foreign forces can temporarily uproot their enemies in both Iraq and Afghanistan. Less clear is whether those forces will outstay the insurgents to provide lasting security and reliable governance for the local population. It won't happen in Iraq and seems even more unlikely in Afghanistan, the age-old "graveyard of empires."

My immediate concern is to illustrate the current state of the conflict, or whatever narrow slice of it I can witness. I've chosen OP Kunjak for its harsh cinematic beauty. Afghanistan is a rugged country rich with soaring mountains and dramatic deserts. Since 2007 I've done several embeds in Kandahar Province and have learned that the smaller and more remote the base, the better the access and the stronger the pictures. It doesn't get much more remote, or basic, than OP Kunjak.

A flayed Afghan flag snaps in the wind on a wooden pole atop the outpost's only solid structure, a single-room mud hut housing half a dozen Afghan police. The Marines sleep outside on camp cots, their boots and weapons within reach. The hum of a diesel generator powers a tiny command post, or Combat Operations Center (COC), sheltered under an open-sided tent. The COC's crackling radio is the only link to the main base at Musa Qala District Center a few miles and a world away. There's no running water, only bottled water for the mandatory Marine morning shave, usually conducted in the reflection of a cracked wing mirror salvaged from a damaged military vehicle. There are no showers. Many of the Marines will go months without washing. Wet wipes get the job done. There are no toilets, only a jagged metal piss tube buried into the earth and "wag bags"—disposable plastic sacks that fit over a folding toilet seat. Food consists of self-heating ration packs. Marines eat out of one bag and shit into another. Waste is thrown into a smoldering burn pit. The base isn't much, but at least it's not out there, beyond the wire, where the threat of Taliban attack is as constant as the dust.

In the evening TJ tells me a bit about his Iraq tour and alludes to his role in the 2004 battle of Fallujah. He quizzes me about where I'm from and why I'm in Afghanistan. I knew this was coming. Embedded journalists are always grilled by members of the military trying to gauge our motives and assess whether we're a liability. I've anticipated such a moment and hand TJ several cartons of Marlboro Red cigarettes and a dozen cans of Copenhagen and Grizzly chewing tobacco I picked up for a few hundred bucks at the PX in Kandahar. It's a transparent ploy to ingratiate myself, but it seems to work; good tobacco is like gold at a base like this, where the PX truck will stop by once or maybe twice during an entire deployment. TJ tosses the cartons of cigarettes and the tins of dip to his squad members, keeping a single pack of Marlboros for himself. The sleeping area is soon thick with smoke. As an ardent nonsmoker raised by a medical oncologist mother, I'm once again baffled by people's willingness to slowly kill themselves by puffing and dipping. Then I remember where we are. There are quicker ways to die out here.

As TJ pulls on a smoke, I explain how the week of 9/11, I had just quit my staff job at a Canadian newspaper and was en route to my first free-lance posting as a "superstringer" working for Reuters. I was to be based in Kinshasa, the capital of the Democratic Republic of Congo in Central Africa. On the morning of the attacks on New York and Washington, I was in southern England on the second day of a "hostile environment" course, a weeklong boot camp of sorts for journalists. Most major inter-national media outlets send their staff and contractors for such training before deploying them to conflict zones. Run by former members of the British army, the course taught journalists how to administer first aid, identify threats and different calibers of weapons, navigate roadblocks, crowds, and riots, and behave in hostage and kidnapping situations. The exercises involved wearing full body armor and included simulated am-bushes, abductions, and scenes of mass casualties. I was in a Land Rover being driven to a forest obstacle course "booby-trapped" with trip wires connected to harmless flash-bang explosions, camouflaged snipers, and other simulated "deadly" threats when our instructor told us he'd just heard over the radio that a plane had hit the World Trade Center. None of us on the course took the news seriously. I assumed it was part of the scenario setup for the pending exercise. Only after we'd been "blown up" half a dozen times on the forest obstacle course and returned to the class-room at our countryside base did we see the television footage of the col-lapsing towers. Once my initial shock subsided, I grasped that everything had changed. The world had just entered a new era of global conflict. There was no predicting what shape or form that might ultimately take, but one thing was certain: Western media would focus on the Middle East and Asia for years to come. Africa would receive even less coverage than usual (at least until it too was drawn a decade later into a frenzy of revolutions and wars that would allow violent Islamic extremism to spread across North Africa and to destabilize huge swaths of West, Cen-tral, and East Africa).

I tell TJ that I was initially tempted to change direction and to try making my name as a journalist covering the inevitable war against the Taliban in Afghanistan. But I knew Central Africa had a massive, sprawl-ing, and underreported conflict of its own, with Congo at its center. I figured the Reuters gig could still offer a different kind of opportunity to carve out a career as a foreign correspondent. I've never enjoyed being part of the pack mentality that so often drives journalism. I much preferred to work on lower-profile stories in the hope that my reporting would add something to the conversation rather than getting lost in all the noise.

Or so I told myself. Part of me perhaps didn't feel ready to step onto such a big global stage. I'd spent a year backpacking through Africa after university, and it felt less intimidating than Afghanistan. As one of three international agency reporters based in Kinshasa (the others being a British BBC stringer and a Belgian freelancer for the Associated Press), I would have a more significant role covering Congo's violence—and the deadliest conflict since the Second World War—than I would have competing with the world's top journalists swooping in to cover Afghanistan (and later Iraq). My decision to cover Congo kept me living and working across Africa for more than a decade.

I moved from writing toward photography in 2005, I explain, as a more immediate way of telling stories from a region where images often have a more emotional impact than yet another dispatch on the latest round of tribal clashes or ethnic killings. My interest in Afghanistan began in 2007, when much of the world was still preoccupied with Iraq. At that time Canadian troops were one of the main fighting forces in Afghanistan. As a Canadian I wanted to know what they were doing there. I'd also grown accustomed to covering African conflicts and wanted to push myself further, both personally and professionally. I felt ready to test myself in another theater of war, though that's something I've always kept to myself.

I went on a series of embeds with Canadian troops in 2007 and 2008, and my first assignments landed me in the midst of heavy fighting in Kandahar's insurgent strongholds of Panjwaii and Zahri districts, the heartland of Mullah Omar, founder of the Taliban, who still enjoyed the loyalty of much of the local population. I also spent several weeks with the U.S. Army, flying dozens of missions with medical evacuation, or MEDEVAC, units using Black Hawk helicopters to collect the dead, the wounded, and the maimed from Afghan battlefields. Aware that the other Marines are listening to my conversation with TJ, I rattle off a few well-worn war stories about firefights and close calls while trying to sound nonchalant. I finish up by joking that there's one big difference between my past embeds and this stint with the Marines.

"Your living conditions really suck," I say, but the Marines are indifferent to such a truism.

While with the Canadians, even at remote forward operating bases (FOBs), I had enjoyed fresh food prepared daily by a field kitchen, endless supplies of fresh coffee, ice-cold soft drinks, toasted bagels and cream cheese, salad bars, and even small tubs of Häagen-Dazs ice cream in the evenings. The troops slept on comfortable mattresses in air-conditioned bunkers or "C-cans"—armored shipping containers fitted with bunks—and had access to hot showers, TV, wireless Internet, and washing machines. My weeks with the U.S. Army MEDEVAC units had been even more luxurious, with much of the downtime spent watching action movies on a giant HDTV screen with surround sound. The MEDEVAC units stationed at Kandahar Airfield (KAF) performed essential, lifesaving work while enjoying the comforts of a base resembling a small American city grafted onto the Afghan landscape. KAF had about ten thousand troops from NATO countries, plus support staff, and fully equipped gyms, basketball and volleyball courts, a ball hockey rink, and a half-square-mile boardwalk featuring massage parlors, ATMs, an AT&T call center, and shops and restaurants, including TGI Fridays, Burger King, Pizza Hut, Kentucky Fried Chicken, and Subway. A Green Beans café served gourmet drinks under the motto "Honor First, Coffee Second." The base has even had celebrity visits, including from Bradley Cooper, David Beckham, and Robin Williams (who joked that the bearded Special Forces looked like heavily armed Amish).

When I told the Army MEDEVAC crews that I was heading to Helmand for an embed with the Marines Corps, they warned me, "Get ready for the Marines. Those guys live rough."

No kidding. The greatest luxury at OP Kunjak is usually a book or a months-old magazine, maybe a battery-powered video game or some real coffee.

When TJ and I finally bunk down for the night, the aluminum rails of our camp cots are inches apart. I can hear the breathing of the other squad members stretched out nearby. They're listening to my conversation with Brennan without saying much. I sense no hostility, just fatigue. I may have found the kind of embed situation I've hoped for—but I still detect a hint of skepticism from TJ. I'm aware I'm entering into the closed sphere of a small group of men who have trained hard for months and then spent the last few weeks living side by side. They rely on one another to stay alive. I have yet to find out whether they will accept an interloper. As I drift off, shooting stars skim across the darkness through a veil of camouflage netting.

The next morning I'm forcing down lukewarm breakfast rations of beige scrambled eggs and gray sausage when TJ tells me I can join his squad's foot patrol into the nearby village of Nabu Agha, a sprawling web of mud compounds and alleyways stretched across a few square miles of rugged desert. I've been on a patrol into the village with another group of Marines a few days before, and I know it's a place mostly devoid of people, except the kind who shoot at you. I put on my flak jacket and helmet (both were the media's preferred navy blue until I spray-painted them beige to better blend into the landscape) and sling three cameras over my shoulders, then fall into line as TJ's squad heads out.

We're moving up a narrow alleyway about half an hour into the patrol when a machine-gun muzzle flashes from a corner about 150 feet ahead of us. I turn and duck behind Navy Corpsman Donald "Doc" Howard, using him for cover as TJ orders his squad across the lane. I follow. The curved alleyway is two blocks long with high mud walls and it's barely wider than a car. We are stuck halfway along it with only the wall's contour as cover. The machine gun sounds like one of the Russian-made, belt-fed PKMs favored by the Taliban and capable of firing 650 rounds per minute. Our attacker fires in controlled bursts, ricocheting bullets off the wall in an effort to strike us. There's no way to move forward or back along the alley without getting hit. We're pinned down.

Marines "break contact" by moving. Remaining static is the worst thing to do in a firefight. Brennan radios in a contact report and orders one of his men to fire a 40 mm fragmentation grenade toward the attacker's position. Lance Corporal Dustin Moon kneels in the middle of the alley under a burst of covering fire and lobs the grenade forward. As an embedded photographer and a noncombatant, I concentrate on taking pictures as bullets gouge the mud wall above Moon. Having something to do in such situations helps contain my fear. My shutter whirs as a projectile from Moon's weapon makes a distinct "plunk" sound, followed moments later by the *crump* of the explosion.

Word comes over the radio from Marine snipers providing overwatch from a nearby ridge that more insurgents are moving into positions around us. The snipers tell TJ to push back into the line of fire. "Oh, so you want to use us as bait?" He replies. "Thanks a lot!"

The Marines kneel in the middle of the lane and fire up the alleyway, drawing return fire. Moments later a volley of .50-caliber rounds from the Marine sniper's Barrett M82A1A semiautomatic sniper rifle whooshes over our heads. The Taliban machine gun falls silent. Another nearby team of Marine snipers maneuvers to hunt the insurgents, but as usual the Taliban have vanished like ghosts into the warren of compounds and alleyways, hauling their dead or wounded away with them. All they leave behind are the metal casings of spent bullets.

Back at OP Kunjak after the patrol, I ask TJ why he waited so long in the alleyway instead of maneuvering and attacking.

"Why are you asking?" he snaps. He seems to think I'm questioning his judgment, but I just want to understand the military strategy in such situations. I don't have the training he does. He says the idea was for his squad to remain in place to keep the attackers engaged while other Marines outflanked and killed the insurgents. It makes sense.

"So that's what you meant about using us as bait?" I ask.

"Yeah, basically," he answers. It's not always easy to persuade patrol leaders to add a journalist to their list of concerns, so I thank TJ for taking me along and for watching my back.

"Yeah, well, I could tell you'd been shot at before," he says. "You didn't freak out or get in the way." He's also worried about how much trouble he'd get into if something happened to me. "You know how bad it looks to get a noncombatant hurt?" he tells me later. "That's so much paperwork." I laugh, but he's only half joking.

Although I've just finished a two-week embed with U.S. Army MEDEVAC crews in Kandahar, today's firefight is the first I've photographed in a while. It's also one of few occasions when I've actually seen the Taliban during battle. Usually they're too far away or I'm busy taking cover, but this time I saw the machine gunner's face when he opened fire. Even though their roadside bombs and mortars and rockets can strike at any moment, the danger often feels abstract. Not anymore. The war now feels personal. And then I get an e-mail from a colleague with the subject header "Joao's been wounded."

Joao Silva is a forty-four-year-old photographer for the *New York Times*. We both spent the previous week in Kandahar waiting for our embeds. When we parted, Joao waved me off with the words "Stay safe." The e-mail says Joao was out on a patrol with American soldiers near Kandahar when he stepped on an IED that blew off both his legs. I can't believe it. Joao is a legend among photojournalists, the last working member of the famous "Bang-Bang Club," a group of South African photojournalists who covered the violent last spasms of apartheid in their home country. He has produced some of the most memorable photographs from the Iraq war. In 2004 he embedded with the Mahdi militia, loyal to Shia cleric Moktada al-Sadr, as they battled American forces in Najaf and Baghdad.

Joao seemed fearless and invincible. The machinery and muscle of war offer an illusion of safety. Photographing combat involves a degree of cognitive dissonance; you're aware of the risks while also denying them. Journalists are increasingly targeted in conflict zones, but I cling to the foolish notion that our good intentions should protect us from harm, and this news shakes me badly. Joao's injury is a sharp reminder of the indiscriminate nature of violence, and it cuts a chink in my armor of denial. I'm even more relieved than before to still be in one piece after the alleyway firefight—fate has brushed closer than usual, but it still touched someone else. Then I feel like an asshole for having such thoughts. Most of the Marines I'm with would take a bullet or absorb a bomb blast themselves before they would allow one of their comrades to be hurt or killed. And here I am feeling glad that I'm not the one who got maimed today. I make an oath to myself to visit Joao in the hospital—assuming he survives—only half aware of how much this is just to assuage my own feelings of guilt and cowardice.

When I return to the sleeping area, TJ asks me what's up. "Sorry to hear it," he says, then tells me he once searched for a friend's severed leg at the scene of an IED blast in Iraq. He's matter-of-fact about it, and I'm reminded that Marines have to keep doing their jobs when their friends get hurt or killed. Grief is not an emotion to be indulged on the battlefield.

We talk about injuries and photography. What would I do if anything happened while we were out on patrol? he asks. It's a delicate question. I say I would do my job and take pictures but that I would follow military restrictions and withhold publication of images of dead or wounded Americans until after their families have been notified. TJ says that stories about the mundane yet deadly risks Marines face daily are rarely publicized in the media. Then he tells me that if anything happens to him, he wants me to report it.

"People back home don't give a shit about this war, or Afghanistan. So yeah, if something happens to me, I want people to know about the sacrifices I've made."

On patrol the next day, there's a brief volley of gunfire nearby. TJ detains an Afghan suspected of being the shooter and escorts him back to the main base at District Center. After handing the prisoner over and submitting the paperwork, TJ has a few minutes on a computer with Internet. He later tells me he Googled me. He doesn't have time to read much more than the first line of my Wikipedia page: "Finbarr O'Reilly (born 1971 Swansea) is a Canadian photographer, who in February 2006 won the premier award of the 49th annual World Press Photo contest."

"You didn't tell me you were a big-time award-winning photographer," he says back at OP Kunjak that afternoon. "I thought you were just some schmuck with fancy cameras."

"So you're Google-stalking me now?" I ask. "That's creepy. But aren't you glad I'm here to make you famous?"

The days at OP Kunjak settle into a routine: wake up around 0600, wash, eat breakfast, make coffee, do chores around the outpost, go on foot patrol through the nearby villages or across the wadi, return to base, eat lunch, kill time reading or playing cards or dominoes, clean dust from gear, sit around, heat more rations for dinner, work out at the makeshift gym (consisting of a chin-up bar and a few weights), turn in for the night, lie in bed chatting or reading until falling asleep. TJ and I pass slow evening hours reclined side by side in our racks talking, the glow of his cigarette hovering in the darkness. He's curious, always asking questions about what I do and what makes me tick. As a Marine he can't fathom the idea of traveling alone into hostile environments without a weapon or a support system. I can't understand why anyone would choose a profession that's about killing other human beings, though I keep that thought to myself. Instead I tell him I could never tolerate military constraints and conformity. I'm baffled by the upturned moral universe of the military, where service members can be disciplined for adultery, drinking alcohol, or minor uniform infractions but where killing people is not just fine—it's the goal. TJ clearly finds comfort in the structure and the bonds the military provides, but occasionally he appears to think beyond the confines of the Marine Corps. Sure, he smokes, is easily seduced by talk of trucks and guns, and shares a toilet sense of humor with the other Marines, but he confides that he used to enjoy writing back in high school, and that he misses it.

Our conversations are an escape for him from the drudgery of deployment. For me, having someone to talk to at the end of each day is a comfort, even if the divide between us sometimes feels like a chasm. TJ is a warrior, an active player in the war. I'm a professional witness. He has a gun; I have a camera. He's trained to follow orders; I'm programmed to question authority. He seems to believe in God; I'm an atheist. He's a fan of George W. Bush and a follower of Fox News. I'm not. He pulls a trigger; I press a shutter. We're like opposite ends of a pencil, lead and eraser, one creating, the other destroying.

One evening, as we lie on our backs in our camp cots, the generator humming in the background, I mention how Joao Silva had embedded with the Mahdi militia fighting American forces. TJ pauses to consider the idea that a photographer for an American newspaper risked his life on the front lines working side by side with an enemy battling U.S. troops.

"I guess that would be like you embedding with the Taliban now, huh?" he says. It's something neither of us can imagine, though the idea is tantalizing. He then asks whether, given the chance, I would interview Osama bin Laden. His question catches me off guard. There's no good answer, and I sense it's a test of sorts. If I say yes, I'll be giving voice to America's sworn enemy and would know the whereabouts of the man Special Forces has been hunting for years. I deflect the question and say something vague about its being too risky. TJ needles me. "What kind of journalist are you? I'd take that interview in a second."

Maybe the chasm between us isn't so wide after all.

Within a few days TJ and his squad seem to have accepted me, or at least tolerate my presence. TJ shares his supply of Starbucks coffee and lends me his charred metal canteen cup each morning. TJ alludes to things he did in Iraq, but the only clues I have to his most troubling experiences are inked across his body in a map of cryptic tattoos. The most prominent one curves downward across his chest like a necklace of thick Gothic script. "Only God Can Judge," it reads.

"Yeah, we did things over there that civilians would never understand," he says. "People called us baby killers and shit, but what the fuck do they know about war?"

We reinforce our tiny sleeping space by stacking cardboard ration boxes in a shoulder-high semicircle around the bunks in an effort to deflect the constant wind coating us with layers of fine dust. This makes our ramshackle corner of the outpost even more cramped but also makes it feel cozier.

The daily routine is broken one afternoon when the mail truck arrives. Boxes of care packages and letters are unloaded and torn open by Marines eager for news and goodies from home. The delivery sets off a round of trading and sharing among squad members. Socks are exchanged for magazines, chewing tobacco for cigarettes, and coffee for candy.

I don't get a care package, but one of the squad members tosses me a large pack of wet wipes to help keep me clean. The dust has been chafing in uncomfortable places, and I'm relieved when Lance Corporal Benjamin Brickman shares a yellow bottle of Anti Monkey Butt powder. I've never heard of the stuff before, but the silky talc is a godsend. As one of the reviews I later read on Amazon.com says, "My bum feels like a Christmas morning."

Marines find solutions for many problems encountered on deployment, and perhaps the biggest problem of all is the absence of women. Solution? The "happy sock." With no privacy and a lack of water for washing, the happy sock prevents a mess by catching ejaculate when the Marines masturbate inside their sleeping bags, or wherever else they choose. On one occasion I climb up to a lookout post at Kunjak to find one of TJ's squad members rubbing one out into his sock. I turn and leave before he notices me, but it's unlikely he would have been too embarrassed. Masturbation is a regular topic of conversation, and several members of the squad say they plan to jerk off on each of the lookout posts on base. It makes a certain sense, I suppose. Post duty lasts for hours and staring into the desert soon gets boring, plus it's about the only place where a Marine can spend any time alone out here.

Daily conversations revolve around a handful of subjects: sex, trucks, women, guns, bowel movements, music, girlfriends, motorcycles, wives, family, postdeployment holiday plans, tattoos, pussy, and more sex.

One such conversation unfolds as I'm sitting on my bunk writing in my journal. It's a lazy afternoon and the squad is lounging around killing time.

"I read somewhere that the prostate gland is the male G-spot," Dustin Moon, the loudmouth of the group, says to nobody in particular.

"What the fuck?" says Doc Howard.

"Yeah, I heard that too," another chimes in.

"So what the fuck does that mean?" Howard asks.

"Means if you let a chick stick her finger up your ass while she's blowing you, you'll come like a motherfucker," Moon says, grinning with his wad of chewing tobacco bulging under his lip.

"Aw, dude, that's fucking disgusting," says Howard. "You gotta be kidding me."

"No joke," says Moon, laughing.

"Get the fuck outta here."

"Seriously, man. Some dudes will even let a girl stick her tongue up their ass," says a third Marine.

"No fucking way I'd ever let my girl do that," TJ says. "I've seen what comes outta my ass. I'd never be able to look her in the eye again, never mind kiss her."

The military has its own distinct language, littered with acronyms, slang, and derogatory terms. Above all for the Marines is their Latin slogan, "Semper Fi," short for "Semper Fidelis," meaning "Always Faithful." Helicopters are "birds" (never "choppers"), the MEDEVAC birds are known as "dustoff," and "fast air" is a fighter jet. A firefight was a TIC (for "troops in combat," and pronounced "tick"), "fobbits" are the chumps who hang back like hobbits at forward operating bases (FOBs) without ever patrolling "outside the wire," which means beyond the safety of the bigger bases. These types are sometimes also called "REMFs," rear-echelon motherfuckers. If a Marine gets his bell rung by an IED or an explosion, he is said to have "got blowed up." Interpreters are "terps," an improvised sleeping quarter is a "hooch," and the repetitive cycle of days where little seems to change makes for another "Groundhog Day." Sometimes it's just a week of Mondays—the shittiest day of the week. And of course there is the running joke about photographers bearing the acronym for "camera unit, non-tactical."

In addition to TJ's squad, OP Kunjak is home to a combined antiarmor team (CAAT), a platoon of about twenty Marines with four armored vehicles and a sleeping tent. Their role is to provide vehicular and heavy-weapons support during ground missions or to escort convoys and make supply runs. They are often on the move for days at a time and make frequent visits to the main base at District Center. This means they have access to hot showers, Internet, and laundry. They often bring back stashes of soft drinks, fresh fruit, and snacks, but they hide those luxuries from TJ's squad and are reluctant to share, even while enjoying them in plain sight. They also refuse to share their satellite phone or to bring chewing tobacco or cigarettes for TJ and his men. This does not sit well with TJ's squad. The two groups sometimes have words, but for the most part resentment simmers, and rarely more so than on the night of October 29, when a rainstorm lashed the outpost, leaving TJ and his squad soaked. I managed to take shelter under a motorcycle tarp and woke in the morning in time to take a photo of TJ lying in his bunk smoking, a dripping camouflage tarp draped over his head, his personal gear scattered beneath him in the mud. He was not a happy Marine. I snapped a picture of him smoking and looking grim in his bunk.

Headquarters promised TJ a tent for the squad ahead of the winter rains, but, like much of their cold-weather clothing, it has yet to arrive. Together we scrape together fifty dollars of crumpled dollar bills and send them with one of the Afghan policemen stationed with the Marines at OP Kunjak to the Musa Qala bazaar in search of a tarpaulin. He returns with rolls of clear plastic sheeting. We use bits of scrap wood and metal to prop up a shelter of sorts, but the wind soon shreds the plastic and the sleeping quarter ends up looking like an aborted Christo sculpture. Meanwhile the CAAT guys produce a thick blue tarp and fashion a dry living space outside their tent. TJ scribbles a bitter handwritten letter home to Mel that evening.

"So today was the most miserable day I've had in Afghanistan yet," he writes. "I woke up at 2 a.m. to get rained on all night and day. It's pretty miserable. We took spare crap from all over our outpost and pieced together a shanty house of sorts. It is ghetto as hell. Part of Maddie's drawings got erased by the rain. . . . Today was just such a crappy day. We couldn't do anything because the ground was too muddy for the trucks to be able to drive. They just kept sinking. . . . It's so shitty here. Everything just turns to muck and you sink to your ankles."

The picture of TJ soaked in his bunk gets published in the *New York Times*'s *Lens* blog's "Pictures of the Day" selection, but this only adds to his woes. Battalion headquarters sees the image online and dispatches Captain O'Brien to discipline TJ for poor leadership. HQ wants to give him a nonjudicial punishment, which means his pay could be docked and his service record could earn a black mark, but when O'Brien arrives and sees the grim living conditions, he relents and gives Brennan a verbal lashing instead. A commander at another base is less forgiving and prints out the picture and posts it on a bulletin board with the inscription "This is what a turd Marine looks like."

Command is upset because they believe Brennan smoked inside a tent, but there was no tent. They also believe Brennan's weapon was not being cared for, but the first thing he did when it began to rain was cover it to keep it clean. I showed Brennan the picture before publishing it, and he had no issues with the scene it portrayed. Marine Corps public relations back in Washington seems to agree. Shortly after this ruckus hits, I receive an e-mail from a major who is the deputy director of the Marine Corps Community Relations Branch at the Pentagon.

"Dear Mr. O'Reilly," the e-mail reads, "We would like to feature a photo you took in a newsletter we put out for the Marine Corps. The photo is of Sgt. Brennan after a night of rain, sleeping outside, smoking a cigarette. Would you be willing to allow that?"

I'm wary of causing TJ more trouble and reply asking how the picture would be used. I inform the major that TJ's superiors dislike the photo.

"What did his command have an issue with?" the major writes back. "Am I missing something unauthorized in the photo? Looks pretty hardcore and motivating to me."

I feel bad for creating problems, but TJ isn't too bothered by the fallout. "Don't worry," he says. "It's just Marine Corps bullshit."

Chapter 3

Ambushed

I spit in a bamboo viper's face
And I'd be dead, but by God's grace.

—Johnny Cash, Vietnam War song "Drive On"

Finbarr, Nabu Agha, November 1, 2010

On the morning of November 1, 2010, TJ tells me to prepare for an overnight operation into Nabu Agha. Every time the Marines venture into the deserted town they get into a firefight, and they expect the same again. It's not a question of whether they will be ambushed, only when. The plan is to infiltrate the village and occupy a designated compound for the night. A team of four Marines will then head out the next morning at sunrise to act as bait and lure the Taliban into an attack. The rest of the Marines will be in position for a counterattack, with air support and artillery, if needed.

I copy the Marines as they "rat-fuck" the ration packs, picking out only the best contents and stuffing them into overnight bags while throwing away the rest. As the squad checks their weapons, I ensure my camera batteries are fully charged, then layer on my kit—a journalist's version of the hardware the Marines wear, including Kevlar helmet, flak jacket, kneepads, heavy boots, gloves, eye protection, and clothes made from natural fibers that won't melt onto my skin in case of an explosion.

By midday the sun warms the flak vests strapped to the chests of fifteen Marines. TJ surveys the men as they shoulder their weapons and packs. Each has a flame-resistant uniform and boots, a plate carrier with four armored Kevlar plates, a four-liter CamelBak filled with water, chest pouches stuffed with 180 rounds of 5.56 mm ammunition, two M67 fragmentation grenades, night-vision goggles, and an M4 carbine rifle with an advanced combat optical gun sight and PEQ-16 laser. Their packs are laden with extra batteries, more ammunition, rations, and gear for an overnight bivouac. TJ's point man, Lance Corporal James Roche, uses a combat metal detector, a broom-sized minesweeper that beeps at the slightest hint of metal buried below the surface. Two Marines each carry a THOR, a frequency jammer with a large antenna poking up to block enemy radio or phone signals used to trigger hidden bombs. The phallic shapes of the antennae earn nicknames—the French Tickler and Black Thunder. TJ also carries maps, five smoke grenades, three colored signal flares, demolition explosives, and a radio. He makes sure all his men are wearing regulation gloves and ballistic eye protection and then does radio check.

"Kunjak, Kunjak, this is Able 3-4 requesting permission to depart friendly lines with one-eight packs." The reply squawks back, "3-4, this is Kunjak. Permission granted."

One by one the Marines file past the outpost's wire gate, each sliding the bolt of his M4 carbine rifle and ramming a green-tipped round into the chamber as he goes. I march in the middle of the column, behind TJ. Apart from the sweat already soaking my shirt and running into my eyes, and the usual twinge of trepidation when heading out on patrol, I feel comfortable as OP Kunjak recedes behind us. The patrol crests a ridge and the outpost disappears from view. Pushing down past the first compounds into Nabu Agha, the streets are empty, as usual. The place is a ghost town. Civilians have fled the frequent fighting. The only Afghans in sight are the four policemen patrolling with us in ragged formation, weapons slung over their shoulders, caps askew. The patrol reaches a crossroads about a mile into town and spreads out to cover each direction, with Roche, the sweeper, securing the left flank. Corporal James Edward Orr, a beefy twenty-year-old from Eufaula, Alabama, pushes to the front of the column, treading on hard-packed dirt to avoid loose stones and soft earth that could conceal an IED.

Orr approaches the corner of an alleyway and calls out, "I see someone!"

"What's he doing?" TJ asks.

"He's turkey-peeking," Orr answers, meaning the figure is poking his head in and out of sight. "What should I do?"

"Does he have a weapon?" TJ shouts back.

"Yeah! He just ran across the road with an AK! Do I shoot?"

"Fuck yeah, shoot the motherfucker!" TJ orders.

Gunfire erupts and the Marines stack up against a wall. TJ directs his men into position; some face rear to make sure they are not outflanked. Staff Sergeant Ysidro Gonzalez Jr., a brash Texan with a scuffed rocket-propelled grenade round strapped to his pack, leans around the corner and lays down suppressing fire as he runs across an alley. Gonzalez is a rank above TJ and the senior Marine at OP Kunjak. Gonzalez is not part of TJ's squad, but he's along for the mission. He takes a position behind a mud pillar half the width of his body as incoming rounds smack into it two feet from his face, kicking up tiny puffs of dust.

"Fuck you! You can't hit me, motherfuckers!" Gonzalez shouts as he fires back, the muzzle flash from his rifle leaving black marks on the pillar. (Gonzalez had previously shown me a bullet hole in his trouser cuff and said it was from a round fired by a Taliban sniper. "Asshole tried to shoot me, but he fuckin' missed.")

Gonzalez calls Roche and Lance Corporal John Chun over, and Roche and Gonzalez alternate firing rounds as Chun crouches in the alleyway and aims his rifle-mounted M203 grenade launcher slightly upward. Again the distinct *plunk* of the grenade lobbed from the barrel is followed moments later by the round's explosion. Again I snap photographs and catch a frame showing the blurred projectile shooting from Chun's weapon.

TJ barks into his radio over the noise. "Able COC, this is 3-4. Stand by for contact report."

"Send it, 3-4."

"Be advised, we have just taken enemy contact from one military-age male in the vicinity of building forty-three."

Gonzalez holds his firing position as Brennan orders his men forward up the alley in a tactical column, with each Marine close on the heels of the man in front of him. I follow, snapping pictures on the move. Roche peers around the next corner, stops, and calls TJ forward. An open one-acre field of parched mud lies ahead, too exposed to cross.

TJ, Nabu Agha, November 1, 2010

Roche and I peek around the corner and scan ahead, looking for a way forward. I weigh my options. I spot a doorway up ahead and decide the compound would make a secure staging point, but we'll have to blast open an entry point. It's time for some magic. I pull a doughnut charge from the drop pouch hooked to my belt, attach a blasting cap, and creep forward along the wall into the open field. After ten paces I stop at a blue sheet-metal gate with a green triangle painted in the middle. It's locked. I pause for a moment, aware my back is exposed to enemy positions across the field. My gloved fingers are thick and awkward as I fumble to cinch the charge onto the padlock. It slips and clanks against the metal door. The sound echoes behind the door and across the field. I wince and look over my shoulder, expecting to be shot at any moment. I grasp the fuse igniter, pull the safety pin, push the plunger deep into the cylinder, turn it ninety degrees, and, with a swift snap, pull back on the plunger. The fuse sizzles. I have eight seconds to get to safety before the charge blows, but it always feels like less. I bolt back to my squad and brace myself against the wall. We open our mouths so the pressure from the blast won't rupture our eardrums. The explosion sends a shock wave through our chests and we immediately move, using the dust kicked up from the ground to mask our entry into the compound. Magic. The door has vanished. I guard the entrance while others clear the rooms, moving with weapons raised through the garden, past a rusted oil drum, an overturned wheelbarrow, a pair of black rubber boots, a yellow plastic jug, and a rickety wooden ladder leaning against the ten-foot wall.

"Room clear," my Marines call over and over.

Fin is surveying the compound's small orchard and the green grass, but I can find little time for horticultural appreciation. Bullets are flying and the Canuck is on a nature walk. I have to put the battlefield puzzle together: Machine gunner goes there, grenadier over there. As my Marines move into position, more gunfire erupts. Rounds kick up dirt along the walls and hiss overhead. Fire is incoming from three directions. We are nearly surrounded. Whether it was intended or not, we've been lured into the very attack and counterattack scenario we were hoping to deploy against the Taliban. The puzzle has shifted.

My Marines and the Afghan police lay down a flurry of machine-gun fire toward the muzzle flashes coming from across the field. A woman and child walk out from behind a Taliban position.

"What the fuck? I nearly just shot a woman and a kid!" shouts Corporal Clarkson, who is lying prone on the ground just outside the compound and using a pile of dirt for cover. "They just walked right out from behind that wall. What the hell are they doing?"

It sometimes seems that, after decades of war, Afghans have become inured to the violence swirling around them like dust. I've been in firefights and seen farmers plowing their crops in an adjacent field, kids playing soccer nearby, and civilians weaving their motorcycles through crossfire. Combat is almost like a spectator sport here, but the people on the sidelines seem indifferent to the outcome.

I order Roche and Orr to bound ahead to the next alley and they take off under our covering fire. *BOOM!* The ground shakes. A cloud of dust and smoke rises from Roche and Orr's position around the corner, just out of sight. The shooting stops and suddenly, there is quiet. Fuck. Despite weeks of intense fighting and the constant threat of IEDs, none of my Marines has been hurt. Now I fear I may have just ordered two of my men to their deaths. My chest tightens as the dread of failure grips me. I stare out the gate into the cloud of smoke and dust, begging for Roche and Orr to emerge. Nothing. Then they stumble back into view. They have their arms and legs. As they stagger closer, I scan them for injuries and blood. None. They collapse into the compound and fall against a wall, blank stares and ashen faces. A Taliban RPG struck the wall beside Roche and Orr and knocked them off their feet. They are concussed, but with the RPG's lethal blast range of twelve feet, and a much wider radius of flying shrapnel, Roche and Orr are lucky to be alive. RPGs—originally designed as an antitank weapon—were responsible for more than 3,600 deaths and almost 31,000 injuries of U.S. troops in Iraq and Afghanistan between 2001 and 2009 alone.

Doc Howard examines Roche and Orr and finds their response time is slow and they have trouble seeing. I'm pissed. My men have been injured—nearly killed. I study their stunned faces. My squad is flanked by Taliban. Marines are trained never to give up ground. We have to keep pushing forward. If we don't do that here, we are at risk of being trapped inside the compound. The only way out is for us to fight. Fin snaps pictures of Gonzalez as he calls in to report our casualties. I grab Chun and order another volley of fire downrange as we sprint forward along the wall to the position Roche and Orr abandoned. Chun sweeps left to hold security down the alley. I'm between my men and the enemy. I've secured our next position so we can continue maneuvering toward the Taliban fighters. I look back toward my men a few meters behind me. "Set," I call out—telling them I'm in position and ready for us to maneuver toward the men shooting at us. The CAAT Marines are still loading into their vehicles back at Kunjak to head toward our position. The plan was for them to hit the Taliban once we lured them into attacking, but we were far from the location of our planned operation when they ambushed us. The CAAT team is more than a mile away. My men and I are alone. Thirteen Marines. One Corpsman. One photographer. Three cameras.

I sprint into the alley toward Chun and join him on the corner. He's only a few feet away, but it's as if there were miles between us, like I'm enveloped alone in this noise of battle. This is the first sustained heavy combat my squad has seen, and I'm scared of how they'll react with shit fast going sideways. We're getting lit up and we're already at a disadvantage. Two men are wounded. Two more are caring for them. I have nine men left and at least six enemy rifles and a grenadier trailing us. We've never been this deep into this town before. With every pull of our triggers, our supply of ammunition is depleting. We have no reinforcements. We have no resupply. The closest Marines would take fifteen minutes by vehicle to get within reach, but we'd still have to fight our way through half a mile of narrow alleyways to get to them. I question my decisions that got us here, but I can't afford to dwell on that now. I need to get us out of this mess. I can't afford anyone going "black," getting that look in their eyes, that look that means they've checked out and can no longer function. A mental casualty. This is make-it-or-break-it time, the moment when I find out whether I can trust my Marines. And whether they trust me after all the training and punishment I've put them through.

Chun and I check the alley for signs of IEDs. It's a painstaking process and usually a guess. We scan for any visible anomalies—unusual patterns on the ground, stacked rocks, or wires and plastic protruding from the earth. I notice something sticking out from the ground and carefully probe around it with my knife. It's the first suspected IED I've located under fire. I don't have Roche to help. I lean around the corner and holler to Gonzalez about what I've found.

As I look back, I see the Afghan police commander in charge of the three local policemen accompanying us on the mission. He's kneeling and holding an RPG launcher just outside the gate of our staging compound and exposed to incoming Taliban fire. The police officer's aim is too low to shoot the projectile across the field, and when he fires, the weapon's muzzle is aimed directly at Chun and me. I see the warhead wobbling toward me. I don't hear the explosion.

My head throbs as I look up from the ground. Smoke and dust float around me, but I don't know why. Rays of light make the sand floating in the air glimmer and shine. I look around and see a figure running through the cloud toward me, a figure with a weapon. He is wearing gear and camouflage. A Marine. Gonzalez.

"Brennan! Brennan, are you okay?" Gonzalez shouts.

I'm not sure. I struggle to understand where I am or what I'm doing. I remember the grenade and hitting the dirt, then nothing. Where is the warhead? There should have been an explosion. Slowly I realize the blast must have knocked me out. I grab my balls—still there. Hands and feet. Check. Then I remember Chun. I spin around to see him trying to stand and checking himself for injuries.

Gonzalez reaches us. "Brother, I thought you guys were dead. Get up! Let's go!"

Finbarr, Nabu Agha

I snap photos of TJ after the RPG hit, trying to run, teeth gritted, toward the compound entrance as his men open fire across the field. At the gate he falls to his knees. Gonzalez grabs him by the elbow and steers him up against a wall inside, where TJ collapses and pukes. He says the scene around him is spinning. He can't focus, his speech is slurred, and he shields his eyes from the sun's rays, saying the light feels like needles piercing his brain. I pick up TJ's sunglasses and hand them to him and move him into the shade. I take a few more photos as he sucks on a cigarette while leaning back against the wall. One of the images shows him leaning back, eyes closed. Once I have what I need, I stop photographing.

Everyone inside the compound initially feared TJ had triggered an IED. We are relieved it was only the RPG, but the blast from such a warhead still forms a ring of death: Anyone inside a twelve-foot radius will likely be torn to bits. Those outside the circle are still vulnerable to flying shrapnel and the invisible force of the blast wave. The power of the explosion decreases almost immediately as it moves away from the epicenter, but at close range the blast wave can crush bone and amputate limbs. Farther away it inflicts less visible damage. Its movement through human tissue is enough to force gas pockets inside the body to contract and to send blood and fluid sloshing into spaces that are normally empty. Organs can be knocked out of place. Most susceptible to such a pummeling are the inner ear, the lungs, and the brain—that three-pound mass of fat and protein that makes us who we are, and that responds most poorly to hard hits. TJ was just far enough away from the explosion to avoid the lethal blast radius, and the shrapnel somehow missed him, but the shock wave from the RPG still ripped through the delicate wiring of his brain like a baseball bat smashing a computer circuit board.

Incoming bullets are snapping overhead. The compound walls offer protection, but the Marines need to move out. With four men down, they are "combat ineffective." The mission is a dud. They have to evacuate the injured, but there's no safe landing zone for helicopters. Gonzalez radios for armored vehicles to drive up the wadi to transport TJ, Chun, Roche, and Orr back to OP Kunjak. To rendezvous with the vehicles, the Marines will have to navigate several hundred yards of alleyways. One of the vehicles hits an IED en route. Nobody is injured, but the truck has to limp back to base, delaying the convoy. Eventually, during a lull in the shooting, the Marines abandon the compound, egressing back the way they came. The injured Marines are scattered along the column and walking unevenly. Toward the rear, TJ struggles with each step. I'm behind him and close the gap to make sure he doesn't stumble off track. He's delirious and almost dragging his weapon, stopping every few minutes to lean against walls and vomit. I hook my hand under his damp armpit and steer him forward as he mumbles incoherently. As the squad reaches the wadi, the vehicles exchange fire with Taliban gunners shooting from a row of mud compounds on the edge of town. We wait for a lull before moving TJ and the others across a hundred yards of open ground to the convoy.

Once the four injured Marines are loaded into the armored vehicles, I join the remaining members of the squad for the thirty-minute slog back along the edge of the wadi toward OP Kunjak.

TJ, Nabu Agha–OP Kunjak

Inside the vehicle I remove my helmet and am examined by a Corpsman I don't know. He keeps asking what happened and if I know where we're going. The ride back is less than a mile, but the grinding of the diesel engine and the jarring shocks as the MRAP bounces over the stony riverbed make it seem much longer. I try to rest my head on the butt of my downturned rifle, but the Corpsman smacks my face and tells me to stay awake. Despite the rough ride, I float in and out of consciousness. I vomit the remnants of a fruit medley onto the lurching floor. I feel like an asshole and start heaving into my upturned helmet instead.

Our squad rarely works with vehicles, and not having to trudge up the hill to OP Kunjak is a relief. I'm in no shape to do that on my own. As we pull up to the outpost, the back door of the MRAP creaks open and Marines help me climb down the vehicle steps. While waiting for the helicopters to arrive, I walk to my bunk to pack a bag of essentials. I take my iPod, but also crossword puzzles, coffee grounds, and a single dirty sock, choices I will later wonder about. (My wife later jokes that I was just making sure I had my "happy sock" and that, even injured, I was as horny as ever.)

As two Black Hawk helicopters circle overhead, I swing on my body armor. The weight almost knocks me to the ground. Without thinking, I put my helmet on, forgetting I'd thrown up in it. Vomit oozes down my face. I toss the helmet on the ground and wipe the puke away. The helmet rolls downhill and fills with dirt. I pick it up and put it back on. The weight bears down on my skull and makes my eyes feel like they're about to burst. I shout at Chun to hurry up, then wince from the sharp pain caused by my own yell. At the foot of the hill below OP Kunjak, the rotor wash pelts me with dust and sand. The pulse of the rotors makes me stumble as I stagger through the red signal smoke marking the landing zone. Air Force medics pull me and Chun aboard.

Finbarr, OP Kunjak

The MEDEVAC units pride themselves on being able to extract the injured—civilian or military, foreign or Afghan, including insurgents—and getting them to a state-of-the-art field hospital within an hour of the initial injury, often less. Their ability to operate under fire while scooping up victims who have lost limbs or suffered other severe injuries from IED blasts, firefights, or motor vehicle accidents accounts for unprecedented battlefield survival rates. When the convoy reaches OP Kunjak, the injured are led from the trucks. Black Hawk helicopters are inbound to evacuate TJ and Chun to a combat hospital at Camp Leatherneck (Roche and Orr are not as seriously concussed and are driven to the Musa Qala District Center for medical observation at a field clinic). TJ's and Chun's injuries are deemed not potentially fatal, though, and the MEDEVAC birds respond to more urgent calls first. I arrive back at OP Kunjak with the rest of the squad, exhausted and sweating. TJ is sitting beside the central mud compound, having just been handed a satellite phone.

"Call your family and tell them you're alive," Gonzalez says. TJ struggles to remember his wife's cell phone number. She answers with a cheery "hello" that makes him smile.

"Baby, I've got my legs, I've got my arms, but I got blown up. They're taking me to the hospital. I love you and I'll call again as soon as I can." The exchange is short and, after hanging up, TJ drops the phone on the ground.

Someone helps TJ remove his equipment and strips him of his serialized gear. His ammunition, weapons, and maps are all accounted for. Even as TJ and the other injured Marines struggle to find their bearings, there is a procedure to follow, an overseeing military machine to be served.

But I'm also here to do a job. I upload photos via satellite to a Reuters feed every night, or more often, and I'm facing a deadline. Military restrictions prohibit me from publishing images of Marines who have been killed or injured without their permission, or before their families have been notified. Without wanting to be callous, I need TJ's permission to use the photos. I know I might not see him again for days or even weeks, if at all. By then the photos will have little news value. I assume, because he has called Mel, that his family will know what has happened.

It's late afternoon and the sun is softening.

"You okay with me using the pictures from today, or you want me to wait awhile?"

"Nah, fuck it. Use 'em," TJ says.

"You sure?"

"Yeah, what's the difference? Go ahead."

When the helicopters land at the foot of the hill, I walk down beside TJ. He's staggering as he walks through the rotor wash and is pulled aboard. I take a few frames of the helicopters spiraling upward, silhouetted against the sinking sun, the feet of the MEDEVAC crew dangling free from the open side doors of the Black Hawk as it banks away. And then they're gone.

Walking back uphill to OP Kunjak, my body and head ache. My ears are ringing from the gunfire and explosions. I still have to edit, process, caption, and transmit my pictures. I replay the day's events on my computer screen and feel the familiar twinge of disappointment. The challenge of combat photography is translating the kinetic energy of a firefight into static images. It's a rare photo that captures the drama of combat—indeed perhaps only a handful in history have managed to do so, which is what makes them so memorable. Robert Capa's grainy black-and-white images of the D-day landing on the beaches of Normandy are one example.

My images have none of the noise, heat, and fear I felt in the moment, to my eye. During the firefight, my senses were in overdrive—I heard and smelled and saw everything acutely. My mind processed stimuli at warp speed and time seemed to slow down. Pumped full of adrenaline, my mouth was dry and my breathing was fast. My fingers were clumsy on the dials of my camera. I was hyperaware of what was unfolding around me, and yet it seemed like a video game. Only after TJ was hit did the gravity of the situation sink in. I felt odd taking photos of him in pain. I'd photographed injuries before, but this was the first time that the subject was someone I knew. I kept photographing until it didn't feel right to continue. I drew the line at photographing him vomiting. I focused instead on trying to convey the concern among his squad mates for his well-being. Looking at my computer screen, however, I feel like I've failed to capture something important, even though such incidents are just a variation of what happens daily in Afghanistan. But maybe that's the point: The battle will not change the course of history, nor of the war, but it will change the lives of those who were involved. And if history is made up of the lives of those who live it, then I want to capture not only a record of events but also something more, something lasting. I haven't succeeded. I hit the "send" button, unaware of the impact my images will soon have on TJ's mother when she clicks on a link directing her to photos of her injured son.

I shut down my computer and crawl into my sleeping bag. The outpost is quiet. For the first time in two weeks TJ's cot beside mine is empty.

Chapter 4

Walking Wounded

The human brain has 100 billion neurons, each neuron connected to ten thousand other neurons. Sitting on your shoulders is the most complicated object in the known universe.

—Physicist Michio Kaku, *The Future of the Mind*

TJ, Camp Leatherneck Field Hospital, Afghanistan, November 2010

As the Black Hawk banks up and away, I watch Kunjak shrink below. My flight is a cascade of noise and light and disjointed words and thoughts and emotions and memories as the altitude tightens a vise on my skull. My ears pop when the bird finally lands on the tarmac at Camp Bastion—one of the largest coalition field hospitals in Afghanistan. Two female British army nurses are waiting to escort us into the hospital. The nurses smell of body wash and perfume and seem like the most beautiful women I've ever seen.

"You smell so good, this is almost worth it," I tell them. They laugh. These are the first smiles I've seen from women since, well, I can't recall.

As we are escorted into the emergency room, blood is pooled on the floor in a trauma bay behind a blue curtain. I stare at the crimson splashes and the gauze and bandages strewn about. At least they didn't leave any severed limbs lying around. It's eerily quiet and not what I expected during our flight. I thought the hospital would look like a scene out of *M*A*S*H*—the 1970s television show about an Army surgical unit during the Korean War, where green vinyl tents with minimal supplies were the norm for treating casualties. Instead it's a steel building outfitted with top-notch medical equipment—MRI and CT (computerized tomography) imaging, surgical wards, and electricity—the latter a comfort I'm no longer used to. If anyone else is being treated, we can't tell.

Chun and I remain under observation for several hours and are made to perform a battery of simple cognitive tests. The U.S. Navy Corpsman asks my wife's name. I pause before I answer. The sailor then asks me my daughter's name. I can't remember. I struggle, and weep.

During my CT scan, I almost fall asleep on the table. The technician tells me it doesn't look like I have a brain bleed. But the CT scan does not measure brain function. No piece of machinery in Afghanistan can determine whether I might have any long-term brain damage.

After the CT scan, Chun and I remain in the emergency room under observation for a few more hours. When we step outside afterward, the stars are gleaming. We are brought to a concussion rehab and recovery ward with recreation room, office, canteen, computers, TVs, phones, and sectioned-off sleeping area. Half the fluorescent bulbs have been removed from the overheard tube lighting to make the room dimmer and less abrasive for patients. I walk outside and call home to Mel, but I'm barely coherent and repeat the same conversation. Mel, a nurse back home, is alarmed by my list of symptoms and makes me promise to report my twitching eyelids to the doctor.

When I go inside, my entire body aches. It feels like I've been cross-checked by a professional hockey player. As I sit down on a bench outside the showers, my back burns and my knees pop. The hospital staff at Camp Bastion has removed my camouflage blouse and rigger's belt, along with my plate carrier, Kevlar helmet, wallet, and knives. The only personal item I have with me is a St. Michael medallion my grandpa, World War II sailor John Nugent, gave me before my first deployment to Iraq. Generations of veterans claim that there are no atheists in foxholes. Raised Catholic, I lost faith in religion as a teenager. My belief in a God is something I've always struggled with, but as I stare at the medallion, I begin to question my belief in the existence of any kind of deity. No God would allow their creation to even contemplate war.

I put the silver chain back in my pocket and examine my worn boots as I hunch toward the floor. My fingers fumble with the laces. I know exactly what I need to do to untie my boots, but my fingers won't cooperate. It's like my hands aren't listening to my brain. I begin tearing at the laces, becoming so frustrated that I cry. I feel helpless and don't know why I'm so emotional since the blast. I calm myself down and try to untie them more slowly. I talk to myself as if I were trying to teach my two-year-old daughter something. I remember her name. Maddie. I laugh at the thought of her having to untie my shoes for me when I get home.

I must sound like a lunatic—a twenty-five-year-old man laughing, cursing, and crying because I can't untie my boots. I do lots of cursing. I tell myself that nobody is tying or untying my boots for me as long as I have both my hands. I finally get my boots off. I take my first hot shower in more than two months. Holding my head, I'm disgusted by the dirt and skin and hair and filth curling down the drain. I change into freshly issued sweatpants and a sweatshirt. My skin is so dry my whole body itches. A U.S. Air Force medic tells me I will be woken every four hours to check for vital signs, but after collapsing into a metal-frame bed with a soft spring mattress, I remember nothing more from that night.

When I wake the next morning, I'm initially unsure of where I am, or why. Stepping outside for a cigarette, I catch myself scanning the gravel pathway for IEDs even though I know I'm safe. With every step I fear an explosion will rip my legs off. I feel lost and vulnerable without Roche to clear the path in front of me. It's the first time I've walked anywhere safe in more than ninety days. Despite the cool morning air, I'm sweating. Chain-smoking, I struggle to recall events from the previous day. My mind skips from memory to memory, from Iraq to Afghanistan, from life to death, from family to enemy. It wasn't the enemy that blew me up. It was an ally. Had the Afghan policeman fired on me intentionally, or was he really that poorly trained? Was I to blame?

Back inside the recovery room, I discover a white archway spanning the center of the hall. It's the width of my arm span, eight feet high, and covered in hundreds of signatures. Chun explains that every patient who passes through the concussion ward signs the arch upon leaving. As Chun searches for his own name—this is his third trip here—I study the clutter of colored handwriting. Each scrawled name represents an invisible scar carved inside a human skull, a brain rattled, a mind scrambled, a life altered. For all the high-tech weaponry of modern wars—the jets, the artillery, the digital surveillance drones, the laser-guided missiles, the tanks and armored vehicles—it is the simple roadside bomb that inflicts the most damage on the American military and its psyche. Usually fashioned from plastic jugs or kitchen pots, mobile phones or speaker wires, and using explosives made from fertilizer, the roadside bomb is effective not only at killing and maiming but also at instilling a profound level of psychological stress from constant fear. It doesn't even have to be there to be effective. It takes a toll on the human mind through the mere possibility of its presence.

Traumatic brain injury (TBI) is the signature war wound of both Iraq and Afghanistan. More than 357,048 U.S. service members have suffered traumatic brain injuries. The annual number increased every year from the invasion of Afghanistan in 2001, when 11,619 TBIs were recorded by the Department of Defense, through to 2011, when 32,625 TBIs made it the worst year on record (the annual number of recorded TBIs remained steady, averaging around 25,000 per year from 2012 to 2015, when most U.S. forces withdrew from Afghanistan). The injuries and symptoms range from mild—such as language, balance, and mood problems—to severe, debilitating brain damage. If treated early and well, sufferers can experience varying degrees of recovery. But all the research indicates that those with a TBI are far more likely to succumb to depression, post-traumatic stress, and suicide. We will also live with a higher likelihood of being afflicted with dementia, Alzheimer's disease, Parkinson's disease, and other degenerative neurological disorders. Even if we don't forget something in the immediate aftermath of the blast, residual effects might cripple our minds with age. We were told a bit about brain injuries during training, but most Marines, including me, paid little attention. It wasn't a priority, until now.

I'm summoned into a psychiatric nurse's office. There are chairs, a couch, and a bed. I'm unsure where to sit and assume the confusing array of furniture is some cruel psychological test. I move to a corner where I can observe the entire room, including the door. Sitting diagonally across from me, the nurse asks a series of uncomfortable questions about what happened and why I'm here. I'm in no mood to talk. Who is this woman, anyway? Has she ever seen combat, seen friends killed and maimed? No fucking way am I going to tell some desk jockey what I'm really thinking, or share the emotions tearing at my insides. When she asks how I feel about my men being wounded, I break down in tears.

"I hate this psychobabble bullshit," I say as I stand to leave. I tell the nurse I'm neither suicidal nor homicidal and insist I do not have PTSD. "I'm not a pussy," I mutter. I say there is no point in discussing combat with someone who has never experienced it. The nurse sits calmly as I open the door. Then she tells me I won't be allowed to go back to my men if I don't talk to her. I release the handle and the door clicks shut. The nurse says she may not empathize with me, but she can sympathize, and that she would like for me to sit down and talk with her.

"But," she says, "if you want to leave, we can try again tomorrow."

Desperate to return to duty, I relent, turn, wipe the tears from my face, and walk back to my chair, forcing a poof of air from the cushion as I sit.

"How do you think I feel about getting my guys hurt?" I ask. "I feel like shit. I feel like a failure."

I spend the next hour answering the nurse's questions, my face growing more flushed with each round of query. I feel tears roll down my cheeks as I recount the extreme brutality of things I saw and did in Iraq. *Fuck it*, I think. *If she wants to hear about combat and loss, I have stories to tell.* Too many stories. But the more I reveal, the deeper she digs. I wonder whether she is taking some perverse pleasure in making me cry. It takes nearly the entire session, but I realize she's just letting me ramble, and I'm the one delving deep into disturbing memories. When we are finished, I shake the nurse's hand and she tells me to come back anytime. But all I want to do is leave.

My spirits are lifted when I'm moved the next day to the wounded warrior barracks at the adjacent base, Camp Leatherneck. It's the green vinyl *M*A*S*H* tent I expected in place of the hospital on Camp Bastion, except we have televisions, video games, Internet, and heaps of fat-kid food. I'm one step closer to returning to OP Kunjak, and I feel reassured when I'm not shipped to another base for more serious treatment. Still, I know I'll need to mask the difficulty I've been having finding my way around the base. Navigating from bunk to bathroom is a challenge.

During a doctor's appointment, I admit to having severe headaches, balance problems, and memory lapses. The doctor assures me these symptoms should pass after a few days' rest and asks about prior concussions. I tell him I was shot in the helmet with a pistol round in Fallujah. For days afterward my ears rang, I had headaches, and I was often confused. During the same operation, an RPG exploded nearby, causing more severe symptoms. And as a demolition specialist, I'm often exposed to blasts.

By carefully calculating overpressure—the strength of an explosion's blast waves—infantry assaultmen like me are able to stand very close to steel-shattering explosions, often just a few feet away. It's one way I get to confront death and come out on top, as long as I do my math correctly. It's one of my job perks.

The doctor explains that I've probably suffered at least three serious concussions in combat throughout my career. No shit. It's not like I forgot that part. In the early days of the Iraq war, those of us with concussions were often returned to duty without time to recover. In Fallujah an RPG exploded near me and my team leader, leaving both of us dizzy and sensitive to light. We were returned to duty the same day and were engaged in heavy fighting for weeks afterward. No medical team ever evaluated us. It was only as the wars dragged on, and the number of head injuries mounted, that the military began to recognize that concussions required greater care and attention. As TBIs emerged as a growing problem, new protective measures were implemented, removing the concussed from the battlefield for observation and treatment. Anyone with more than three concussions was automatically relieved from combat duty for the remainder of that deployment. I'm scheduled for an automated neuropsychological assessment metrics (ANAM) test to evaluate my brain function and reaction time. The doctor also informs me that the results of my predeployment ANAM test have not been sent to Afghanistan, so there is no baseline for a comparison. I wonder how the extent of any brain damage will be measured.

I'm given Motrin for the headaches and ten milligrams of Ambien to help me sleep. Drugged up in my bunk, I try to relive the firefight in my mind. It plays like a flip book with too many pages missing. I don't remember the blast or walking toward the wadi to be medically evacuated. I remember throwing up in my Kevlar and calling Mel, but not what I said to her. I know two of my men were wounded—Roche and Orr—but I question whether sending them into that alley was a mistake.

The doctors tell me I'll be fine and make a full recovery, but I begin to worry about whether my men will trust my leadership once I return to duty. I hope it's just the drugs that are making my mind foggy and lethargic—many of the other wounded Marines and Corpsmen in the recovery ward complain about the same things—but I've got enough mental clarity to know something isn't right. It seems as though all of us are equally confused, but we all want to get back to our men.

For the next few days I call Mel and Maddie between my marathon sleep sessions and surf the Internet and Facebook to see what's happening back home. I'm not surprised that Iraq and Afghanistan are mere blips for American media and public. Miley Cyrus's birthday is coming up, and one of the deadliest months of the Afghan war can't compete with things like that. The online universe is populated with silly videos and memes, news of the latest Madonna scandal, and warnings of a financial apocalypse.

I fail the ANAM test several days in a row, which leaves me frustrated and depressed. I try to cheat the test and lie about my headaches and bouts of dizziness. I don't report my reduced depth perception or my eye twitch. When I'm monitored during a one-mile run on a dusty track behind the clinic, my head pounds, the road appears to lurch in front of me, and I lose my breath, but I tell the medical staff I'm just out of shape from lying around for several days. Eventually I pass—barely. On November 8, one week after the explosion, I finally get some good news, which I share in a Facebook post: "I passed my brain scan today. Although many of you would beg to differ, it turns out I do have a functioning brain inside of my skull. I'm cleared to return to the fight!!"

Weather and full flights delay me five more days, but eventually I secure a ride back. As I sit shivering on the flight line waiting for the helicopter, I consider returning to the clinic and admitting I lied to pass the tests declaring me fit for duty. But I'm afraid of being reprimanded or, worse, of being considered a coward. I already worry that I've lost the respect of my men by getting myself—and them—injured. It's not the time to show weakness. Even though my mental lapses could put my squad at even greater risk, I decide the best thing for us is to be reunited. I vow to myself that if my ability to lead them into battle is genuinely affected, I'll resign as squad leader, no matter the cost to my career or my reputation.

Chapter 5

The In-between

You get paid to travel to the most interesting places at the most interesting times. What do you lose? Each time you lose a little bit of your heart.

—Rory Peck, freelance cameraman killed covering the 1991 coup in Russia

Finbarr, Afghanistan, Paris, Tunisia, and Afghanistan, November 2010–March 2011

On November 2, the day after the ambush, I receive an e-mail from an editor at the *New York Times* photography blog, *Lens*, which published the photo of TJ looking miserable in his bunk three days ago. *Lens* has published another photo of TJ in its "pictures of the day" selection, this time showing him sitting injured in the compound after the explosion.

"I was very struck by the fact that we have now run your pictures, back to back, of Sgt. Brennan: first, in his makeshift quarters last week; yesterday, after he was injured," reads the e-mail from the editor. "Among other things, it suggests to me that one of the toughest things about being a photojournalist in your position is getting to know people who are, first and foremost, in harm's way. I'm assuming you have some kind of rapport with Sgt. Brennan to have been permitted to take the rather intimate picture you took last week. And then to watch him suffer a concussion just a few days later—this is really something difficult to fathom. I'm wondering if you would have a moment now to share some thoughts on this subject for a post on the Lens blog. Also, do you know of his current condition?"

I respond and send a draft of the story through to TJ on Facebook, detailing how I see things from my side of the lens and what life looks like with a squad of infantry Marines.

"Living in such close quarters—and the intensity of being shoulder-to-shoulder during combat—forges a rare level of kinship and loyalty among men. As a journalist, you are not exempt from this bond, which makes remaining entirely objective difficult."

I mention sharing the traumatic experience of drinking Marine Corps coffee, converting files for Marines' iPods, how getting to know the Marines only made it harder to photograph TJ when he was wounded, and how, as TJ puts it, "in the scheme of things, a concussion was a favorable outcome."

When TJ logs in from the field hospital on November 4, he approves the story while reiterating his desire to get back to work.

"It feels really surreal and I'm having a really hard time trying to piece it all together in my head," he writes to me over Facebook. "It doesn't feel like I'm really a victim of the incident. I feel like I abandoned my guys at Kunjak. . . . It just feels like I shouldn't be here right now. I need to be out there with my guys."

A few days later, I'm waiting for TJ when he arrives by helicopter back at Musa Qala District Center, his battalion's main base. I want to catch him before he hops on a convoy for the half-hour drive to OP Kunjak. I track him down in a transit tent, where he's sitting on a camp cot. His mother, who has yet to tell me the story of seeing my photos, has e-mailed me and asked me to give him a big "mommy hug." We embrace. It's kind of awkward, but we laugh.

We have a few hours to catch up over lunch before his ride to OP Kunjak is due to depart. We bypass the Marine chow hall and instead share an overpriced meal of fresh grilled chicken and greasy fries cooked by an Afghan vendor allowed on base. Things could have been much worse on the day TJ and his men got hurt. The mission was a bust, but all the Marines, including TJ, survived the blasts with no limbs lost or other obvious physical injuries. All returned to duty. Still, I wonder. Winter is closing in, and though the intensity of fighting will ease until the warmer months of spring, the threat of IEDs increases as the insurgents turn to hit-and-run tactics. The unpredictability of roadside bombs and the lack of a visible enemy only ratchet up the psychological stress levels. Helmand Province is as deadly as ever.

When it's time for TJ's convoy to leave, I see him off. He's wearing a borrowed helmet that's too big. It flops down over his forehead and he tilts his head back to peer under the brim. He has no weapon—his rifle was kept at OP Kunjak when he was medically evacuated. I photograph him as he climbs up into the armored hull of the MRAP vehicle. He grins back. "Do you ever put that camera down?" he asks. "Or would you be totally lost without it?"

We say our good-byes and the heavy door slams shut. With a low grinding of gears, the convoy pulls away toward the compound gates.

The intimacy required to do my job often makes leaving a place difficult once the assignment is over. And this assignment has been more intimate than most. TJ and I talked over the weeks about my career and about the parallels between our unconventional lives: the months away from home, the living in foreign lands, the routine threat of bodily harm. Still, the parallels go only so far. He's a Marine, bound by his oath, and honor, and the rule of law, to take orders and follow a chain of command, even unto his own death. And I'm a photographer—bound by my own codes and contracts, sure, but ultimately free to come and go as I please. TJ says he envies that freedom. He has openly wondered whether the regimented life of a Marine is still something he wants.

But things have happened, and are still happening, that will set us both on unpredicted courses. Beneath TJ's skull, the aftermath of the grenade blast is still unraveling; it will ultimately churn a golf-ball-sized section of his right frontal lobe into a lump of dead matter—a brain injury of life-altering proportions.

And outside, beyond Kunjak, the world is churning too. The impending chaos of the Arab uprisings is about to make the coming year one of the deadliest yet for frontline journalists.

I leave the base the day after TJ. It's mid-November. I fly out at night on a darkened Chinook helicopter that lands and then takes off as tracer fire arcs through the night sky. It's impossible to know whether it's hostile or just celebratory fire from a wedding or funeral in Musa Qala town, but the bird fires decoy flares to ward off any surface-to-air missiles just in case. I'm transported over invisible deserts in the glowing green belly of the clattering hydraulic machine to Kandahar, where I board a flight to Dubai. Less than twenty-four hours after leaving Helmand, I'm spread out on the soft cotton sheets of a five-star hotel, ordering a burger and a beer from room service after my first proper shower in more than a month. I stand for ages under the stream of hot water and scrub myself with floral soaps. I still don't feel clean.

The next day I travel to France and arrive just in time for Paris Photo, an annual photography festival described by an editor friend as a strange event combining absurdity, talent, and boredom, not necessarily in that order. Helmand's dirt is still wedged under my fingernails as I make my way through the streets. My hypervigilance and IED paranoia are handy when it comes to avoiding the ubiquitous *crottes de chiens*—the piles of dog shit that litter Paris sidewalks. Every year in France some six hundred and fifty people are hospitalized for injuries (usually broken collar bones) sustained by slipping on dog shit and falling. Not exactly as dangerous as an IED, but before my first trip to Afghanistan in 2007, I often trod in the vile stuff. Not anymore. I'm now expert at minding the path in front of me.

The festival is being held in a sprawling exhibition space beneath the Louvre. I find it crammed with booths and books and prints and people. Crowds mill about and conversations unfold around me. I run into two editor friends; they comment on my long beard, asking in jest which side I've been embedded with. They say I look gaunt and disoriented. I try chatting, but I can't focus on what people are saying. The conversations seem trivial and my mind keeps skipping back to Kunjak, wondering what's happening there. Eventually the crowd is too much. I feel smothered. In the middle of a conversation I walk away.

On my way to the door, amid the chatter and the kaleidoscope of showcased images, I notice one picture in particular, a 1972 black-and-white photograph taken in Martinique by the Hungarian photographer André Kertész. It shows the shape of a solitary man silhouetted behind a frosted pane of glass and looking out to sea. The clean and sharp composition is like a beacon of tranquillity. The image lingers in my mind.

Photography can be a strange pursuit. It requires intense engagement and the ability to withdraw and go unnoticed. I've always been naturally withdrawn and solitary. I can be social, but I'm most comfortable within my own space. Photography has been my excuse for interacting with others, an introvert's key to an external world. The vanishing act photographers must perform in pursuit of their craft is captured by the American novelist Hanya Yanagihara in a 2016 essay for the *New Yorker*.

"If love belongs to the poet, and fear to the novelist, then loneliness belongs to the photographer," she writes. "To be a photographer is to willingly enter the world of the lonely, because it is an artistic exercise in invisibility. The person with the camera is not hiding but receding. She is willfully removing herself from the slipstream of life; she is making herself into a constant witness, someone who lives to see the lives of others, not to be seen herself. To practice this art requires first a commitment to self-erasure."

War has been imprinted upon my mind and it always takes time to fade. By the time I met TJ in Afghanistan, I'd spent nearly a decade covering wars, famines, refugee crises, ethnic conflicts, plane crashes, and natural disasters. Readjusting to the "real world" always takes time. I know my mind needs to recalibrate itself, and for days while walking down Paris streets or riding the London Underground I feel like I'm watching myself from above as I drift through crowds of commuters. There's a powerful sense of disconnect. I'm at once detached and hypervigilant. My mind fades in and out of this out-of-body state for up to a week before I settle back into the modern world of high-tech distractions. The temporary detachment isn't unpleasant, but I know from experience that there's a longer-lasting and more troubling fallout to be reckoned with. I've seen other journalists become strung out and unable to adjust to normal life, always rushing off to cover the latest upsurge of violence in some distant land, as if solace can be found amid the bullets and bombs. I'm as guilty as anyone of chasing misery and war. It's not that the adrenaline is addictive but that it's easier to adapt to extremes than to tedium. After the intensity of war and combat, everything else feels irrelevant. When leaving a place like Afghanistan, it's difficult to switch off. The temptation is to keep the motor running, to keep producing images, getting the instant gratification of publication, and basking in the thrill of living on the so-called cusp of history.

Afghanistan is just my latest stop on a continuum of conflict, and ironically, that's one of the reasons I wanted to go there—the risks seemed more manageable compared to Africa, plus the military would take care of all the logistics, including food, transport, and security—my version of a holiday. Even as I left Kunjak, I was angling for an assignment to Haiti to work on a project marking the anniversary of the 2010 earthquake that killed some 200,000 people. Violence has become a regular part of my life. I've begun to wonder how long I can keep up the pace.

I've been based in Dakar, Senegal, since 2005, and my area of responsibility in West and Central Africa is often in crisis. Journalists joke there's a template of unrest that rotates around the region. On my first assignment as a photographer in 2005 (I'd been working as a text correspondent in the region since 2001), I covered disputed elections in Togo. There were running street clashes between opposition supporters and security forces. I was in a slum when election results were announced on the radio, confirming that the incumbent had won. Crowds of angry opposition youth armed with machetes tried to pull a South African photographer and me from the battered taxi we had hired. We shouted at the terrified driver to smash through burning barricades and over a railway line to escape the bloodthirsty mob as it closed in and hurled chunks of concrete and stones at the car.

It was a fitting welcome to West Africa. The years that followed are a blur of conflicts and challenging assignments. I soon lost count of all the times I'd been teargassed, stoned, shot at, spit on, detained, and harassed. It's part of the job. As a Western journalist I at least enjoy a level of protection local journalists and civilians do not. I always have the option to leave; they don't. Mostly the hassles are just that—a nuisance to be dealt with. But then there are days when the violence boils over.

One of those days came on July 27, 2006. It was the final day of election rallies ahead of Congo's first democratic elections. The United Nations had invested half a billion dollars in the historic vote. The country had endured a century of colonial exploitation, forty years of brutal dictatorship, and a decade of regional war that had killed more people than any conflict since World War II. But the legacy of violence was too strong for outside forces to dampen. The philosopher Frantz Fanon once observed the African continent is shaped like a gun, and Congo is the trigger. On that day I felt it being squeezed.

With a handful of other local and foreign journalists, I was covering rising tensions between the incumbent president, Joseph Kabila, and the former warlord and opposition presidential candidate, Jean-Pierre Bemba, in the capital, Kinshasa. Confrontations and shoot-outs between Bemba's militias and Kabila's bodyguards were common, and skirmishes between supporters of both sides were escalating. Then, on July 27, things got out of hand. Tens of thousands of Bemba supporters rampaged through the streets, looting shops and houses and overrunning riot police. Several policemen were captured, doused in gasoline, and set on fire, and their corpses were dragged through the city, charred bones poking through blackened flesh. Women were attacked and raped on broken sidewalks.

Smoke rose from a burning church across a dusty road from the Tata Raphael Stadium. A tide of Bemba supporters pushed through the stadium's rusted metal gates, overwhelming Bemba's own security detail of militiamen, who carried AK-47s and wore ill-fitting khaki uniforms. The crowd filled the concrete stands and spilled over onto the parched field.

I fought my way into the stadium through a surge of people pulling at my clothes, taunting, grabbing. On the balding pitch, sweating youths held up trophies salvaged from the murdered cops—a cracked helmet, a torn police jacket and what looked like part of a hand.

I had lived in Congo for two years and was used to navigating the sweltering heat, the insecurity, and the daily hostility from Bemba supporters who accused Western powers of backing President Joseph Kabila. But something felt different that day. Something had been unleashed.

A call came through on my mobile phone from my friend Marco Longari, a photographer for Agence France-Presse who had been following Bemba and a swelling mass of supporters headed to the rally.

"Get out of the stadium," Marco's voice crackled over the din of the crowd. With no outlet for their rage, a generation of angry, unemployed youth was venting its frustration on the only Westerners they encountered—foreign journalists. "You have to get out of there now," Marco said. "They will kill you."

But there was no way out. The seething crowd had clogged the entrances to the stadium. This was the same stadium where Muhammad Ali outslugged George Foreman on October 30, 1974, during the "Rumble in the Jungle." Back then, Congo was known as Zaire. The capacity crowd of thirty thousand that rainy night included James Brown, Norman Mailer, and the dictator Mobutu Sese Seko, who had orchestrated the event. It was also the place where Mobutu's henchmen tortured political prisoners in the dark tunnels beneath the stands. Some prisoners were said to have been executed and buried beneath the soccer pitch.

Word raced around the stadium that a bomb had exploded at Bemba's headquarters and that several people had been killed, including a woman and a child. Wild rumors spread through the mob of Congolese, who are always quick to blame the former colonial power, Belgium. The West. The whites.

The crowd's focus narrowed on us, the seven foreign journalists trapped in the middle of the field. Images of the mob parading the dead policemen's clothing and body parts flickered to mind. I looped my camera's shoulder straps across my body, rather than letting them hang loose for easy use, and braced for the onslaught. It wasn't my cameras I needed to worry about. I had a metallic taste in my mouth, my stomach tightened, panic rose in my chest.

"You! You whites!" a man in the crowd screamed. His spittle sprayed my face. "You support Kabila! You are criminals, spies, liars! We will kill you and eat you." Those around him cheered. Another man swiped his finger across his throat, the whites of his eyes flashing fury and hate. The crowd closed in. Fists pummeled my head and shoulders. I broke away, but only for a moment. There was nowhere to go.

There is no negotiating with an angry mob. It becomes a singular living thing with a will of its own. Psychologists say crowds are the most dangerous human phenomenon. Individuals feel less responsible for their actions when others around them behave the same way. Add to this an absence of the rule of law and a moral fabric eroded by decades of deprivation and war, and it's easy to see why the stadium had become a cauldron of aggression, and why our faces paled despite the heat and sun. The noose tightened.

There was a commotion at the far corner of the stadium and the crowd's attention turned to a motorcade carrying the hulking Bemba, triumphant, into our midst. The swarm of hands plunging into my pockets and ripping at my clothes and cameras withdrew. The dusty ground before me opened up as the crowd surged toward Bemba, who was riding atop an open car. He was built like a tank, with no neck, his shaved head a turret atop broad shoulders. His arrival ended our beating. Bemba too was swarmed as he pushed his way through the throng and climbed onto a makeshift stage at the center of the field. Seeking safety, we journalists gathered close to his security detail.

Our only chance of escape was to leave while Bemba was speaking and the crowd was distracted. I elbowed my way to Bemba's security chief and implored him to provide armed escorts to get us out. He agreed—perhaps realizing a handful of dead journalists would not be good PR for a presidential candidate, at least not beyond these walls.

Four armed escorts led us down broken concrete stairwells into the stadium's labyrinth of tunnels. As we descended deeper into darkness, the roar of the crowd faded, replaced by the stink of stale sweat and urine.

We emerged back into the searing daylight of the stadium's parking lot—and an even bigger, more hostile crowd.

The earlier threat echoed in my mind. "We will kill you and eat you!"

The mob moved in. We were pushed, shoved, beaten, spit upon. We moved forward, elbows up, cameras held tight to our bodies. The crowd threw chunks of brick and stone in our direction. A black plastic bag flew past me and exploded nearby, spraying human shit across the pavement. Our militia escorts pushed us through, racking their weapons and pointing them at the crowd and clubbing people with truncheons. One escort pulled out a hand grenade and held it to the faces of some of those shouting at us—an odd form of crowd control, but it created just enough space for us to break free. Smaller groups pursued us with more stones and bricks, closing steadily.

"Where are your cars?" an escort shouted as he pushed people back. We tried to call our drivers, but they couldn't hear us over the throng. Eventually we saw one of our cars a few blocks away, across open ground. We made for it, a growing crowd following us. Seven journalists piled into the tiny two-door Toyota, some spilling out of the open trunk as the old car limped slowly away under a deluge of fists, stones, and other projectiles that dented the doors and smashed the lights.

From the backseat I shoved a fistful of grubby Congolese bank notes out the window and into the groping hands of one of the militiamen as thanks. The mob collapsed upon him, grabbing the money. And we were away, the crowd and the violence receding in the side mirror, now cracked.

Back at the hotel that night, we sat under a giant banyan tree drinking cold Primus beers, nerves still jangling.

"I knew if I ended up down on my knees, that would have been it. I had to stay standing no matter what," said one seasoned independent photographer who had covered Congo for two decades. "I don't have the heart or the balls for this any more. I'm leaving tomorrow and I'm not coming back."

He did leave, and he hasn't returned. As a staff photographer I wasn't so free to walk away. I was back on the streets the next morning.

I try not to let the grimmer aspects of the job get me down. Like TJ, I've developed a mental checklist of my own—reminders of things to do to keep me grounded: exercise regularly, see friends as often as I can, don't drink too much, create goals that I can work toward, even if that only involves getting out to surf three or four times a week. If I'm active, social, and working with purpose, things tend to be all right. And I'm aware that things often look bleaker than they really are. My situation is different from TJ's. I've witnessed people dying in conflict zones, but I've never done the killing, or been responsible for those who did. I've been shot at, but I've never taken a pistol round to the helmet. Shells fired by the Taliban have exploded close enough to knock me over and shower me with dirt, but I've never had anything more than a headache and a good fright as a result.

There's a paradox to the war photographer's existence. We put ourselves in positions of danger and discomfort, but usually for limited amounts of time. We endure hardships knowing they'll soon be over and that we can return to the comforts of "normal life," to our newsrooms or favorite restaurants, to dinner parties or cafés, to the beach or the mountains, to our friends and families. That's part of the appeal of the job. The lifestyle is a passport to unlimited excitement, brushes with mortality, and immediate gratification; and, after the self-imposed deprivations, simple pleasures become amplified. Food has more flavor, bedsheets feel softer, a hot shower is sublime. Few things taste better than that first beer after leaving Afghanistan. At Kunjak TJ fantasized about being home and pulling on a pair of jeans fresh from the dryer, the denim still warm and snug and smelling of fabric softener, the zipper and metal studs hot to the touch. As for sex, well, the softness and warmth of a woman's skin, or the smell of her hair, is beyond compare. Men may go to war to prove themselves and to become brothers-in-arms, but they come home for the women. Brennan's description of dressing in warm jeans is nothing compared to the colorful fantasies Marines (and journalists) share about their women—wives, girlfriends, exes, and one-night stands.

Flitting from one war zone to another is like having multiple lovers; it feeds the ego and fulfills a desire for excitement and conquest. But it can be equally superficial and leave you feeling empty, alone, and adrift. The violence of war becomes normal and anything else seems disorienting and unsettling, even unbearable, which helps explain why so many service members reenlist and return to war after failed stints back home. For me the emotional disconnect upon returning home is countered by the hyperarousal of the physical senses. Somewhere between is a layer of guilt. Enjoying life after war somehow feels wrong.

Living a mostly solitary lifestyle far from close friends and family leaves me without the kind of social support network that helps with decompression and transition after being at war. Depression creeps forward and things go numb. When I first started covering conflict, I coped well with the aftermath of violence. I was never reckless or particularly brave, but I worked well under pressure and moved comfortably through precarious situations. It was easy to separate personal involvement from the job at hand and to keep my emotions in check. That worked just fine for years. I could handle covering lethal clashes in Togo, interviewing gang-rape survivors in Rwanda and Congo, or photographing starving infants in Niger and Sudan as they exhaled their final breaths. It was disturbing, sure, but I always moved on. The most upsetting images would sometimes linger, but eventually they would fade or be replaced by fresh ones. All in all, it didn't seem so bad.

But 2007 marked a gradual shift in that attitude. The year started well enough with an assignment to cover New York Fashion Week, followed by presidential elections in Senegal, Mauritania, and Nigeria. During the first week of May, I was back in New York on vacation and partying hard with friends. A few days later, I was in Cameroon covering a plane crash in a fetid swamp. All 114 passengers and crew had been killed. Among them was an Anthony Mitchell, a Nairobi-based Associated Press correspondent who was returning home to Kenya after an assignment.

The smell in the mangrove swamp hit me first. Tropical heat meant bodies rotted quickly. The plane had come down nose first, creating a circular crater filled with black oily water. Corpses pulped on impact were hard to distinguish from the muck. As masked salvage workers picked through the debris, I photographed a wallet, a mobile phone, a digital recorder, a laptop computer, and a passport. Some items felt too personal to photograph—smiling family pictures, birthday cards, intimate letters, and identity documents. From the beginning, my presence felt like an intrusion; we all slow down at the scene of an accident, gazing at someone else's misfortune. Was I just feeding the public appetite for the macabre?

On the way to the crash site, I'd met Kamal Shah, a thirty-two-year-old Kenyan whose wife, Meera, thirty, was on the plane on her way home from a short business trip. With family members banned from the crash

site, I'd helped Shah pose as a journalist to gain access. As I busied myself
with work, Shah slowly and silently picked his way through the stinking
mud, twisted metal, tree roots, scattered clothing, a dead snake, and
other debris. After a while, he came up to me, covered in mud and sweating. Somehow, he'd recovered his wife's wallet from the mess.

"It means a lot just to find this, to see her smile on her photo ID," he
said, his lips and hands trembling.

I left Shah to make a phone call back to the news desk in Dakar. Leaning against a tree, the ground was soft underfoot. Looking down, I saw
that I was standing on a disintegrating corpse. I left the crash site soon
after. Since that day, the smell of jet fuel always transports me back to
that sweltering swamp. It wasn't the grisly scene that bothered me so
much. I could handle that. What affected me was the uncertainty about
my role. Shah had a reason to be there. I just felt like a parasite. It was,
perhaps, a crack into which later traumas would become wedged.

Toward the end of 2007, during my second trip to Afghanistan, I spent
five weeks on foot patrols and covering combat operations in Kandahar's
kinetic Panjwaii District. One ambush in particular shook me up pretty
good for a few weeks afterward. I was in the hamlet of Howz-e Madad in
Kandahar's Zhari District with Canadian and Afghan forces planning an
operation similar in design to the one that would get TJ injured a few
years later. The soldiers planned to set up a roadside checkpoint as bait to
tempt a Taliban attack in an area where vehicles were frequently being
targeted along the main road between Kandahar and Lashkar Gah, the
capital of Helmand Province. The idea was to then ambush the Taliban
with a counterattack. We moved overnight into concealed positions on
the rooftop of a mud compound overlooking the hamlet, and the checkpoint was set up on the road, but a few hours after dawn the Afghan
army picked up radio chatter that the Taliban knew where we were.
They would not fall for the trap. The planned operation was abandoned.

We were egressing across an open field when the first Taliban shell
exploded about five meters from where I was walking with four Canadian
soldiers. A cloud of dust and smoke from the blast enveloped us. We

scrambled for cover behind a mud wall, shielding us from Taliban positions on the opposite side of a field. I focused on taking pictures of an Afghan army soldier shooting his heavy machine gun from a nearby ditch. Another shell from an 82 mm recoilless rifle exploded just in front of him and he disappeared in the flash of light. Sand blasted my face and pelted my body armor and helmet as the shock wave knocked me over. I was sure the Afghan soldier was dead, or at least wounded. A moment later he bounded out of the ditch and ran toward me through the smoke, the machine gun now blazing from his hip, Rambo style. Then a third shell punched through the solid mud wall where Canadian sergeant major Paul Pilote was crouched, sending him sprawling backward. There was a moment of stunned silence, and then shouting and shooting resumed. With blood spilling from his nose and mouth, Pilote crawled away from the explosion on hands and knees and tumbled into a ditch. I was about thirty meters away and kept taking pictures through the haze. Under fire, two Canadian soldiers ran to help Pilote. I moved back from the wall taking shell hits and rolled into a ditch and lay low, snapping the occasional picture as the battle raged. Then I realized the Afghan troops had pulled back and the Canadians were busy with Pilote on the other side of an open dirt road in the direct line of fire. I was cut off and alone in the ditch. My heart was already thumping from the adrenaline rush, but I felt my chest constrict and a wave of nausea envelop me at the thought of being left behind in the chaos of battle. I dragged myself, prone, toward the wall of a nearby compound, then clambered over it and moved through a garden with delicate purple flowers blooming from green vines creeping up one of the walls. The blossoms seemed unbelievably bright and vivid and for a moment I felt safe, concealed from view and from fire by thick mud walls, the flowers so pretty and delicate. In my adrenalized state, everything had a crisp, sharp quality. Time seemed liquid and slow. Then a crackle of gunfire accelerated it, and I was catapulted back into the present.

Still separated from the Canadians by a road taking heavy fire through a gap in the mud wall lining the field, I was trying to figure out how to reach them—make a run for it and risk getting hit or worm my way across the road on my belly?—when a Canadian RG-31 armored vehicle raced into the gap and opened up on Taliban positions with its roof-mounted .50-caliber machine gun. I ran behind it toward the wounded Pilote and the others.

"Get back behind the RG!" shouted one of the Canadians. I turned and ran back, stumbling and falling as my legs gave way beneath me. I clawed in the dirt as I struggled to get up, my cameras dangling from my shoulders, my legs numb, and wondered for a moment whether I'd been shot. But I staggered upright and climbed into the vehicle with the rest of the Canadians and we retreated to a nearby base, where we heard the sound of heavy fighting as another company came under attack. We dropped off Pilote, who had minor shrapnel wounds and hearing loss, to be MEDE-VACed. Then we headed back out into the fray. It was the last thing I wanted to do. I was ready to call it a day, to stay within the safer confines of a base, but this wasn't the base where I was embedded and my ride was leaving. I couldn't risk being left behind, possibly for days without my laptop, sat phone, and other gear. When the soldiers dismounted to rejoin the battle, I stayed inside the vehicle, my mouth so dry that no amount of water seemed able to slake my thirst. I couldn't force myself out of the vehicle to work. Instead I shot pictures through the scuffed bulletproof glass.

I always tried to brace myself for the worst, and this was hardly my first experience of violence or combat—I'd spent much of that summer in the same area during the height of the fighting season. But the suddenness, the size, and the proximity of the explosions were more frightening that day than anything I'd experienced. More troubling than nearly being blown up, though, was the humiliation of feeling cowardly. None of the soldiers seemed to notice, and they may have been glad I remained in the vehicle—one less thing to worry about—but for the first time I just wanted to curl up and be somewhere safe, to drive away from there and leave everyone else behind, to never put myself in that kind of situation again. Maybe the incident only confirmed what I'd already known; that I'd been trying to disprove some personal weakness by confronting risk. Or perhaps I'd just learned one of war's dirty secrets: Few if any of us can live up the heroic ideals we're fed growing up. When TJ was ambushed in Nabu Agha three years later, he too was less bothered by nearly being killed than he was plagued by guilt for feeling like he'd failed his men, and possibly himself. Perhaps he was also forced to confront uncomfortable inner truths.

Ironically, I took the best combat pictures of my life that day in Howz-e Madad. One photo, showing the wounded Pilote crawling on hands and knees through the aftermath of the explosions, was splashed across the front pages of Canadian newspapers the next morning. I was told Prime Minister Stephen Harper called top military brass in Kandahar to ask what the hell was going on. War, mostly, was the answer.

By the time I left Afghanistan nearly a month later, I'd managed to shake my sense of shame from the ambush. I'd gone out on dozens more foot patrols and several combat operations and filed strong news pictures that were widely published. The validation restored my bruised ego. And finishing any embed was always a relief. As my flight took off from Kandahar Airfield, I sat in a window seat with the sun glinting off the silver wing. I felt pretty good. I would soon be reunited with my girlfriend, Uma, for a few weeks' holiday in Zanzibar. My romantic relationships over the years had often been transient or nonexistent, but I'd met Uma in Dakar earlier that year. An American, she was working as a researcher for Human Rights Watch and then as a reporter for Voice of America. At twenty-four, Uma was twelve years younger than I, but she was tall and striking, with a commanding presence. She carried herself with a calm sense of confidence and worldliness and had a spirit for adventure, a sharp wit, and a quick laugh. Over the summer of 2007, our romance evolved into something more profound and lasting.

"Age did matter in the beginning, but now it doesn't," she told me as we grew closer. "I don't want to consider anyone seriously if I can't see the possibility of something larger. I think superficial relationships are a waste of time and a drain on the spirit. I'm appalled by stupid, destructive relationships, unnecessary drama, and overly sticky romance. But I *am*, weirdly, a bit old-fashioned, if it's old-fashioned to want to be with someone and have it mean something."

We settled into our own version of domestic bliss, which was as unconventional as the rest of our lives. Each time I returned from assignment, I knew I'd be returning to her, not just to an empty house. We hosted parties, danced late into the night, went swimming and snorkeling on the islands around Dakar, did weekend road trips, and watched movies projected onto the wall at home. And even though she hated watching sports, she would bring a book and read courtside while I played pickup basketball with friends. She was smart, social, and funny and usually managed to keep me from taking myself too seriously.

Uma was accepting of my itinerant lifestyle and my long absences on assignments. I didn't have to shield her too much from the realities of my job, but that didn't mean she was unconcerned. When she read my first-person account about the ambush in Howz-e Madad a few weeks after it was published, she sent me one of her oddly punctuated e-mails, knowing I was by then enjoying the safety and luxuries of Kandahar Airfield and on my way to meet her for our planned holiday.

> hello. so THIS is NOT okay: *WITNESS—Ambushed by the Taliban in Afghanistan.* gawd. i'm glad i hadn't read it til today, when you're tucked safely into your burger king massage parlour base. yes, okay, let's go to zanzibar. quickly.

A few months after we returned home to Dakar, I began to notice a change. In addition to those brief out-of-body experiences, I became increasingly irritable. I couldn't tell whether my mood was affecting my work or whether it was the other way around. I got into a dispute with my bosses when I was sent to cover the Africa Cup of Nations football championship in Ghana instead of to Kenya, where postelection violence was tearing the country apart along ethnic lines, ultimately killing more than 1,000 people and displacing 350,000 more. I'd spent a lot of time in Kenya over the years, helping out at the regional bureau there. I'd also lived in and covered some of the most difficult and unstable countries in Africa and had been instrumental in shaping our pictures coverage from the continent. So I took it personally when Reuters photographers were flown in from elsewhere to cover the biggest Africa story in years while I was stuck in a desolate, flyblown town in northern Ghana photographing second-rate football in a half-empty stadium. It drove me half crazy, and I sent angry e-mails to my boss, only to receive responses that made things even worse.

"I understand that you are frustrated in Ghana and maybe shooting soccer is not at your expectations," I was told. "But not all assignments are glorious, some can be very dull and totally unattractive, they are also part of our job and we have to do them."

I was furious. When I returned home to Dakar, I was miserable company for Uma. Rather than spend time with our friends, I withdrew and preferred to remain at home, reading or watching hours of TV. I dreaded dinner parties and social events, unless I could drink myself into a stupor. I was of course also making life miserable for her as I tried to avoid the growing list of things that irritated me.

"When you didn't like something, or weren't in the mood for something, you tended to kind of ruin it for me," Uma told me months later. "And your very specific comforts seemed almost more important than anything else. Silence, when you're in the mood for it, is so precious to you that it's ruined quite a bit of music for me, which I can't now hear without thinking about your almost painful irritation. And after a while I just wanted to scream. But I didn't. I held it all in. All those times I was frustrated with you, disappointed because you seemed so unwilling to be open to things I liked or wanted to do. [I was] living for months within your boundaries."

I didn't know what was wrong with me or why I was so glum I could see only myself, and my misery seemed to be feeding off itself. In March I came across an Associated Press story citing an Army mental health report that said U.S. soldiers fighting in Afghanistan were suffering increased levels of depression as violence there had worsened. Nearly a third of the soldiers fighting in Afghanistan were experiencing anxiety, depression, and postcombat stress, according to the research, and these problems were linked directly to the amount of exposure they had to combat. I e-mailed the story to Uma, with an explanation saying, "Maybe this is why i'm so mopey lately." She replied, "oh, fin. i'm sure that's part of it. . . . how could it not be. i'm sorry."

My assumed immunity had been of course an illusion. The years of working under stress in difficult and dangerous places were finally catching up with me. And yet I wanted to keep returning to such places because I felt more able to function there than at home. I resisted assignments such as covering sports or African Union summits attended by fat-cat politicians and heads of state. I loathed such assignments even though they were part of my responsibility. But each time I had to cover something I deemed pointless—which at that point was pretty much everything—I grew more irritable and depressed and complained to my boss.

I didn't have the courage to quit, though, and despite my miserable outlook, Uma did her best to make me feel better. One night she persuaded me to go out to Duplex, one of Dakar's glitzy nightclubs. As usual, I wasn't in the mood, but I went along anyway. Inside, the music was thumping, the crowd was sweating, and strobe lights flashed in painful pulses. As I stood at the bar trying to order yet another drink, an older Senegalese man in a suit leaned on me and elbowed me, asserting himself more than necessary within the confined space. Already annoyed at being somewhere I didn't want to be, I leaned and elbowed back. Things escalated and words were exchanged. After some pushing and shoving, the man spit in my face. I wanted to punch him but knew that would only make things worse. I backed down, again feeling cowardly, and walked away, furious and humiliated. I found Uma, took her hand, and insisted we leave. Driving home, I swerved in and out of traffic. When we pulled up to my house, my guard was not there to open the gate. Still seething, I yanked on the hand brake and climbed out of the car to open it myself. A mangy street dog that often lurked outside greeted me. I kicked it as hard as I could in the ribs, sending it twisting through the air yelping before it scampered off whining. I threw open the gate and climbed back in the car to find Uma staring at me, aghast. To her I was a gentle, sensitive person not prone to violence. We ended the night without saying much. The next day Uma urged me to seek professional help.

The media is generally more open than the military when it comes to offering psychological support to its members, but that doesn't mean journalists are any more willing to admit their problems. I sure wasn't. But after much hesitation I made a call to the confidential hotline provided by Reuters. I was initially referred to a Senegalese doctor, but my visit to his open office in a noisy and crowded hospital hallway, and his conclusion after a fifteen-minute conversation in French that I should just take Prozac, left me feeling even more dispirited than before. I called the hotline again and insisted on access to a psychiatrist who spoke English, and preferably one who was more familiar with the kind of problems associated with my work. I was then referred to Anthony Feinstein, a South African psychiatrist who had served in the military and who had written a book titled *Journalists Under Fire: The Psychological Hazards of Covering War.* Dr. Feinstein, a professor of psychiatry at the University of Toronto, has done the only extensive research on journalists and trauma, finding that most journalists, like soldiers, cope just fine in the face of adversity and that the majority do not succumb to PTSD, depression, or anxiety. A smaller number, estimated to be around 20 percent, fare less well when working in war zones for years or even decades. The findings of his research speak to the cumulative effects of prolonged exposure to danger and violence. I knew Feinstein's background and research would allow him to understand my situation and help me manage it. He lived in Toronto, but I was headed there for a visit and we agreed to meet. In his office he ran me through the standard twenty-two-point PTSD questionnaire and a similar screening for depression. In his research Dr. Feinstein discovered that the symptoms most reported by war journalists who responded to the twenty-one-question Beck Depression Inventory included sadness, a perception of past failure, loss of pleasure, guilty feelings, self-criticism, loss of interest, irritability, and a reduced libido—all symptoms familiar to me.

"The list demonstrates the extent to which those with depression experience symptoms other than sadness," Dr. Feinstein wrote in *Journalists Under Fire.* "And it helps explain why depression can be such a debilitating illness."

During our discussion Dr. Feinstein diagnosed me with major depression. I had skipped from war to disaster for years, but I could no longer outrun the gloom that would envelop me whenever I stopped moving.

"Resilience in the face of adversity is not synonymous with immunity,"

Feinstein said. He prescribed medication and said it would take around ten days to kick in, but after months of feeling trapped in a fog of unhappiness, just taking that first step lifted my spirits. I understood for the first time that there wasn't something fundamentally wrong with me. I was afflicted by an illness that could be treated. Labeling what I was feeling eased the burden. I'd shaken off the stigma attached to asking for help. I walked out of Feinstein's office and floated across the parking lot, finally feeling hopeful for the first time in ages. When I got to the car, I had a parking ticket.

Of course, there was no magic cure. The medication improved my mood, but things were still challenging, both at work and at home. The 2008 financial crisis meant that travel budgets tightened and fewer of my proposed assignments were approved. During a monthlong solo assignment to eastern Chad, I ended up in the middle of heavy fighting along the Sudanese border and was shot at and briefly captured in the desert by a ragtag band of rebels who beat me, my driver, and a human rights researcher I was traveling with before they abandoned us and stormed off across the dunes to ransack a nearby town. I filed dramatic pictures and frontline reports. Another harrowing experience became another good story. I was fine in the midst of the chaos and felt alive creating pictures under threat of violence and the stress of deadlines. By contrast, my increasingly long stretches in Dakar spent managing administrative tasks became unbearable, and I blasted off impetuous messages to my bosses.

"I'm tired of conversations about pointless objectives and bureaucratic nonsense that wastes everyone's time," I wrote at one point. "I'm extremely discouraged with such an unproductive and unfulfilling year that in my view has illustrated a lack of vision, leadership and commitment on the part of Reuters. I'm supposed to be a photographer, but I have had exactly one meaningful assignment this year, to Chad, which was a great success on all fronts. My firm belief is that to be of any value, I should be doing these kinds of profitable and worthwhile assignments on a regular basis, not once a year. My journalistic skills are not being put to any good use. This destroys morale and makes me wonder what kind of future I can expect with the company, if any."

The In-between

In truth, Reuters was being as supportive as po[ssible?]
conditions, including the uncertainty of new corpo[rate?]
Reuters Group had recently been acquired by the Th[omson?]
Despite my occasional outbursts of frustration, I [was well?]
looked after, and more opportunities would come my way once things sta-
bilized. But by then Uma would be gone. She earned a full scholarship to
do a master's in religion at Yale and, after much deliberation, accepted the
offer and left Dakar for New Haven. We maintained our relationship for
another ten months, but by the spring of 2009, distance had amplified the
cracks, caused mostly by my wavering mood and selfish behavior, and
circular conversations about our problems got us nowhere.

"finbarr, i can't teach you what it means and looks like to love someone,
you're supposed to know that by now," Uma wrote as things unraveled.
"and i don't think i can keep doing this, either, rehashing all this stuff. i
can't take it, i'm sorry. it feels really, really awful. the worst feeling is that
the more we talk about this stuff, the more i confirm that you don't know
me at all. there's so much i couldn't show you, or lean on you with, because
in the end, it always becomes about you."

She was right. We ended our romance. Though we ultimately remained
friends, at the time there was a deep feeling of loss. That year, 2009, I did
lengthy trips to Congo, Afghanistan, Sudan, South Africa, and refugee
camps on the Somali border in Kenya. Reuters organized a big exhibition
of my Congo work in France, then sent me to work for a month in New
York. I was back on track workwise, but after each assignment I returned
home to an empty house.

The e-mail from my boss comes with the subject line "Tunisia." In the
body of the message are four words: "Do you fancy it?" It's January 17,
2011, my fortieth birthday.

Violence has been escalating in the North African country over the
past month. A street vendor named Mohamed Bouazizi doused himself
in gasoline and set himself alight in protest after a policewoman in the
town of Sidi Bouzid confiscated his vegetable cart, insulted his father,
and slapped him in the face. Protests over Bouazizi's humiliating

ment and then his death on January 4 spread to the capital, Tunis. scalating protests and riots called for the end of President Zine al-Abidine Ben Ali's twenty-three-year reign, which was marked by authoritarianism, corruption, and the ruling family amassing fortunes against a backdrop of simmering poverty. Defeated, Ben Ali fled the country on January 14. Violence, looting, and street protests filled the power vacuum left in his wake.

During one of the riots on the day of Ben Ali's escape, a policeman fired a tear gas canister directly at a group of photographers covering the demonstrations. The gas canister struck thirty-two-year-old French photographer Lucas Dolega in the head. He died in the hospital three days later.

Still, it's an easy assignment to accept and a good excuse to knock back a few birthday glasses of Scotch with my friend Marcus, a British photographer, before heading off to a Muslim country, where alcohol will be in short supply. We're used to such fleeting, alcohol-soaked reunions. Marcus and I met in a hotel bar in Kinshasa in 2001 and have been friends since, squeezing in holidays and visits between assignments, sometimes collaborating on stories in Congo. A bottle of whiskey is usually involved and often finished in a single night. As with TJ, shared experiences in difficult places anchor our friendship. Neither of us is the kind of hard-driving daredevil sometimes found in our profession, but when we say good-bye at the end of the evening, we hug and Marcus offers our familiar farewell, reserved for when one of us is headed into a situation of unrest.

"Take care, mate, and don't take any risks," he says. "Remember, I can't drink with dead heroes."

I spend a week covering clashes and political protests in Tunisia before returning to Paris. I didn't know Dolega, but I join fellow journalists attending his funeral at the Père Lachaise Cemetery, where his conflict photographs are mounted and displayed on easels. Whereas I understand the sentiment, particularly in France, where war photographers are regarded in a heroic light, I can't help thinking that if ever such a service were to be held for me, I would not want my images of war on display. Maybe I'm reading too much into it, but the images seem to suggest that photography is more important than life. I struggle to reconcile that idea. For a long time any risk I took seemed worth it. But now I'm beginning to wonder whether there's more to life than building a career chasing war. I leave the funeral feeling unsettled.

Chapter 6

Human Triggers

But there are other things which a man is afraid to tell even to himself, and every decent man has a number of such things stored away in his mind.

—Fyodor Dostoyevsky, *Notes from Underground*

TJ, OP Kunjak, November–December 2010

When the convoy of trucks pulls up at Kunjak, I swing the armored door open and am met by the smell of burning trash from our always-smoldering burn pit, stale urine, and months of accumulated sweat and filth. I'm home. Several members of my squad are waiting and welcome me with hugs, handshakes, and slaps on my ass.

"How'd you like Camp Cupcake, Sarge?" Roche teases. Serge joins in and jokes about how it looks like I've eaten well. I have.

My squad fills me in on what happened while I was away. Three Marines from another squad were sent to replace Roche (who has since returned to duty), Orr, and Chun, the trio who were injured along with me. There have been some firefights during patrols. One of the replacement Marines was shot in the forearm in the same alley where we were pinned down on that first patrol with Fin. The bullet severed an artery and shattered the bone, but the Marine survived.

After a few minutes of catching up with my men, Staff Sergeant Gonzalez, the gruff Texan, pulls me aside. "You good to go?" he asks.

"I'm fine," I say.

Gonzalez tells me he will be leaving Kunjak immediately and that I will assume command of the post. I'm stunned. Command of an entire outpost such as Kunjak is generally the work of an officer, or at least someone with a higher rank than sergeant. I worry that I'm not experienced enough under the best of circumstances, much less with my head still fuzzy and incomplete. Out here there's always the dread of making a mistake and getting one of my men hurt or killed. Now that fear is more acute than ever, and the worry about making a mistake and being punished for it is part of what makes life miserable in a place like Afghanistan.

"You fuck up, they scream at you," Ben Fountain writes in his Iraq war novel *Billy Lynn's Long Halftime Walk*. "You fuck up some more and they scream at you some more, but overlying all the small, petty, stupid, basically foreordained fuckups looms the ever-present prospect of the life-fucking fuckup, a fuckup so profound and all encompassing as to crush all hope of redemption."

I can't bear the thought of such a fuckup. I choose instead to see my new role as an opportunity. The outpost needs work to make it safer. The best offense is a strong defense. Reinforcing the roofs of our posts will help to protect us from mortar fire. Having a pit to store our ammunition and explosives will ensure that any mortar strike doesn't trigger our stock of explosives and kill us with our own ordnance. Many of the HESCO barricades on our base that should be filled with dirt are filled with trash. And they're only four feet tall. Right now we look weak and vulnerable. We need to make our lines of defense more imposing. I begin making a mental list of what needs to be done.

On November 16 one of our battalion's Marines, twenty-six-year-old Staff Sergeant Javier Ortiz-Rivera, is on a foot patrol a few miles from Kunjak when an IED detonates and kills him. That evening I receive the news over the radio that yet another of my friends is dead. I scribble my nightly note to Mel. I tell her about being back with my squad and about Ortiz-Rivera, who was on his third tour of duty—one in Iraq and then two more in Afghanistan—and who left behind a wife and three young children.

The guys were happy to see me and I'm very happy to see them. I also ran into Finbarr at District Center where he did an audio interview with me. It was fun and I hope you get to see it and hear it. He took some more photos of me (go figure) and said he was going to send them to you. I guess he is going to try and come back in February to spend some more time with us. We'll see. I'm not sure if he is just saying that to appease me.

It's 8 p.m. We just found out that SSgt Ortiz with 2nd platoon got killed about an hour ago. He hit an IED while on patrol. I feel horrible. I have three of my assaultmen with that platoon. . . . I feel bad for those guys and wish I could be there for them. He was a really great guy. I feel so terrible for his wife and children. How is there a God when stuff likes this happens? . . . What the fuck? It's so depressing being surrounded by death all of the time.

I go to bed wondering when my head will feel less foggy and when things will get back to normal, as the doctor said they would. I still have four months left on deployment and am worried I won't get any better. I want to believe the doctors, but I'm skeptical. I tell myself I'm just paying too much attention to what is happening in my mind.

I wake up the next morning and brew a pot of coffee. It's as awful as I remember. I'm told over the radio to prepare for an afternoon patrol, my first since my injury. As I sip my coffee, my palms begin to sweat. My heart pounds. It isn't because of the caffeine. To calm my nerves, I start cleaning my weapon for the first time in two weeks. I perform my prepatrol ritual, just as I've done countless times before, scrubbing the compensator free of rust, lubricating the bolt, scraping loose and wiping away the carbon residue from the firefight on the day I was injured, then dusting off the exterior. The routine calms me, but as I run through my mental checklist, I find that I still can't remember how to recite the standard nine-line casualty report used for calling in a MEDEVAC. I think for a few minutes, trying to remember the sequence and the many mnemonic techniques to recall each step—something the Corps teaches us in case we're "as dumb as a box of rocks" or need something explained "Barney style"—but I fail. I pull out my notebook and read:

Line 1. Location of the pick-up site

The remaining lines flow back, and suddenly I'm able to recite them one by one:

Line 2. Radio frequency, call sign, and suffix
Line 3. Number of patients by precedence
Line 4. Special equipment required
Line 5. Number of patients
Line 6. Security at pick-up site
Line 7. Method of marking pick-up site
Line 8. Patient nationality and status
Line 9. Nuclear, biological, and/or chemical contamination

Okay, a little rusty, but not too bad. Still not good, but I'll keep practicing until I get it. But there is something else. Every Marine has a ZAP number, used to identify him in case of injury or death. Before my concussion I knew by rote the numbers of everyone in my squad. Now I can barely remember half of them. I didn't think of any of this between doctor's appointments on Camp Leatherneck. I was more concerned with clicking a mouse or pressing the space bar on a keyboard each time the screen flashed. I didn't think about what matters most. Again I pull out my notebook, glance at my handwriting, and wonder how I could forget something so critical. And again I chalk it up to being as rusty as my weapon was. Too much downtime has dulled my memory, I tell myself.

Dreading that I might forget something crucial under pressure or make a mistake on my first patrol back, I run through my prepatrol checks dozens of times. I pull on my gear and walk to the gate, pressing the button on my radio.

"Kunjak, Kunjak, this is Able 3-4 requesting permission to depart friendly lines with one-five packs."

Part of the patrol's objective is to distribute food to Afghan villagers. I'm on edge as we head out. The doctors at the hospital didn't tell me that symptoms caused by blast-induced concussions include problems with memory, concentration, planning, judgment, and impulse control; anxiety; and dizziness. My crappy memory worried me before the patrol and still does, but out in the field I have to contend with other cascading problems. As we hand out food packets, the men and women and children gather closer and closer around me until I feel swarmed.

"Tell them to back up," I tell my interpreter, HB. "Tell them to back up or I'm going to start hitting people."

I bring the patrol back to Kunjak earlier than I normally would. I blame it on the "ungrateful bastards" who can't wait patiently for free shit. "Fuck them," I say. I call them "animals," refer to them as "subhuman," and throw my gear against a HESCO. I'm not happy. I slip on the headphones to my iPod and write another letter to Mel.

"On our patrol today we had to hand out rice and corn. My anxiety was so bad I almost had a panic attack."

A few nights later I'm still working through my concerns. Another letter home, but this time I explain my fears, and a growing sense of disillusionment.

Nov. 23, 2010. Chun isn't with us anymore, and with Ortiz and Johnson [another Marine in our company] dead I'm just really scared, not of me dying or getting hurt but of me getting one of my guys hurt or killed.

Taking them out on patrol is just such a huge weight on my shoulders. How can there be a God if he takes [Ortiz] and Johnson away from their kids? It's just so sad. They lost their lives trying to help a country that doesn't care. Oh well, right? Everything happens for a reason. I just can't wait to get home.

I can't share my worries or reveal my mental lapses to my men. They have to trust my judgment. Winter has set in, and with fewer Taliban fighters around, the insurgents rely even more heavily on roadside bombs, not only to maim and kill but also to instill a constant state of fear. We despise such chickenshit tactics and the Taliban's unwillingness to face off against us in a fair fight. But there is no questioning the disruptive effect of roadside bombs. For coalition forces in Afghanistan the threat dominates military strategy, slowing patrols and movement while consuming resources employed to detect and dispose of them or deal with the aftermath when bombs explode, hurting or killing troops and innocent civilians. My Marines and I are reduced from being an effective fighting force pitted against a clear enemy to being a wary band of human triggers wandering the desert, waiting to be blown up. The shadow of uncertainty is even more stressful than combat.

Roche's metal detector is often triggered by mineral-rich clumps of rock, but two or three times each week the pinging detector signals the battery pack of a detonator linked to an IED. His skill reassures the squad, but the Taliban has started to use wooden pressure plates that will not register on Roche's machine. I remind my Marines not to lose focus. Over and over I tell them complacency kills.

One brisk December evening a few weeks later, my men and I are patrolling near Post 1, the easternmost Afghan National Army (ANA) position at the farthest end of Nabu Agha. While searching a nearby compound, Roche identifies a cache of more than five yellow jugs packed with homemade explosives, nearly a dozen pressure plates, and battery packs. I call in an explosive ordnance disposal (EOD) team to destroy the jugs and examine the pressure plates for fingerprints. Watching controlled detonations always gives me an uneasy feeling. Here's the creepy way my mind works. If one of my men triggers an IED, I hope he will suffer only amputations and not be killed. It would be hard, but I could deal with it as long as he survived, even if he wound up needing prostheses. I can't bear the idea of another funeral back home, and another family I couldn't apologize to. As the EOD team works, my squad and I share sugary tea and a hot meal of beef, bread, and vegetables offered by the Afghan soldiers manning Post 1.

When the disposal is finished, the EOD convoy leaves and I thank the ANA commander for his hospitality. We prepare to make the hourlong march back to OP Kunjak through falling darkness. Roche sets off first. Within fifty paces outside Post I can hear the metal detector squealing. Roche stops, bends down, and gingerly sweeps away the loose dirt. He looks back at me.

"Oh, come on!" he yells. It's going to be a long night.

I radio in that we have discovered another IED, and I'm told the disposal team has already been called to detonate another cache elsewhere.

I'm ordered to mark the IED location with glow sticks and instruct the Afghan soldiers not to approach the area. I do as I'm told and set off once again. I steer my squad through the wadi, which means the final approach to base involves a long uphill slog. The worst part of any patrol is the last five hundred meters. The finish line is in sight, but the weight of weapons, ammunition, and packs seems to increase with each step. Sometimes, climbing the hill at the end of a patrol, my men are doubled over with fatigue. If they reach out their arms, their fingers will touch the ground. This is one of those times. Finally I radio ahead to request permission to reenter friendly lines. As the confirmation squawks back, an orange fireball ignites the darkness near Post 1 more than three kilometers away. Seconds later comes the hollow *whump* of the explosion.

I know what has happened even before the sound reaches me. What kind of dumb soldier would step on an IED marked with more than fifteen chemical-light glow sticks? I strip off my gear and head to the COC to report the explosion, then go to the eagle's nest, a sniper position that offers the clearest view from OP Kunjak. In the distance blue and red lights flash across the wadi as Afghan soldiers from Post 1 speed toward Kunjak. I order Doc Howard to be ready to treat any casualties. When the truck peels up the hill toward the entry control point, a dozen Marines meet the Afghans, curious to see the carnage. Skidding to a halt, the distraught Afghan soldiers fling open the tailgate. Inside is a mangled torso ripped in half. In an effort to provide first aid, the Afghans have tied a ratchet strap around the victim's waist and cinched it tight just above the gaping wound, squeezing the man's intestines, liver, and kidneys onto the corrugated flatbed. Blood drips off the truck into the sand as the Afghans beg Howard to save their friend. Howard tells me the man has no pulse. It's more blood and guts than Howard has ever seen. From the bed of the truck Howard snaps off his gloves and jumps to the ground. He tells me there's nothing he can do. No shit.

Through my interpreter I tell the Afghan soldiers the man is dead. The Afghans weep or stand in shock. They eventually climb back onto the vehicle and speed off toward District Center, lights still flashing as they career through pebbled canals. The scene sobers my Marines and leaves us standing together in silence as we stare at the bloodied ground. If Roche hadn't found the IED that killed the Afghan, one of us would have walked over it on our way back to Kunjak. One of my Marines cuts the tension by joking that the dead man's intestines looked like soggy spaghetti spilled all over the back of the truck. The others laugh. So do I. For the next few weeks, whenever the squad sets off on patrol, someone always fucks with Roche about "making spaghetti today." When heating ramen noodles or spaghetti dinners, someone always makes a quip about eating it off the back of a pickup. A young man's disembowelment becomes part of the repertoire in our battlefield humor. It gets you laughing, but it also acknowledges that you've seen things that never quite leave your mind.

On December 10 I'm hunkered in front of the radio giving my nightly counts—how many beans and bullets we have to keep us alive while we kill the bad guys. Each of my company's seven outposts does this, and in return the hierarchy of the company passes on intelligence briefs and details about operations, and Captain O'Brien gives our two-hundred-man unit his nightly summary of what we've accomplished or will do in the upcoming days. O'Brien tells us that Staff Sergeant Stacy Green, one of the most well-liked Marines in our company, has been killed. His voice sounds pained as he recounts the details: Green stepped on an IED during a firefight. He never felt anything. (I later find out the Marines with him couldn't even recognize him from the remains.) The smile, sense of humor, and compassion I admired in Green are gone. And now I have to tell my Marines. It's never easy doing this. I last did it when Staff Sergeant Ortiz-Rivera was killed last month. When we are done on the radios, I walk to where my men are lying on their racks. I'd be an asshole if I walked in and told them callously. And it's insulting to anyone who dies. My men deserve more than a matter-of-fact explanation. I tell them what Captain O'Brien told me—he stepped on an IED and died. He didn't feel anything. I remind my men that I'm here if they need me. It's not the first time I've said this to them, nor will it be the last. We're three months into our deployment. Each of my Marines has come to me in confidence to talk about something. I can now expect this to join the list. I may not know the answers to their questions, but if I can tell them their friends are being killed, I can share how I've dealt with the same thing myself: Talk with your buddies here inside our sleeping quarters, tell each other stories about them, honor them and remember them, but pull your shit together as soon as we step outside, and watch one another's backs. We still have a mission to do. Stacy Green is gone. It's another wake-up call, as if we needed one.

It is well into the month of December by the time our cold-weather clothing is delivered to Kunjak. It's like an early Christmas present. For weeks my Marines and I have shivered against bone-chilling winds and cold nights. Temperatures continue to plummet, and cotton USMC sweatshirts just don't cut it anymore. I've been wearing the same crusty boxer shorts for nearly two weeks. My men and I muse about how good it feels to have clean underwear brushing against our balls. It's the simple things in life.

The delivery also brings spare uniforms, allowing us to change out of our grease-stained trousers and sweat-encrusted tops. Putting on a clean outfit feels magical. It almost makes me cry. The clothes have the aroma of fabric softener, of Mel, of home. Everything smells fresh and safe. I think about how one month earlier I nearly lost my life, how close I was to never again enjoying this smell. *Four more months*, I tell myself. Each day brings me closer to my goal of getting my men home alive, and with all their limbs.

The next day is Christmas Eve and I wake up as the mail truck churns uphill toward the gate. For Marines the mail truck is both a blessing and a curse. It brings not just letters and notes from home, when most of us don't have access to e-mail, but also care packages and goodies sent by family, friends, and sometimes well-wishers and local community organizations. To the best of our knowledge the letters and personal items aren't censored. I'm supposed to scan my men's mail for contraband—alcohol, drugs, pornography, weapons—but I have no interest in invading their privacy. They've done nothing to suggest I need to. Once opened, the boxes and letters unfurl a painful longing for home that often leaves us feeling even more homesick and depressed than before.

The socks and snacks are always welcome, but it's my daughter's drawings and the photographs showing life back home that I cherish. I enjoy the gifts, but it also troubles me that on deployment my life seems to stand still while things back home continue apace. It's something they warn us about before we deploy, but it never makes sense until we're here. Each picture brings a new kind of pain, but each new picture also makes me smile. Just as Fin's pictures tell our Afghan story back home, the pictures sent by my girls do the same in reverse. The pictures are reminders of the days, weeks, and months passing by. They carry me home by showing me that at the moment Mel drops them in the mail, I'm on her mind, I'm missed. But the pictures also make me wonder how often people really think of me back home. Perhaps not thinking about me is easier.

I add my daughter's artwork to my family shrine and kiss each photograph of Mel and Maddie before I tack them onto the HESCO wall. I've been gone only four months, but I can see Maddie is growing up without me. Her drawings are getting better, more accomplished. This makes me proud, both of my daughter and of my loving wife, but it saddens me that I'm missing out while Maddie flourishes. I worry she might miss me as much as I miss her and become sad or anxious. I worry she will resent me for leaving.

That night I spend my shift on radio watch reading news from home. The delivery time lag means that the letters were written a month ago. Mel wrote that Thanksgiving hadn't been the same without me. Now it's Christmas Eve, and I feel a wave of sadness that Maddie will awake on Christmas morning without me there.

My shift over, I pack up my boxes and letters and head back to my hooch. Five minutes later my replacement on radio watch comes and tells me I will be picked up at 0600 and transported to District Center. I'm advised to wear clean camouflage utilities, not the flame-resistant utilities issued for patrols. I'm also told that I need to have a fresh haircut and a clean shave. I can't figure out why I'm being summoned to battalion headquarters, especially on Christmas morning. I sleep poorly and wake at 0500 feeling edgy. *Well, this is it, I guess.* I'm about to be disciplined for the photograph that got me into trouble for smoking in my bunk. There is no other explanation. I try to calm my nerves, but my mind races.

When the trucks arrive to pick me up, my company commander, Captain

Daniel O'Brien, is in the convoy, which makes me even more nervous. The only thing that puts me at ease is that I'm under someone else's command. It reminds me of Iraq and the easier days before I was charged with the responsibility for other men's lives. I was a dumb boot before Fallujah. I graduated from the School of Infantry in March of 2004. I did two week-long training events—one in fighting holes in the woods of Camp Lejeune outside a mock village and the other at an abandoned Air Force housing complex in California known as Camp Matilda—a wasteland of asbestos and lead-based paints, broken glass, and tetanus. After two months with my senior Marines I went on thirty days of predeployment leave in Boston, trying to get laid as much as possible before I deployed. I returned to Camp Lejeune in June and deployed to Iraq. I'd known the men I was heading to war with for only three months, but I trusted them.

By the end of June I was driving down highways in Al Anbar Province, Iraq, in an unarmored military vehicle as a driver for my platoon commander—a lowly minion in a squad of Marines. I was encouraged to think on my own, but I mostly followed orders. There is a hierarchy for a reason—instant and willing obedience. To learn to lead you must first learn to follow. I did as I was told. At Kunjak the roles were reversed. I made decisions that could cost life or limb and my men had to deal with the consequences.

When we arrive at District Center, it looks different. It's tidy. The motor pool where the vehicles are parked is free of trash and debris. Marines and sailors are in clean clothes and have fresh haircuts. I relax. Unless the entire battalion is going to attend my punishment hearing, something else is planned. As we climb from the trucks, I have my first proper conversation in weeks with O'Brien. The captain asks how I'm doing postinjury and comments on how much better Kunjak looks with the improvements I've made during the last few weeks. The suggestion is that I'm doing my job well and should be proud. I finally ask O'Brien why I've been summoned to District Center on Christmas Day.

"The commandant of the Marine Corps is coming to present you your Purple Heart," O'Brien says with a smile. "Congratulations."

I'm relieved I'm not in trouble but feel awkward about being singled out for recognition. Our battalion has already lost six men and even more are recovering in amputee wards stateside. They deserve a ceremony, not me. It's the first time my invisible injuries make me feel unworthy of saying I'm wounded. I look fine. And I don't feel as though I rate the Enemy Accuracy Medal—a joking term for the Purple Heart, awarded to all U.S. service members killed or wounded in combat. The helicopter transporting General James Amos coats the nearly one hundred Marines waiting for his arrival in a thick layer of dust as it lands. So much for being clean. The ceremony is brief—and thankfully the Taliban in our area aren't keen on using mortars—but my mind races. I think of Marines lying crippled in bed at Walter Reed with no legs, no arms, sometimes no limbs at all. I imagine the commandant giving them the same medal he's just pinned to my chest. I wonder how I could deserve the same medal as a quadruple amputee. I haven't been through the same heartache, the same pain, or the same trials. But I'm expected to wear that medal, and to wear it with pride. How does not ducking quickly enough warrant a medal? As the crowd disperses, I remove the Purple Heart from my chest and place it in my pocket, where I massage the cloth and thumb the metal until it is warm to the touch. When I imagine telling my men back at Kunjak about the medal, I feel ill. Will they think I rate it? Or will they mock me behind my back? I don't want to be viewed as a medal chaser.

The trucks roll up Kunjak's hill under moonlight. The outpost is quiet. Nobody is at the makeshift gym or pacing the base. The guards are on post, but the rest of the squad is hunkered around the fire, cooking a turkey that we purchased weeks earlier and that my guys slaughtered fresh for the occasion. I ask why they are eating so late. Dinner is usually cooked during daylight so we can see what we are doing. Instead they're using flashlights. One by one they each stand and congratulate me on my medal. Some slap me on the ass, others hug me, but most pat me on the back. I don't bother asking how they know, and I'm happy it's a surprise. They've waited for me to get back so we can eat together. It wouldn't have been Christmas dinner without me, they say.

Chapter 7

Limbs Lost and Skull Tattoos

Love is a battlefield.

—Pat Benatar

Finbarr, OP Kunjak, February–March 2011

In February 2011 I land at Kandahar Airfield on the day British photographer Giles Duley is dropped off at the base by an army MEDEVAC helicopter. Duley stepped on a land mine while out on patrol with American forces earlier in the day. He has lost both his legs and his left arm. The immediate aftermath of Duley's injuries and his MEDEVAC flight have been captured on film by another embedded Canadian journalist, Dave Bowering, who strapped a GoPro video camera to the medic's helmet before the MEDEVAC crew took off on the mission that rescued Duley. Dave offers to show me the footage and I make the mistake of watching it. On the video Duley is wide-eyed with shock, asking, "Am I going to live?"

Those MEDEVAC choppers. Their hydraulic whir and the *whump-whump-whump* of rotors, the smell of jet fuel mixed with pools of blood from limbs severed, torsos disemboweled, and scrotums shredded. Blood hosed off the decks after missions, a pink trickle of truncated lives. These air ambulances save lives and limbs, but after weeks of riding dozens of missions, I've grown to dread their damaged human cargo. The fear of ending up as one of their mutilated passengers can be hard to shake. I've photographed enough casualties to grow somewhat numb to the sight of their pain, but it's unnerving in some wholly different way to see a fellow photographer staring back into the camera.

People often ask whether war photographers get scared. Of course we do. On risky assignments I'm scared most of the time, always calculating odds, weighing options, anticipating what might go wrong and how I'll react when it does. Fear is constant. It keeps us alive. There are two frames of mind I use to manage fear. They are diametrically opposed and I never really know which one I'm subconsciously employing. One version is a state of complete denial, a belief that bad things happen only to other people and that "this is me; I'll be fine." The other is a total sense of resignation; I'm going to get hurt and I just hope it isn't too bad when it happens. Both are flawed ways of thinking, but they help me manage my fear. It's always a bad idea to imagine the worst that can happen, but now I don't have to imagine it; I've seen it.

Each foot patrol or vehicle convoy is a game of Russian roulette. Spin the chamber, hope for the best. On a combat operation with the Canadian army in November 2007, I wanted to play it safe and, instead of joining the soldiers on foot, I hung back to ride in an armored personnel carrier bringing up the rear. There were several Light Armoured Vehicles and I hopped into one at random. A few hours into a kinetic operation that killed at least twenty Taliban fighters, word came across the radio that one of the other vehicles had hit an IED. The blast killed two Canadian soldiers and their Afghan interpreter, and three other Canadians were injured. On another occasion with Marines in Helmand, an IED struck the vehicle behind the one I was traveling in. Nobody was seriously hurt, but it's easy to drive yourself half mad riding around waiting to get blown up. One minute you're alive, a living, breathing being, a son, brother, friend, or lover, and then you are not, you're just a hunk of meat, a memory. It almost makes me wish I believed in an afterlife. The random immediacy of an ever-pending doom is enough to make my brain ache.

Despite the sobering effect of Duley's injuries, I'm looking forward to getting back to TJ and his squad. As the armored vehicles churn their way up the hill toward Kunjak, the outpost looks more imposing than before. The ring of HESCO barriers has doubled in height, obscuring the inside from view. Coils of concertina wire add another defensive layer. When I climb out of the vehicle, a few of TJ's squad members greet me with handshakes, grab my gear, and haul it through to the main compound, where large tents have been erected and a cinder-block building has sprung up, consuming the area that was previously open space. The dusty ground has turned into muddy clods from winter rains. One of the men directs me to a large tent housing a dozen Marines. It's dusk, and a warm light glows from behind the door flap as I pull it back. TJ sits on his bunk wearing headphones and playing a video game, a cigarette tucked behind his right ear.

"Holy fucking shit," he says. "I heard a rumor you were coming this way but nobody told me it was today."

I dump my gear on a nearby camp cot.

"Cold-weather gear this time, I see, huh?" TJ says. "How you liking old OP Kunjak? Looks a little different, doesn't it? The stench is still the same, though."

TJ fills me in on events since my last visit. He has overseen the reinforcement of the outpost, but his proudest achievement is the opening of a tiny school at the foot of the hill. Several times a week, four Marines gear up in full battle dress, march five hundred yards down the hill, and stand guard as a bearded Afghan teacher leans a whiteboard against the outside wall of a mud house, where he teaches the Koran to about two dozen Afghan boys in ragged clothes who sit on the ground repeating verse after verse.

"Yeah, okay, so there are no girls at the school and we're probably training future jihadis, but at least it feels like we're doing something worthwhile out here in the middle of nowhere," TJ says. "Some education's gotta be better than nothing, right?"

His comment reflects a deeper sense of unease. At this stage of his deployment, TJ feels his squad should be securing gains and trying to win over the local population. Get busy taking care of "hearts and minds," even if the running joke is that the best way to do that is with bullets: two in the heart and one in the mind. TJ wants to stay put and focus on that, but battalion commanders want to push farther into Taliban-controlled areas to gain additional ground. This more aggressive approach aggravates TJ. What's the point of risking more Marines being killed or injured just to gain a few more square miles of pseudocontrol in a vast expanse of stony desert?

Like many of the foreign troops I've encountered in Afghanistan, TJ believes the war is mostly a senseless waste of resources, with life and limb being sacrificed for a resentful population that only wants them gone. To stave off growing feelings of disillusionment, TJ focuses on leading his squad, keeping them safe, and exerting a measure of control over the outpost. It's clear, however, that morale among the Marines is down since my last visit. They bicker and some of them talk trash while out on patrol. Just as TJ has begun to question his orders, his own men have begun to resent their duties. It's hardly surprising. They've been confined to the outpost and its privations for months, with only the same handful of guys as company. It's the hazard in a long deployment. Pretense gets stripped away, nerves get rubbed raw, and everyone is seen for who they really are. And that Marine buddy you love and rely on to stay alive is sometimes just an asshole.

While out on a patrol one afternoon, TJ wants to buy a goat from Afghan villagers to barbecue fresh meat for the base. Kunjak chicken is good, but it's time to expand the menu. Through his interpreter TJ negotiates with some Afghan farmers over the price, which should be between $100 and $150. But accustomed to generous handouts from the Marines, the Afghans instead ask that water pumps be installed throughout the village in exchange for a goat. The Afghans are good-natured and smiling throughout the discussion, trying to see what they can get, but TJ becomes agitated. He turns and strides away from the elders midconversation, without the customary farewells.

"'We'll give you one goat if you give us ten hand pumps,'" he mutters as he brushes past me. "Fuck you."

With the seasonal ebb in fighting, villages around the outpost are quieter than before. Life at Kunjak slows to a routine of daily patrols (with the latent threat of IEDs), odd jobs around the base, watching videos on laptops, and spending nights sitting around the campfire cooking chicken and talking. It's the wartime equivalent of being in the Boy Scouts. With the slower pace I have more time to get to know members of TJ's squad and one of the things I'm curious about is their near universal affinity for ink. I'm especially interested why so many of them have images of skulls.

To me skulls seem hackneyed, but in talking about their tattoos, the Marines reveal more about their lives and their fears about returning home than ever before.

Corporal Brian Scearse is so quiet that it takes me awhile to even notice he's part of TJ's squad. The twenty-two-year-old from Kentucky keeps to himself and seems most comfortable existing in the background. As the base mechanic, he busies himself fixing things, including the ever-faulty generator. A sleeve of tattoos covers Scearse's entire left arm, with skulls representing every person he knows who has been killed during the past eleven years of warfare. There are thirty-two skulls.

"It's a pretty high number," Scearse says. "Only two on here are family. Most are friends I met through the Marine Corps that got deployed when stuff in Iraq got pretty rough, and also here. I know a few people who have lost as many or close to the same number as me."

One of those he lost was his cousin, Jason Boswell, who died in Iraq in 2006. Scearse was sixteen at the time and got the news when he came home from school one day. The two were close growing up, and Boswell's death rattled Scearse. The skull for Boswell is now etched at Scearse's elbow, near the word "family," which forms part of another tattoo that reads, "For Faith For Family For Honor"—ideals by which Scearse says he lives his life. On his right forearm is a tattoo of a sword and shield with the initials of his two-year-old niece, Lillian Grace, who lives in Jacksonville, North Carolina, with his brother.

"It's a personal reminder what I have to be for her as she grows older," he says. The sleeve of skulls often prompts inquiries from strangers. "I don't get too many questions after I tell them what they stand for. It's something that I look at every day and it just reminds me of what I'm here for and what I signed up for."

Duty bound, as a good Marine should be, but like everyone at Kunjak, Scearse's mind has turned toward home as the battalion's deployment enters its final weeks. Each Marine has begun to indulge in fantasy cravings. These include wearing freshly laundered clothes, ordering Chinese food, using a flush toilet, and hitting a supermarket to fill a shopping cart with "nasty food." One Marine tells me he wants to stand in the open doorway of a fridge to feel the blast of cold air on his face. Another can't wait to hear the sound of traffic and a lawn mower. "Holy crap, there ain't no grass out here. Hearing a lawn mower—that's going to be weird." For Scearse it's cookies-and-cream ice cream. And his Kawasaki ZX14R.

"Riding my motorcycle calms me down," he says. "It clears my mind. It's a good stress reliever."

Back home in Kentucky he takes off for seven or eight hours at a stretch, cruising through the Appalachian Mountains and across the state's open plains. The bike will be waiting for him when he gets back to Camp Lejeune, and he can't wait to explore North Carolina alone. He's less enthusiastic about discussing his Afghan tour with people back home.

"I remain mostly quiet around here. It's going to be weird getting back to talking about things with my family and everybody else. I don't normally like to talk about my issues with anybody. My mother likes to find out what's going on in my life, and that can get a little aggravating. I'll explain it to them the best I can if they have questions. It's gonna be rough at first, talking about it and not just clamming up."

Such reticence has long been part of the warrior conduct and psyche. The only way to keep functioning during war is to shut things out, be tough, move on. I've seen this time and again. Suppressing emotions is easier than confronting the reality of one's fears and the pain of loss. First Battalion Eighth Marines has lost Staff Sergeants Ortiz-Rivera and Green to IEDs. While their deaths have shaken TJ's squad, not much is said around the outpost.

Such surface stoicism barely masks emotions swirling beneath the surface, as TJ's letters home to Mel reveal. Staff Sergeant Scott Wilkie, a twenty-eight-year-old veteran of Iraq, admits his fears about the daily risks only when pressed.

"The psychological stress, maybe we just become numb to it, [but] it's hard to walk and look at the ground and to look to your right and look to your left," he says. "You don't know if you're going to get shot from over here or ambushed from over there or if there is an IED sitting three feet in front of you. You might be lucky enough to step over it, but the guy behind you might not be lucky enough to step over it and there goes his life.

A lot of us will just deal with it when we get home. Not so much here—this isn't the right place for it. We still got a job to do; we still got a couple of weeks left. We gotta stay the course."

Wilkie too, though, is thinking about home. He longs to take his six-year-old daughter fishing, and he has a two-month-old son whom he has yet to meet.

"I don't even know how he looks," Wilkie says. "I heard him cry a few times over the phone. Dive in and change some diapers. It's gonna be a good time. I can't wait for that."

The Marines at Kunjak have been living in close quarters for months and are beyond sick of one another's faces, voices, stories, and behavior, but even as they count down the days—maybe even the hours—until they ship home, they all acknowledge that the one thing they'll miss about being on deployment is one another.

"There's nothing about Afghanistan I'm going to miss whatsoever. Nothing," says Wilkie. "I ain't gonna miss the people. Nothing. It's the Marines. My platoon, we didn't come here for anyone but each other. That's our primary goal: Come here, do our job, and make sure everybody gets home. Why do you decide to become a grunt and go halfway around the world from your families for so long? We don't really know; we just do it. It's a weird kind of love, I guess, when it comes to the Marine Corps."

Such sentiments of kinship and loyalty are what has always held warriors together through the stress of combat and deployment. Patriotism, youthful doses of testosterone, or in some cases a lust for revenge in the aftermath of 9/11 drove many of the men at OP Kunjak—including TJ—to enlist. Once out here in the dirt and the dust, though, amid the bullets and bombs, the larger purpose of the mission is replaced by the daily realities and the instinct to survive. Grunts don't worry about whether the war is being won or lost; they just want to get through it. Few of the Marines I meet seem hell-bent on destroying the Taliban, except to keep themselves and their comrades alive. This isn't the Good War against Hitler and the rise of fascism or the Bad War against communism in Vietnam. Iraq and Afghanistan may as well be the Ugly Wars, intractable conflicts with undefined lines and a tendency to spread like a virus across regions and reach across continents, with no foreseeable end and the mission long forgotten. So however futile the war may seem to the men fighting it, and no matter how shitty the conditions, the one thing Marines can fight for is one another. And when things go wrong, it provokes feelings of failure and guilt, just as it did for TJ after he was injured.

The Israeli military psychologist Ben Shalit asked Israeli soldiers immediately after combat what had most frightened them about the experience. He expected the responses to be fear of injury or death or capture on the battlefield. Instead the greatest fear expressed was that of "letting others down." Shalit contrasted those findings with surveys of Swedish peacekeepers who had not experienced combat. They gave the expected responses about fearing death and injury. Shalit concluded that experiencing combat reduces fear of death and injury. His study also suggested that the greatest psychological burden placed upon warriors is the fear of being unable to meet the obligations of combat—namely, the responsibility toward fellow fighters. Failing them—or believing you had failed them if they got hurt or killed—was one of the most significant factors contributing to psychological injury and breakdown. It may also play a role in the challenges soldiers face upon returning home, for such bonds are hard to comprehend beyond the battlefield.

"Many combat veterans are denied compassionate understanding by civilians, because so many people cannot understand a love between men that is rich and passionate but not necessarily sexual," writes Jonathan Shay, a psychiatrist who works with veterans, in his book *Achilles in Vietnam: Combat Trauma and the Undoing of Character.* "Veterans need to voice their grief and love for their dead comrades if they are to heal. However, many have learned to keep quiet because of their culture's discomfort with love between men that is so deeply felt."

After witnessing friends killed and injured in Iraq, TJ got a tattoo on his right bicep of military boots, a rifle, and a helmet—the traditional memorial image to honor the fallen.

"Some of the stuff we did in Iraq, none of it was war crimes, but it's bad memories," he says one evening. "I've done some things in my life that I'm not quite proud of and I've dealt with them. I've moved past them."

But here in Kunjak TJ knows he hasn't really dealt with the things he did in Iraq. He hasn't moved past them. He's only suppressed those bad memories to be able to function in Afghanistan. Eventually those memories will creep back to torment him. The invisible brain injury lurking inside his skull will make the challenges even greater. And it will be almost three years before TJ can reveal to me the details of what did happen in Iraq.

When I leave Kunjak for the second time, both TJ and I know there's a good chance our paths may never cross again. We've shared the experience of combat, instant coffee, ration packs, and the joys of wag bags, and we've spent many late nights talking. But I'm not a Marine. TJ has a wife and child and lives on a military base in North Carolina, a place as remote and foreign to me as my life as a journalist in Africa is to him. Neither of us imagines our lives will become so intertwined.

PART TWO

After Afghanistan

Chapter 8

Witnessing War, Living Through Loss

Trauma (n.), from Greek, literally "wound."

—Oxford English Dictionary

Finbarr, Libya, March 2011

Libya's front line worries me before I even get there. I've watched the first three weeks of the anti-Gadhafi uprising unfold on news reports with wild scenes of untrained rebels scattering under government air force and artillery bombardment. Friends and colleagues already on the ground are filing dramatic combat pictures taken along a ribbon of road slicing through miles of golden sand dunes. I land in Cairo and travel fourteen hours across a lonely desert to the Libyan border, then through rebel-held territory to Benghazi, where the uprising began and where the rebels are headquartered. It's ten days since I left TJ and his squad at Kunjak; one war exchanged for another, like some global game of hopscotch, with IEDs.

It was inconceivable when I covered Tunisia's swift and unexpected revolution two months ago that it would spark uprisings across the Arab world, topple dictators in Libya and Egypt, and plunge the Middle East into years of crisis and civil wars. Nor did anyone imagine that the spreading conflict would produce one of the deadliest few months ever for journalists. An Egyptian television-producer colleague in Tunisia watched the revolution there unfold with a hint of derision. "This is amazing," he said as we covered the protest movement ousting a longtime Arab autocrat. "But such a thing could never happen in Egypt."

I arrive to find Benghazi in a celebratory mood. Thousands of jubilant

Libyans gather almost daily outside the main courthouse on the city's seaside corniche. There's a sense of joy and ownership over a future that ordinary Libyans are shaping themselves for the first time in decades. It feels like the beginning of something, and not just in Libya. A monumental shift is reshaping the Middle East as autocratic regimes in North Africa tumble during the first months of 2011; Tunisia in January, Egypt in February. Now it's March. Gadhafi's grip on power is slipping. The country is split in two. The revolutionary fervor sweeping the Arab world is ripe with hope and innocence. It is doomed to falter and plunge Syria, the Middle East, and much of the rest of the world into a long downward trajectory, but not just yet. For now, Benghazi's residents welcome journalists, offering us free food and rides in their cars. It's hard not to be seduced by the thrill of the moment. Such events are intoxicating, irresistible. It's not just the buzz of being on the world's biggest news story. It's about trying to capture the weight of a huge piece of history in a fraction of a second, to interpret and filter the visual noise for some meaningful image to commit to our collective memory. There's treasure out there, and everyone wants a piece of it.

I meet up with other members of the Reuters team already installed at the Al-Nouran, a small downtown hotel buzzing with foreign journalists and their local drivers and fixers. They're all milling around a small lobby with a café that serves strong coffee. Cigarette smoke clouds the air as news of the war plays in Arabic from a wall-mounted TV with the volume cranked high. Our Reuters crew of several reporters, photographers, and video cameramen has been here for weeks along with Sam Jamison, our security man from Belfast. Sam, a retired British soldier, is our safety manager, our unarmed adviser, our logistician, and, if need be, our medic. He provisions food, fuel, and vehicles, secures accommodation, and manages drivers and fixers, allowing us to focus on journalism. He has the final call on our movements, but he consults with us and has a reputation for being sensible and fearless under fire. It's the first time I've had a security adviser in the field, but it seems like a good idea. The Arab uprisings are forging a new post-embed era where the media is no longer under the restrictions—or protection—of the world's most powerful military machine. Throngs of international journalists who covered the downfall of Hosni Mubarak in Egypt have flowed across the border into eastern Libya. Access to the front lines is unfettered, unlike in Iraq and Afghanistan, where it's controlled by the U.S. military and allied NATO forces. Gadhafi's trained troops are equipped with rockets, aircraft, tanks, and mortars, while the rebels are mostly civilians who have recently quit their day jobs to take up arms. It makes for messy and lopsided fighting but provides compelling photographs as theatrical young rebel fighters do their best to emulate Hollywood screen heroes in front of their friends and the media. The action on the front line is lethal but absurd, with youths sometimes running into battle armed with little more than a rolling pin or a bike helmet. Crowds of Western journalists—some of us also acting out our own cinematic versions of ourselves—have followed the ebb and flow of fighting along Libya's exposed desert roads, so far remaining unscathed as local morgues and hospitals fill with Libyans killed and wounded in the mayhem.

Before Sam has time to brief me, I run into Bryan Denton, a towering American freelance photographer. We've crossed paths before, in Afghanistan. The rangy Californian usually exudes a relaxed vibe, but now his face is pale as he describes how a hunk of shrapnel narrowly missed him after a nearby explosion earlier in the day. Another photographer barely pulled him out of the way. It wasn't his first close call on a fluid front line about two hours' drive from Benghazi. In recent days Bryan and dozens of other photographers have come under withering fire and bombardment from Gadhafi's helicopter gunships, warplanes, and artillery. His hand is bandaged and his camera is broken.

Bryan was among the first Western journalists to enter eastern Libya, just as an oppressed and isolated society suddenly tasted freedom. Now, a few weeks on, he's feeling spooked and thinking of getting out. He recently saw a young man suspected of being a Gadhafi loyalist summarily executed by rebels on the roadside outside the city of Ajdabiya.

"We were maybe a hundred and fifty meters from the checkpoint where it happened. By the time we got down there it was over," he recalls.

The killing is a stark reminder of human nature's brutal tendencies and a harbinger of the mistrust and score settling that will later shadow Libya in the post-Gadhafi era. Such extremes—from the initial euphoria to such muddy truths blurred by violence—are part of the cycle of revolution and war.

"It's fucking sketchy out there, man. I don't know. Be careful."

I spend the next few weeks following rebels as they charge headlong into daily battle. As far as military strategies go, it's chaotic. NATO bombings have soon wiped out Gadhafi's air force, and the threat of aerial bombardment and attacks by helicopter gunships is eliminated. Emboldened rebels pile by the hundreds into convoys of pickup trucks and cars and speed headlong down the road until Gadhafi's forces open fire with machine guns, mortars, artillery, tanks, and RPGs. The rebels panic, turn tail, and speed back in the opposite direction, high on adrenaline, laughing and firing into the air. Then they wait awhile before repeating their lethal and clumsy dance, with the dead and wounded conveyed back to grieving families waiting at hospitals and morgues. Most of the rebels have no idea how to establish defensive lines and no real knowledge of how to use many of the weapons seized from Gadhafi's abandoned military bases and arms stockpiles.

Packs of journalists—many of them young and inexperienced freelancers hoping to make a name for themselves—follow the back-and-forth fighting along "Revolution Road," driving hours back to Benghazi or Ajdabiya to file, eat, resupply with food and bottled water, and catch a few hours' sleep before repeating the daily journey—and the mad-dash routine. The appetite for news is constant, and the roadside drama usually delivers something to feed the beast, whether a firefight, a mortar barrage, or some event that steals life and, with luck, looks good on camera.

On one occasion I'm riding in the middle of a convoy of rebel vehicles zooming toward government positions when a mortar round hits the car racing beside mine. It explodes into a fireball. My driver swerves away and spins our car around in a cloud of dust as the flaming vehicle rolls to a halt. I'm in the passenger's seat and miss the picture. The explosion was too close and happened too fast. But it's never long before fresh violence claims another victim. Every day there's something. A midnight gunfight outside my hotel. A deserted stretch of road where a vehicle was shot up just moments ago, the driver torn to pieces by shrapnel, the vanished passenger's minced flesh splattered in dark red chunks on the dusty white paint of the car, the injured driver tossed, groaning and eyes rolling, into the trunk of our vehicle and whisked toward some distant hospital. Maybe he'll make it, *inshallah*, or maybe he won't. Or there's the time Sam Jamison grabs our driver by the collar when our vehicle comes under heavy machine-gun fire, and the driver slams on the brakes and tries to escape the car, and I, not wearing my flak jacket, crouch down in the space beneath the glove box trying to put the jacket and the engine block between myself and the incoming rounds as Sam yells at our panicked driver, "Get back in the car and fucking drive!" Day after day, the rattle of gunfire and the hiss of incoming rounds, the *crump* and *boom* of exploding shells drowning out the gasps of expiring lives. On and on it goes.

As we move closer to the front each day, my chest tightens with anxiety. I scan the road ahead, looking for threats everywhere. It's almost a relief when the shooting starts. The daily ambushes are nerve-racking, but my biggest fear along the shifting front line is venturing too far afield and falling into the hands of Gadhafi loyalists. In a firefight I can imagine some measure of control over my actions, as if luck doesn't rule such places. But I dread the thought of being held against my will and the horrific conditions faced by captured journalists. I have no courage for that.

One morning I'm joined at breakfast by the *New York Times* journalists Anthony Shadid and Stephen Farrell. We're all heading a few hours down the road to the city of Ajdabiya, but we're concerned about the town falling to Gadhafi's troops. Farrell was captured by the Taliban in Afghanistan and is not keen to repeat that experience, which ended with his Afghan colleague being killed in a rescue operation. We finish eating and part ways to head out. In Ajdabiya later that afternoon, the rebels begin fleeing back toward Benghazi. Security Sam urges our Reuters team to leave too, quick time. Less than an hour later the *Times* reporters are also trying to escape as Gadhafi troops encircle the city. Shadid, Farrell, and *Times* photographers Lynsey Addario and Tyler Hicks, who for

weeks have both been part of the regular crowd of photographers working the front lines, are stopped at a government roadblock and come under fire. Their driver is killed and they are captured. The four *Times*
journalists are held for more than a week. During their captivity most of
us have no idea what has become of them. When they're finally released,
in Tripoli, we learn they've been subjected to beatings and threats of execution. Another photographer, South African Anton Hammerl, is shot
and killed while roaming the desert with rebels. Two of Hammerl's
American colleagues are captured and held with no outside contact for
weeks. Only when they are eventually released is Anton's death revealed.
His body is never found. After weeks of lucky escapes on Libya's front
lines, the odds have caught up with the media. It will only get worse.

The risks are high, and my pictures are shit. Photography for me is
about getting inside people's lives, telling individual stories, quietly.
Maybe it's the presence of so many journalists on rolling deadlines and
the rapid-fire pace at which the war is escalating, but the story in Libya
seems somehow bigger, louder, and brighter than when I was working
alone in the relative seclusion of a remote outpost in Afghanistan, where
the daily routine mostly unfolded at the walking pace of a foot patrol.
Here things seem cranked up to warp speed, a reality embodied by my
driver, fixer, and translator, Abdel, a chain-smoking, fast-talking hustler
who transports me along the highway at 160 kilometers per hour with a
cigarette in his hand and a shoeless foot on the dashboard as he shuffles
through his music on a stereo system connected to an MP3 player while
answering text messages or shouting conversations into his mobile
phone (sometimes he does both—he has two phones) over the din of Arabic music screaming from the speakers. In this state of high-speed dis-
traction, it's as if he were trying to find yet another way to kill us, or at
least deafen me. Whenever I implore Abdel to slow down and concentrate on driving, he grins and laughs. "No problem, *habibi*. Nothing bad
can happen. God is protecting us," he says, and then he hits the gas. His
faith isn't always so assured, though. During one frontline mortar barrage, I run to where I've left Abdel parked in relative safety behind a hill,
but he has taken off, not just out of firing range but several hundred

kilometers back to Benghazi. His belief in divine intervention seems only to apply when driving at warp speed. I hitch a slow ride home.

I do a series of individual portraits of half a dozen young rebel fighters I meet at a military base, where they've come for weapons training. I'm trying to sketch in the background figures for a global audience parsing a crowded stage of drama. Among them is Ismail, an eighteen-year-old high school student with acne and a black beret, and Tawfig, a twenty-year-old law student with soft lips and eyes and a crisp desert-camouflage uniform. Ibrahim is a chubby twenty-year-old English student teased by the others for being unable to grow a beard. I know nothing more than this about them, other than that they've left their former lives to be part of a revolution they believe will set them free. One by one they pose for me in a room with charred wooden door frames and walls blistered and blackened by soot from some previous battle. They hold their guns self-consciously, as though bearing the weight of expectation. Ismail and another twenty-three-year-old fighter named Azwa share the same AK-47 with red, black, and green tape—the rebel colors—holding together two magazine clips sprouting from the weapon. I want to learn more about their lives, their families, their inner worlds, to better understand this country that has been largely cut off for decades, but a rebel commander arrives and demands to know why I'm taking pictures on a military base. I'm separated from Abdel, my driver. Tawfig, who was posing for photos moments earlier, now blocks the door and grabs my arm when I make to leave. The commander has accused me of spying and I'm being detained. My phone is confiscated, but I keep hold of my cameras. Sam and the rest of my Reuters team are ahead on the front lines and there are no other journalists around. All I can do is wait. The indignity of the situation enrages and scares me. I know it will resolve itself eventually, but I'm concerned about Abdel, whom I can hear being interrogated and roughed up in the next room. The commander tells me Abdel has links to supporters of the regime and asks how I know him. Hours later I'm driven into town under armed guard without Abdel and released at the rebel media center. My guards tell me Abdel will be investigated and "dealt with." This sounds ominous, but Abdel is set free the next day after a flurry of phone calls, a sleepless night, and the intervention of his family. Things are smoothed over with the rebels and Abdel tells me everything is okay. But when he picks me up at the hotel, he gives me a hug and a sheepish look. For weeks he has been boasting about how the rebels will bring freedom, the rule of law, and respect for fellow citizens, but he now admits they wanted to harm him because of a misunderstanding. The incident is another reminder of how quickly revolutions can cannibalize themselves. When we head out for the day, Abdel drives slowly and smokes his cigarettes in silence.

Between the rebels' ragged advances and their even more chaotic retreats, I shoot a quiet series of destruction along the roadside, focusing on the scars inflicted upon the desert landscape and on the smoldering ruins of government tanks and vehicles bombed by NATO air strikes. The remains of Gadhafi's soldiers are burned to a crisp inside or lying in the desert nearby, their uniforms erased by flames and scorched skin stretched over charred bones. Human jerky. I photograph the booted foot of a dead government soldier poking out from under a red blanket, the body lying blackened beside a white plastic chair, one object as inanimate and disposable as the other.

I return from the front on the afternoon of March 24 to find the British photographer Tim Hetherington in the lobby of my Benghazi hotel. We hug, grab a coffee, and catch up. We aren't close friends, but Tim has crashed on my couch in Dakar while passing through Senegal on one of his many West Africa trips. We get along well and have kept in touch sporadically. I agree to give him a tour around town the next day. With Abdel we cruise through the streets and the bullet-ridden military base where the Libyan uprising began. In the afternoon we stop to photograph Friday prayers in the main square. It's bright and warm. I snap a few photos of Tim working in the middle of a crowd waving rebel flags. He looks up into my camera, grinning, his sunglasses pushed back on his head. I shoot another picture. It's a happy moment.

Tim and I travel up and down the road toward the front lines for the next few days. We plan to share a car, but I end up traveling with my Reuters colleagues. Although we're in separate vehicles, we catch up often along the way. Once, I run into Tim after he's spent the night camped in a ransacked coastal hotel amid thieves and looters who rifled through his bag. He has covered chaotic wars in Liberia and elsewhere, but this one is something else—weirdly staged yet unpredictable. Tim doesn't like how the rebels are posing for the media circus or the risks journalists are taking. He's even less pleased with the images he's getting.

"This is ridiculous," he says at one point, just before he cancels his assignment and decides to go home. We spend our last night together in Benghazi drinking a bottle of whiskey in his top-floor room, talking at length about life and work and about his celebrity roller-coaster ride after his documentary film, *Restrepo*, about U.S. troops fighting in Afghanistan was nominated for an Academy Award. I've seen the pictures of Tim on the red carpet with his partner, Idil Ibrahim, a Somali American filmmaker, and he says they are in a serious relationship. He concedes that being in Libya isn't exactly the best thing for his relationship, but oh well, what can you do, right? Being back in a war zone alongside other photographers is like coming back down to earth after his star turn in Hollywood.

"Man," he says, "it just feels like I'm back where I belong."

Tim leaves Libya the next day. I depart soon after and travel to Ivory Coast, where thousands have been killed in battles after President Laurent Gbagbo refused to stand down following an electoral defeat. I shadow Red Cross workers collecting the dead scattered across the main city, Abidjan. Corpses have spent weeks melting in the dripping heat. They fall apart when lifted, spilling cascades of writhing maggots onto the ground, like rice pouring from a torn sack. Flaked skin peels away and teeth tumble from vanished gums.

Then, on April 4, I get an e-mail from Tim (including typos):

hey man -

was great seeing you and hanging out in Libya. hope all is well out there.

am actually thinking about coming back out this week (yeah—crazy I know.).

What's the situation like? Is it much the same? Is access to the front pretty similar.

Ok—Let me know what you think.

Stay safe

I write back, telling him I've moved on to Ivory Coast. We'd discussed meeting up here to cover a war overshadowed by events in Libya. Sixteen days later, at 16:42 on April 20, I'm in my Abidjan hotel filing pictures when a Facebook message pops up from a friend in New York: "Hondros/ Hetherington rumors. Hey, have you heard any word on Tim Hetherington or Chris Hondros in Libya? There are Twitter reports they've been killed."

Like Tim, Chris Hondros is a celebrated war photographer. He's also a friend—not a close one, but for the past two years he has made a point of calling to invite me to his legendary New Year's Eve parties. We missed each other in Libya by a matter of hours.

I spend the next ninety minutes flailing for information, calling and sending e-mails to friends and colleagues, including Yannis Behrakis, a Reuters photographer on the scene at the hospital in Misrata. It's only after hearing from Yannis that I'm able to respond: "yeah, our photographer was there too and is at hospital now. tim dead, hondros hanging on by a thread, but looks like he will not make it. fuck. i feel numb." Chris dies later that day.

It turns out that Tim traveled back to Libya, to the embattled port city of Misrata, at the heart of the most intense fighting, where the real war was raging full force. A mortar explosion that also injured two other photographers felled him and Hondros.

The loss reverberates through our small but tight-knit community of photographers: two of the most accomplished and likable war photographers of my generation, dead. Despite having covered so much death myself, I can't believe they're gone.

In May I attend memorials for Tim and Chris in New York and then Tim's funeral in London. Photojournalism is a competitive industry driven by egos, but having so many of our tribe united for such an occasion evokes a deep sense of camaraderie and kinship. We share drinks and stories, laughter and tears. Looking through old e-mails from Tim, I find one from when *Restrepo* won the grand prize for best film at Sundance. I joked that after winning World Press Photo of the Year and the top prize at Sundance, Tim wasn't going to impress anyone again until he had won a Nobel Prize. He replied: "thanks man—it's been an incredible week. . . . Not sure if i have the energy for more—perhaps it's a good time for me to check out while things are good. . . ."

Of all the experiences faced by journalists working in war zones, the most difficult to process are the deaths of friends or colleagues, or so the experts say. At Tim's funeral the author Sebastian Junger, who was Tim's close friend and his collaborator on *Restrepo*, relates the story of a Vietnam vet who liked both *Restrepo* and Junger's accompanying book, *War*. Junger says the Vietnam vet e-mailed him on the day Tim was killed. "He said, 'I'm so sorry. And I hope this doesn't sound callous, but I do want to tell you this,'" Junger tells the congregation. "He said, 'You guys with your book and your movie, you got really close to understanding war. You got very close, but you didn't get all the way.' And then he said, 'The ultimate truth about war isn't that you might die. The ultimate truth about war is that you are guaranteed to lose your brothers. In some ways, until today, you didn't have the first idea about war. You didn't know the first thing about it until today. And you've lost a brother. Now you understand war.'"

After the New York memorial I make a quick side trip to visit Joao Silva at the Walter Reed military hospital in Washington. I remember that at the moment I learned he'd lost his legs, my initial reaction was one of relief that I hadn't been injured on that same day when I was pinned down with TJ and his squad in the alleyway in Nabu Agha. Guilt and self-disgust soon gave way to sadness, despair, and pity for Joao and for his friends and family. Now I want to see how he's doing and maybe lend a little moral support, or so I tell myself. The truth is that my visit is more for me than it is for him. I'm trying to make sense of things and I imagine he can enlighten me. He's in bed when I arrive. Even though he's been recovering for more than six months, he still looks shattered, as if he's just been in an accident. His face is gaunt and his sunken eyes have dark circles around them. A pair of prosthetic legs rests by his bedside. He climbs into a wheelchair and we head outside to sit in the sun. We talk for a while about his progress and about Chris and Tim. I eventually confess to Joao my initial reaction to the news of his injuries and that it makes me feel like an asshole.

"Nah, man, no worries," he says. "I've been there before myself, so I know how it is."

A well-known female American photographer I once met in Afghanistan told me her male counterparts seemed to enjoy going on military embeds. "It's like you guys get off on living out your fantasies by playing soldiers," she said. "You come here so you can go back home and brag about being at war."

Perhaps she's right. My posture as a chronicler of war has made me feel larger than myself, more important, more real. The job bestows a veneer of cool directly proportional to the air of nonchalance one can project about the experience of danger and the willingness to confront it. I've played the role and embraced the persona, right down to the cargo pants and khaki shirts. I convince myself that the pursuit of an exciting lifestyle rich with purpose is aligned with a noble calling. My sense of self hinges upon the belief that what I do matters. That belief has compelled me to venture far from home, away from friends and family and any semblance of a normal life, and to immerse myself in the lives of strangers in the hope that my work will have an impact and connect people in some intangible way, that I can contribute to some greater good. I've coveted risk and personal challenges in search of this goal. I have even been prepared—on an abstract level—to die chasing something that seemed more valuable than my own life, perhaps because it *was* my life. And what a life it's been. I've traveled for days by wooden canoe deep into the remote forests of Central Africa in search of rare primates. I've been charged by a silverback mountain gorilla and felt his hot breath against the skin on my neck. I've climbed with armed men to the summit of Congo's volcanoes, camped on the smoldering rim, and stared into the caldera's boiling lava lake. I've met warlords and dictators, mass murderers and peacemakers. I've seen dictators fall and history turn. I've sat astride boxes of grenades on rebel aircraft and shared flights with live crocodiles and bleating goats wrapped in burlap sacks while chickens cluck underfoot. I've been stuck in mud like quicksand, covered in a carpet of bees, eaten alive by malarial mosquitos, bitten by enormous red fire ants, and bounced awake on bone-jarring journeys only to find giraffes gliding along gracefully beside my vehicle. The coppery taste of fear has grown familiar, as distinct and memorable as that first cold beer in a luxury Dubai hotel after a month of Afghan desert dust and wet wipes. I've lived in some of the most beautiful and fucked-up places, and I've done so without convention and the comforts enjoyed by most of my friends. What's not to love?

But there's an uncomfortable question within all this: Do the drama and suffering of others amount to more than a backdrop for my own private adventure? Am I guilty of probing other people's traumas in an effort to escape my own? Such a pursuit now feels predatory and repulsive, a betrayal of decency. Standing in New York at the foot of where the World Trade Center once towered, and in the wake of all that has happened, I wonder whether a career driven by ego and adrenaline can be anything more than fruitless and self-serving.

Chapter 9

Coming Home

For most problems, a Marine is issued a solution: If ill, go to sick bay. If wounded, call Corpsman. If dead, report to graves registration. If losing his mind, however, no standard solution exists.

—Jarhead

TJ, Camp Leatherneck, Afghanistan, March 2011

I'm sitting on a concrete barricade at Camp Leatherneck a week before my entire battalion of one thousand–plus Marines and sailors are due to ship out to Kyrgyzstan and then to Ireland en route back to North Carolina. Our time in Afghanistan is nearing an end, at least for this deployment. Home still feels a long way off. Besides the travel, there's paperwork to do, loads of paperwork. Emergency contact forms. Rosters accounting for our gear and personal information. And buried in it is Department of Defense Post Deployment Health Assessment (Form 2796), which every member of the U.S. military must complete at the end of a deployment. The form asks twenty-five questions about mental and physical health. It also asks, "Did you ever feel like you were in great danger of being killed?" and "Did you encounter dead bodies or see people get killed or wounded?" And it asks a series of questions about blast injuries:

> **10.a. During this deployment, did any of the following events happen to you? (Mark all that apply)**
>
> > (1) Blast or explosion (e.g., IED, RPG, EFP, land mine, grenade, etc.)?
> > (2) Vehicular accident/crash (any vehicle including aircraft)?
> > (3) Fragment wound or bullet wound?

•Head or neck
•Rest of body
(4) Other injury?

10.b. *As a result of the events in 10.a., did you receive a jolt or blow to your head that IMMEDIATELY resulted in:*

(1) Losing consciousness ("knocked out")? If yes, for about how long were you knocked out?
(2) Losing memory of events before or after the injury?
(3) Seeing stars, becoming disoriented, functioning differently, or nearly blacking out?

Other questions cover terrifying experiences, drug and alcohol consumption, nightmares, emotional numbness, depression, personal problems such as with finances and relationships, and finally, "Would you like to schedule a visit with a chaplain or a community support counselor?"

I respond honestly, checking "yes" beside the long list of physical ailments, including an aching back, sore knees, and headaches, and "yes" to a question about whether I've been exposed to toxic chemicals, in my case lengthy exposure to burn pits (full of lithium batteries, rubber, metal, shit, piss, and well-worn porno mags). But the next series of questions, about nightmares, intrusive thoughts, and memory loss, gives me pause. I read through the list and realize I have all the symptoms listed: anxiety, agoraphobia, insomnia. And not just from this deployment. I know I should probably check "yes" beside question 22, "Would you like to schedule an appointment with a health care provider to discuss any health concern(s)?"

I check "no." I'm not willing to take any chances. I'm still worried about what my leaders and my junior Marines will think if I admit my problems and doubts. I know my chronic migraines are an issue, but I still believe they'll pass. I've considered "going to see the wizard," as we call it, but I've seen what happens to others who ask for help. Marines make jokes about them behind their back, calling them malingerers. They become pariahs.

After my return from Fallujah, our leaders made us so afraid of speaking with mental health providers that many of my friends self-medicated with alcohol, marijuana, and other drugs. They abused what seemed like an endless supply of prescription narcotics to treat the pain of their physical ailments. The drugs also provided an emotional and mental escape. They were viewed by their peers as mentally and physically weak and were so often reminded of this that they believed it themselves. The military has no place for broken gear. It gets destroyed or left behind.

One of my friends died from a cocaine overdose after he was busted by the military for smoking marijuana. One week earlier, he had been made to stand in front of our company alongside dozens of other Marines who had also tested positive for drug use. In front of us all, the disgraced Marines were told that their lives were over. They would receive no education benefits and no health care through the Department of Veterans Affairs and would never land a federal job. Our leaders had yelled at them, announcing that their lives would amount to nothing. We believed them. At his funeral his family told me he'd overdosed intentionally. By the time I left for my second deployment in 2006, six of my friends had been kicked out of the Marine Corps for smoking weed (as a result, many of them are still ineligible for mental health treatment at the VA and have been unsuccessful in appealing their discharge statuses). Most of them now have part-time or low-paying jobs. Many go without mental health treatment. All of them feel betrayed.

Form 2796 is yet another numbered piece of paper issued to feed the military bureaucracy. Everything has a number, even me. To the system I'm not Sergeant Thomas James Brennan, a battle-tested squad leader with hard tours in Iraq and Afghanistan. I'm ZAP number AB1333. And just like those numbered bits of paper, I'm disposable, replaceable, no need to recycle. I check "no" beside all the remaining questions, indicating that I'm just fine. Then I hand in the form, hope for the best, and wait to board our flight home.

TJ, Marine Corps Base Camp Lejeune, North Carolina, April 2011

Leaving Afghanistan involves a routine similar to our arrival, only in reverse—gear and weapons inspections every few hours, followed by safety briefings. Instead of prepping for combat, we're focused on decompression.

It's not exactly a nuanced effort. Don't kill yourself. Don't kill your wife. Don't kill your kids. And ask for help if you need it. Nobody takes the last part seriously. We joke among ourselves—how could an office shrink understand anyone who splits skulls?—and tell ourselves that we'll be fine. We are lectured repeatedly to "take care of each other." By the time we board our C-130 to Manas, Kyrgyzstan, and then a civilian airliner to the United States, I already miss the simplicity of OP Kunjak. I miss being geographically separated from my leaders. We land near our home base at Camp Lejeune, a sprawling Marine Corps nerve center nestled in the woods of eastern North Carolina. The base and surrounding community include a population of some 170,000 people and generate almost $3 billion annually in commerce.

Everyone from our battalion is eager to reunite with family and friends. Marines often refer to forced marches as "humping" and, as our white bus rolls past the base's perimeter, a welcome-home sign hanging from the chain-link fence reads *If you thought seven months of humping in Afghanistan was rough—just wait till I get you home.* Everyone on the bus cheers. Our conversations are as testosterone driven as the ones we shared overseas—beer, sex, food, sex, more sex. Beside the signs representing a cheerful homecoming are painted bed linens for Staff Sergeant Javier Ortiz-Rivera, one of the Marines killed on our deployment. They read *I love you Papi* by the kids, and *I love you baby! You complete me! Hope you're enjoying heaven!* by Veronica. Between those white and yellow sheets are even more messages for Ortiz—one by a cousin and others by Marines he served with. The scrawls of paint brushed atop the sheets are a sobering reminder that not all homecomings are the same.

The military police officer at the front gate waves us through. The base hasn't changed. The two-lane road from the front gate to the "main side" of Camp Lejeune is a series of wooded fields broken up only by brick buildings and shopping plazas. Just as at the Air Force base in Kyrgyzstan, military vehicles roll down streets lined with Dunkin' Donuts, Wendy's, Subway, and military vehicles. Helicopters and jets soar above neon signs advertising the latest sales at the military exchange and Smokey the Bear telling me that only I can prevent forest fires. Our bus rounds a traffic circle and turns left onto C Street into the same parking lot where we bade good-bye to our families seven months ago. The roar of the crowd and a volley of air horns erupts as the air brakes on the bus hiss and we come to a halt. It's April 16, 2011, about noon. Our bus driver pulls back a lever and the bifold door creaks open. We sling our bags over our shoulders and spill out.

The crowd is overwhelming. We're all wearing our camouflage utilities and I wander through throngs of elated family members and friends, some crying, others cheering, all searching for their Marine in a sea of tan or green. I've lost roughly thirty pounds since I left. During my calls home Mel joked that she and Maddie wouldn't recognize me. I also expect that they have changed. Then I see them. Mel is standing with Maddie and both our families. My parents, Mel's parents, my sister-in-law and her husband, my sister and our aunt, their eyes scanning the crowd, just as I would have done on patrol. I shout, "GOOBS!" and my family turns toward me. Mel runs carrying Maddie and they wrap their arms around me. I kiss Mel for the first time since our fingers slipped apart last year when the bus pulled away. Her hair has changed—it's shorter and more colorful—and she looks tired. She says the same about me. We're all crying. For months I've suppressed my emotions to be able to function in the face of fear, sadness, and anger. Now I'm home and expected to reconnect with my emotions, to feel happy, but I fumble for the switch to turn them back on. For seven months I've been the source of Mel's worry. She feared I would die. I almost did. Her tears feel real; mine just feel wet. It seems surreal, holding them here, in the middle of this crowd gathered on the tarmac.

Our return has been well planned. When our plane landed at a nearby Marine Corps air station, we turned in our weapons, placed our bags on a truck, and boarded our buses. Now our gear from Afghanistan is stacked in rows on a nearby plot of grass. My family helps me search for my bags, all much lighter than when I left. I threw most of my soiled socks, shirts, and uniforms into our burn pit at Kunjak before we left. We have to be back on duty in two days. We'll be given forty-eight hours to spend with our families—a chance to enjoy some good food, catch up on what we've missed over the last seven months, get drunk, and hope to last more than ten seconds with our lovers. Then it'll be back to the grind. We can live at home, but we'll be coming to the base every day for a mandatory thirty-day decompression period and we won't be approved for leave until that's over. A vacation will have to wait. We'll fill out recall rosters—making sure cell phone numbers are up to date, verifying our blood type and a current vehicle registration. We're still on active duty, and my enlistment isn't up until next December. We'll clean our weapons and be given one "safety brief" after another, first by our company leadership, then battalion, then regimental leadership. They'll all tell us how we kicked ass and chewed bubblegum. How we took the fight to the enemy. Then they'll repeat the advice for our return: Take it easy on the booze. Wear a condom. Ask for ID and consent (i.e., don't rape women, and especially don't rape underage girls). More stuff about asking for help if we need it. It will all feel disingenuous, as though our leadership is just ticking boxes. When our thirty-day decompression period is up, we'll get the same speech again, just for good measure: Cover your stump and don't beat your family.

My squad dissolves as quickly as it was thrown together in Kyrgyzstan, each of us drifting off and reuniting with those we left behind. We haul the gear to the car and drive to a nearby beach house my parents have rented so everyone can stay under the same roof. My family knows I was injured and they're all concerned. Everything they know about my injuries has come from me or Fin. The military never contacted them and they're not sure what to expect. They keep asking whether I'm okay and I try to reassure them on my first day home, even though I'm dizzy and disoriented.

Over the next week their excitement and constant presence begin to grate. My mother and Mel argue about whether I enjoy eating licorice—Mel is right, I don't—and about whose brownies I enjoy more and about whether we should stay indoors or go do something fun. I say nothing. After yearning to be with them, suddenly I just want to be alone. I'm asked what restaurant I'd like to go to. I don't care. They think I'm lying or being passive. I'm not. I'm thinking of sitting around the fire with the guys at Kunjak. I've missed playing board games with Maddie and I missed sex with Mel, but now I long for the simplicity of a deployment. No bills. No grocery shopping. No first-world bullshit.

Frustrations with daily life soon begin to mount. I'm impatient waiting in line to pay for groceries, annoyed by noisy patrons at restaurants and by people whining over the latest iPhone being sold out at the Apple store. I seek seclusion. And I yearn for silence. I sit out on the porch at home and smoke. I tell myself it will get better once I reestablish my routine. I'm just not used to being around "normal people" again. Over the next two months we open a second mortgage for a new house, and I trade in my Dodge truck for a Chevrolet Silverado. I hope it will settle me.

Our new home is off base, and I make the daily commute to work. Our house is in a farming community outside town and the drive takes fifteen minutes unless I hit the morning rush, which can stretch the journey to two hours as the line of vehicles crawls past security at the camp gate. Mel, Maddie, and I move our belongings from our old home in Beaufort, South Carolina, our first home after getting married, where we searched for Easter eggs and played Santa, and where Mel rode Maddie's Sit'n Spin toy until she got dizzy.

During those first weeks back from Afghanistan, I manage to convince myself I'm doing okay. I pretend that leaving our South Carolina home doesn't bother me, but I miss its familiar comfort and the fond memories it holds. I have dreams where I'm preparing to fire a rocket into a building before we're attacked or staring down at the body of an insurgent who killed a fellow Marine. I know what comes next. And that's where the dreams turn into nightmares. But I don't think this is unusual. The same thing happened after Iraq, although I was home for months before they began. I tell myself it's just a normal part of decompressing. I tell myself they will pass, as they did before.

I've just spent my entire deployment wondering whether I'd make it home. Now that I'm here, I can't leave Helmand Province behind. I tell myself that thinking about the day I got hurt is normal. Who wouldn't obsess about the day they were almost killed? Gaps in my memory keep me ruminating. I hate not knowing exactly what happened. As I try to piece things together, my mind remains fixated on another place, another time, far from home. That day is a jumbled loop of events and conflicting emotions. Why don't I remember the explosion? Did I make a mistake? What else have I forgotten? "I don't remember" is becoming a constant refrain. So is "Sorry, I forgot." Mel senses my lack of presence and accuses me of being emotionally distant and numb and of not paying enough attention to her and Maddie. My daughter begs me to play dolls with her. I tell her to go clean her room. Maddie loves Golden Books and we have plenty to choose from. Many of them were gifts from my parents—treasures from my own youth, discovered in the attic above my childhood bedroom. But now I struggle to read them to her. I throw the books across the room when the words blur and blend together, causing me to stumble over them. I've always enjoyed reading. Stephen King. Dean Koontz. Hemingway. Now I hate it. Not only do I stammer on single syllables and flip-flop entire words, but I can't even remember what happens in a twelve-page children's book that I've read six times in one week. Getting angry with Maddie is an easy excuse to get away and be alone. I refuse to read to her. She cries upstairs. I cry downstairs.

In our new home I can't bring myself to hang up family photos or decorations. Seeing pictures of events I can't recall angers me. Bare walls ease the burden of forgotten memories. I tell Mel that she has no idea what it's like to almost die. This drives a wedge between us. I blame her for my forgetfulness, accusing her of not reminding me of things. I defend and deflect. But mostly I offend. I say terrible things to Mel. Things I don't mean—that she doesn't love me or that she's prying by asking questions and that she isn't patient about my poor memory. I accuse her of thinking about cheating on me or wanting to find a way out of our marriage. I call her names: liar, cheater, fake. Slut, bitch, cunt.

All I wanted while I was deployed was to be home, close to my girls, away from the sand, danger, and death. Now I'm afraid to connect with them. I don't feel like I should be here. I wonder whether it's better to leave, to be anywhere but here. I wonder whether I should volunteer to be transferred to another Marine unit to join another deployment. Afghanistan seems more familiar than North Carolina, and I'm already nostalgic for the camaraderie of my Marines. In combat, superior fire-power is usually the solution. In marriage, solutions require compromise. War feels simpler.

But at least Mel is trying. Unlike me, she is here. She puts a dry-erase board on the fridge, sends Post-it notes with me to work, and suggests routines to help my memory. She puts my keys where they are supposed to be if I forget to hang them up. She keeps my laptop in one spot. She scatters pads of paper around the house to jot down reminders. I accuse her of being callous and nitpicky, of treating me like a child. The dishes aren't a big deal, I say. I don't need a to-do list of chores on the fridge beside Maddie's.

I stop thinking Mel is sexy. I'm no longer captivated by her walk, her voice, her appearance. Mel and I start to sleep on opposite sides of the bed. We stop cuddling within the first month. Her playfulness irritates me and then bores me. Her working memory infuriates me. I no longer think her shyness is cute. I deny the passion and dedication she has for her job and our family. Her optimism toward life and me becomes a burden. I no longer care about her happiness, and I can't bring myself to allow her to make me happy. Everything that once made me smile, everything I've loved about her for the past six years, no longer matters. I've turned inward. I hate myself, and Mel is getting in the way of my self-loathing.

I keep trying to convince myself that things will be fine. I lie to myself—I'm okay, nothing is bothering me, I'm happy—and in doing so, I lie to Mel. A lot. I don't understand how I feel, so how can she? She just doesn't get it, I remind her over and over.

Our conversations end in screaming matches. I storm off and bury my face in my Facebook feed. Whether it's memes of Grumpy Cat, war footage, satirical political comedy, or a friend's endless rant, the streams of images and information bring me relief, an escape from myself. It's too difficult to say I need help. It's easier to turn away.

I can't admit that the warning signs are mounting. I see it, but hope others don't. I tell myself that Mel sees a difference because she sees me every day. But there's no way anyone at work will notice. They won't see how I treat Mel and Maddie. Or myself.

My day begins before sunrise. I wake, shave, and drive to base. We go on a morning run. Lots of running through the thick, humid air of coastal North Carolina. We've been home for three months now. We plan to train. Play video games. Bitch and moan among ourselves. Boredom is the theme of our days. When infantrymen aren't training or deployed, our schedules breed discontent and stupid mistakes. Some drink during lunch. Others drink all day. Junior Marines are hazed. Senior Marines abuse their rank and disappear for hours on end. We're back to fuck-fuck games. Formations every few hours for accountability. Being treated like children. The responsibility we shared on our recent deployment is stripped from us. Welcome to garrison life. This is what it will be like for the next five or six months until our next deployment.

I tell myself that in uniform I won't let my guard down. But I do. By my second month home, I get in trouble for disrespecting my superiors. One day I'm told I can't plan training with my men for a demolitions range because I'm "only a sergeant." I remind them of my role in Afghanistan, where I was responsible for millions of dollars in gear, a combat outpost, and the two villages we patrolled. None of it matters. We're home. It's a different version of the Marine Corps. I violate orders by getting more tattoos. I make excuses to leave work early. I pawn off my duties on my men so I can sleep in my truck. I stop trying. I don't give a fuck.

Because of my stint at the field hospital in Afghanistan, I'm obliged to do an interview with the base's Deployment Wellness Center—the largest mental health clinic on base. I put it off until the last possible day, fearful that a mental health professional will see that I'm hiding something. Worst-case scenarios flash to mind. I worry about being committed or ostracized. I worry a bad diagnosis will be an excuse for Mel to leave me and to take Maddie with her. Then I think she *should* leave me; she doesn't deserve to be with a damaged man. She deserves someone strong. And I don't want to let her down.

On the day of my appointment, I arrive at 0845 and sit for thirty minutes with other Marines and sailors in the cold waiting room of the mental health center. It's a place where no one makes eye contact or small talk. Nobody wants to be seen sitting here. Just being in this place suggests you're broken. Rumors about damaged gear travels quickly. Eventually a petite, olive-skinned woman calls my name. She looks Middle Eastern. As she escorts me back to her office past a series of key card–secured entryways, I wonder why she would be screening Marines who might be suffering from PTSD after serving in places like Iraq and Afghanistan. Her presence could be a trigger. Or maybe this is just a twisted ruse to bring out the worst in a Marine. As soon as I sit down, I begin to sweat. My fingers are trembling when we shake hands. The woman's gilded diplomas stare down at me from the walls. I'm sure she senses my anxiety. She reviews my personal information and deployment history. Then she asks whether I've ever thought of killing myself.

Holy shit. I don't even know this woman's name and that's her first question? I expected that question to be asked, but not like this. I feel violated and wonder if this is how she treats all patients who have enrolled or been forced into therapy.

I want to walk away. Her lack of tact and apparent indifference revolt me. She seems to have no genuine interest in my well-being. Her questions are cold. The tone of her voice doesn't change. She barely looks at me. She talks at me. It's as if she just wants me processed and pushed through the system. She has other men and women returning from war whom she must see. I feel no shame in lying. This is a tick-the-box exercise for both of us.

I answer "no" in response to her suicide question. The truth is that I've joked about suicide with other Marines, usually during patronizing suicide-prevention briefings. And now I often imagine my own suicide. I have no real desire to act upon my daydreams, but it excites me to imagine a dramatic self-inflicted death. Pulling the trigger in a dark room doesn't seem like a good way to go out. I'd want mine to be memorable. I've thought about gluing my hands to my head and looping fishing line tied to the tailgate of a truck around my neck so that when the truck drives away and decapitates me, it would look like I'd torn my own head off. Ha-ha, right?

But there's no way I'd share any of my suicide fantasies with this woman. If she knew I'd once laughed about the idea of dangling from a rope tied to a Marine Corps emblem at the barracks entrance, I'd surely be committed and put into a drug-induced coma, or so I imagine.

Marines, especially infantrymen, have a dark, twisted humor that doesn't fit well beyond the military. Jokes about homophobia, rape and sodomy, and walking mattresses (female Marines) are pretty standard. Or, as Eleanor Roosevelt put it, "The Marines I have seen around the world have the cleanest bodies, the filthiest minds, the highest morale, and the lowest morals of any group of animals I have ever seen. Thank God for the United States Marine Corps!"

The rest of the interview covers my battlefield injury and any aftereffects. I keep my responses brief and again answer in the negative when she asks about nightmares, intrusive thoughts, or flashbacks to combat. The woman looks down and scribbles notes. It takes her only a few seconds, but as she glances back up, and then down again to write, I fear my lies will be exposed. I don't want her to write me up for being crazy. Then, after about a dozen more questions, I'm given a clean bill of health and dismissed. As I leave, I'm told the door is always open. What a relief. And maybe it's true. If there is something really wrong with me, surely she would have noticed, the system would have caught me. I don't fully grasp that the system relies on honest self-reporting of mental health problems, even though the stigma discourages those in need of help from speaking up. Service members who ask for help are generally stripped of responsibility, given administrative work, and left feeling disrespected. They're often shunned and seen as weak. Broken gear, useless to the mission. All I know is that by lying I've managed to avoid damaging my career and left myself eligible for reenlistment. At first I feel a flush of satisfaction for dodging the system. It's a victory. Yet as the day wears on, a sense of hopelessness sets in. I've just missed an opportunity to get the help I know I need.

Not long afterward, in June, I get my annual evaluation from my platoon commander, First Lieutenant Bradley Mohr. Based on the year we've spent together before, during, and after our Afghanistan deployment, Mohr ranks me as the best enlisted sergeant he's ever served with.

"He is well-rounded and a results-driven Non-Commissioned Officer. . . . His leadership was instrumental in the refortification of his position and the establishment of hundreds of jobs in his area," he writes in my evaluation report. "A consummate professional, he has demonstrated his tactical proficiency within his specialty and proven that his depth of knowledge is far above that of his peers."

So, a few months after returning from Afghanistan, I'm given praise and awards for valor, and yet I feel like a failure, like a "turd Marine." Time to train with my men is limited to a few hours each day because we have endless paperwork to fill out, or because the Navy has lost our vaccination records and we need another hepatitis or smallpox booster. The busy work and fuck-fuck games seem pointless, especially because it has now been confirmed that we're due to deploy back to Afghanistan in six months. I barely see my men aside from our morning run. I get another review, this time from my company commander, Captain O'Brien.

"Resourceful and experienced combat leader whose ability to adapt to a complex combat environment was critical to the company's success. Marine is an exceptional Non-Commissioned Officer with maturity beyond his years," O'Brien writes. "Tactically adroit and exceptionally knowledgeable, he was the only sergeant to command an independent outpost in a forty kilometer area of operations. Unlimited potential. Ready for promotion now. Retain at all costs."

O'Brien's words add to my sense of pride at having successfully completed our deployment and for bringing my squad members home alive. A few were wounded, but we survived. O'Brien's stamp of approval also deepens my sense of confusion. As a good Marine I must show strength and resilience. My leaders and subordinates must be able to rely on me, trust me. I can't show weakness or reveal that I have problems I can't handle. The Corps has taught me to address problems with a solution. But this time I don't have one. They all say I'm that model Marine—tough, resilient, and reliable. Lying in bed at night, I wonder how long it will be before I'm found out.

Chapter 10

Nosedive

I'm sure that I never read any memorable news in a newspaper. If we read of one man robbed, or murdered, or killed by accident, or one house burned, or one vessel wrecked, or one steamboat blown up, or one cow run over on the Western Railroad, or one mad dog killed, or one lot of grasshoppers in the winter, we need never read of another. One is enough. If you are acquainted with the principle, what do you care for a myriad instances and applications?

—Henry David Thoreau, *Walden*

Finbarr, West Africa, May–December 2011

When I return home to Senegal after Tim's funeral, Dakar is tense and I'm uneasy. I used to enjoy returning home after difficult assignments. Despite Dakar's occasional challenges—perpetual power cuts, paralyzing traffic, impenetrable bureaucracy—it has always been an easygoing place. But something within me has shifted. Then the riots start.

General elections are supposed to be held in a few months, and the situation is all too familiar: Rather than retire, an aging African leader wants to remain ensconced in a plush presidential palace. He tinkers with the country's constitution to extend his rule. Such common tactics nearly always spark violence, but Senegal is one of the few West African countries where unrest is rare. As a stable and democratic former French colony, it prides itself on never having had a coup d'état or war. Dakar, the peninsular capital, is usually a sliver of calm in an unstable region, which explains why most of the foreign press corps for West and Central Africa is based here. It has sprawling beaches, excellent restaurants, a vibrant live music scene, and flashy nightclubs pumping hip-hop or local Mbalax sounds until dawn. Many expats, journalists among them, enjoy the bountiful pleasures—including those of the flesh—in a country with a well-educated middle class and a statuesque, catwalk-ready Facebook generation that embraces African and American fashions to create an elegant and athletic style of bling and beauty. For all the local buzz, not much international news originates in Senegal, so it's usually a place to relax, party, and have fun between grueling assignments elsewhere.

Such existential tension marks the lifestyle of the foreign press corps as we peel ourselves away from Dakar's delights to endure arduous travel through Senegal's less fortunate neighbors, covering the region's panoply of coups, droughts, famines, war, ethnic/religious violence, dubious elections backed by foreign donors, natural disasters, and plane crashes, or some badly organized sporting event, international summit, or visit by a global dignitary. So when serious street violence erupts in Dakar, there's a chorus of cheers from members of the international media. No need to tangle with uncooperative embassy staff for expensive visas. No interminable flights on unreliable airlines or jarring journeys on some of the world's worst roads.

"Finally, a local assignment!" one friend says.

President Abdoulaye Wade, who claims to be eighty-five (but who is believed by many to be much older), is seeking to amend an electoral law to allow himself a third seven-year term. This triggers running clashes in the heart of the capital between security forces and stone-throwing antigovernment demonstrators. Riot police fire rubber bullets, tear gas, and water cannons while rounding up protesters and beating them with batons. The National Assembly building, where lawmakers are due to vote on the controversial constitutional change, becomes the scene of a seething standoff. The clashes hardly compare with a war zone. It's small-time stuff, with crowds of angry youths speaking the political language of violence, but it's the first time I've been back in the thick of things since Libya and I'm wary.

As I head out to cover the riots, I'm anxious—fearful even. People can die at these things, like Lucas Dolega, the French photographer killed by a tear gas canister in Tunisia, and I've been thrown in jail before by Senegalese riot police. It wasn't my best day ever, and my mind plays out worst-case scenarios. Still, once in the midst of the burning tires, tear gas, flying stones, and rubber bullets, I settle into a groove, snapping pictures while dodging police truncheons, barrages of projectiles, and clouds of tear gas. My friend Rebecca Blackwell of the AP snaps a picture of me, cameras slung over my shoulders, a fire burning behind me, clouds of black smoke obscuring the shapes of protesters in the background. I'm grinning.

It's a sad replay of countless stubborn efforts across Africa, where the old ruling class so often clings to power and privilege at the expense of disenfranchised citizens. The history of a country, of a continent even, is built on such moments, big and small, and these events need to be documented. The thrill and excitement would once have kept me buzzed for hours, sometimes days, but that kick fades quickly now, leaving me feeling spent and defeated. The novelty has worn off. Covering Africa has begun to feel like an old *Flintstones* or Tom and Jerry cartoon with the same looping wraparound background. The real politics and issues are being hashed out behind closed doors, and the action-obsessed media is probably missing the real story, whatever it is. It's hard to tell.

In the end, President Wade relents, and nine months later he is voted out of office, affirming Senegal's status as a functioning democracy. It's a positive development for the country, but I'm not so sure about me.

When Chris and Tim were killed, my first thought was to honor them by continuing the kind of difficult conflict work they devoted their lives to doing. Now I wonder what that would really accomplish. At the New York memorial I met Tim's partner, Idil Ibrahim, and I had given her a print of the picture I'd taken of Tim smiling in the crowd in Benghazi. We spent more time together in London at Tim's funeral a few weeks later and Idil was dreading the idea of returning to New York, where her memories of their life together felt overwhelming. I offered that if she ever needed a quiet place to escape for a while, she could stay at my villa in Dakar, whether or not I was around.

To my surprise, Idil accepts. She arrives in June and stays three months. She spends her days lying in my garden hammock or sitting on the local beach staring out to sea. Some mornings I come downstairs to find her curled up on the couch weeping, unable to sleep through the night. She is heartbroken. She says the agony of loss feels like every cell in her body is screaming as if being crushed or stretched to the breaking point. We talk, and I mostly listen, but Idil soon becomes a confidante for me too as I begin to share with her my own emotional wounds—my disillusionment about work, disagreements with my bosses, and the complications of my romantic life. I still harbor sadness over the dissolution of my relationship with Uma, who has recently gotten engaged, and I've been trying to maintain a six-month-old relationship with my Parisian girlfriend, Laurence, who is so French she almost makes smoking look elegant. Geographic distance and emotional numbness since Libya have made it difficult to remain fully connected to Laurence, whose glamorous life working for a fashion magazine in the French capital feels far removed from my own. It's easier to relate to Idil's pain. Having another wounded person to care for while I'm also struggling keeps me from feeling too sorry for myself, but there's balance to our dynamic. Idil looks after me too, and a deep friendship grows between us. I'm used to living alone, but Idil's gentle presence is a comfort and makes her an ideal housemate, especially once I teach her how to make a mean coffee. I introduce her to the joys of the *fondant au chocolat* at one of Dakar's upscale restaurants. "Whenever I'm eating one of these, everything just feels okay for a few minutes," she says with a gleeful laugh one evening.

July in Senegal means Dakar Fashion Week. My closest Senegalese friend, Adama Ndiaye, runs the annual event, which features models I've grown friendly with over the years. Adama and Idil hit it off and Idil helps with some of the event planning, including the casting of models. I'm there photographing it all in the midst of long legs, high heels, perfume, and makeup. The unabashed flirting of the models amazes Idil, and she enjoys teasing me whenever I become the target of their attention.

"You better watch out," she says, "those girls are serious!"

It feels good and therapeutic, almost meditative, working to capture telling moments amid a different kind of chaotic energy. Fashion may seem frivolous, but it's a portal into beauty, creativity, and life—the very things that first drew me to photography before ugliness, destruction, and death dulled my view.

And it lets me challenge stereotypical impressions of Africa as a place only of conflict, disease, and poverty. It's a refreshing reminder that there is so much more to cover than war. It's like dressing a wound.

It takes me awhile to realize I've been sliding into another spiral of despair. I'm burned out from countless months of conflict coverage, from the toll of extended travel, and from engaging with a steady stream of violence, sadness, killing, and loss. I've long accepted the idea of putting myself at risk, but there have been too many close calls, too many friends and colleagues hurt or killed doing their jobs. In the end it's a game of odds, and luck. The margin for error is invisible. Step one way and nothing happens; life continues unaltered. Go another way and the universe tilts in an instant, not just for you but for everyone who cares about you. The constant and potentially lethal weight of such mundane decisions now seems too great. Idil's sorrow is proof of that.

When she leaves in September, the buffer of her presence goes with her and my depression deepens. Although I'm still on medication, I feel much worse than before. I just want to lie in bed and withdraw to the comfort, quiet, and safety of my home. I want to rest my mind and remain far from the overstimulating world outside. My coping strategy is internal exile. I've grown increasingly introverted over the years, but this is a new level of hermitism. I ignore the phone and invitations to socialize. I binge-watch TV series, sometimes for entire days. I curse our resident crows for cawing so much they disturb my afternoon slumber. I imagine snapping their necks. I want the noise to stop.

In my sullen cocoon the TV characters on my computer screen keep me company. Whenever a series ends, I feel bereft and seek out the next cast of fictional acquaintances. Without them as an escape, I'm back in my empty bedroom, staring at the spinning ceiling fan or the rust-eaten burglar bars corroding in the salty sea breeze or the torn mosquito nets that I don't have the will to repair. I'm in a trap; only when I'm working and producing and creating do I feel any twinge of enjoyment, but leaving the house has become nearly impossible.

Just as I've learned to operate comfortably in dangerous situations, I've unlearned how to function in everyday life. Using my camera, I can make some sense of war, but less so the peace that awaits me at home—a place where I spend less and less time. The color of my mind fades from the vividness of those purple flowers I saw during the Taliban ambush to the muted and monochrome quality of everyday life away from war. I never planned or expected to do the kind of work I do, but it's drawn me into war's vortex. I'm attracted to unstable places, and front lines in particular. It worries me that at some point there may be no turning back.

My regular assignments have become more tedious or taxing. I travel to Niger, where members of Gadhafi's family are rumored to be fleeing from Libya in vehicles loaded with gold and weapons. I'm supposed to wait on a main road on the outskirts of the capital, Niamey, for a mysterious speeding convoy of black SUVs. It's completely boring. Then I cover Pope Benedict's visit to Benin, a tiny, broccoli-shaped country regarded as the birthplace of voodoo. In the country's largest city, Cotonou, I have to work in huge crowds, which I've always found unpleasant and unnerving, but more so since my experiences in Congo. At one point I'm trapped in a crush as the pope exits a church. I get into a shoving match with the pontiff's chief public relations officer, a nasty man reviled by the media for his arrogance. He shoves me hard from behind and, without thinking, I turn and punch him even harder in the chest, dropping him to the ground. Furious, the Vatican flak calls the police over to arrest me. A Reuters colleague traveling with the pope's entourage intervenes and I use the heaving crowd as cover to slip away. My colleague finds me later and asks me if I'm crazy. I'm beginning to wonder.

Next I travel to Liberia to cover the presidential elections. I use Tim Hetherington's former driver, James, who tells me about their time together during the war there. It's clear the two went through a lot. James introduces me to his daughter, a shy twentysomething. He tells me Tim helped pay for her to attend nursing school and that she will soon graduate. "Oh, Tim," James says, over and over during my stay, often unrelated to anything we're talking about. James has the Liberian habit of dropping the last consonant from his words, so "Tim" becomes "Tihh," a name, and life, abbreviated.

Finbarr moving through a crowd while covering elections in Kinshasa, Congo, in 2006.
(Marcus Bleasdale)

TJ with his parents, Jim and Karen, and his brother and sister, Kevin and Taylor, on the day he graduated from boot camp, November 20, 2003, at Marine Corps Recruit Depot Parris Island, South Carolina.
(Courtesy of Thomas Brennan)

Finbarr photographing government soldiers on the front line in eastern Congo, November 2008. (Marcus Bleasdale)

A suspected rebel prisoner screams while being beaten by government troops near Goma in eastern Congo, November 23, 2008. (Finbarr O'Reilly/REUTERS)

The fingers of malnourished one-year-old Alassa Galisou pressed against the lips of his mother, Fatou Ousseini, at an emergency feeding clinic in northwestern Niger, August 1, 2005. The image won the World Press Photo of the Year, the highest individual honor in news photography. (Finbarr O'Reilly/REUTERS)

After being hit by Taliban shells during an ambush in Zhari District of Kandahar Province, southern Afghanistan, Canadian soldiers from the NATO-led coalition (left) move under fire while an Afghan machine gunner returns fire, October 23, 2007. (Finbarr O'Reilly/REUTERS)

Finbarr returns to a Canadian army base shortly after the unit he was embedded with was ambushed by Taliban insurgents in Zhari District of Kandahar Province, southern Afghanistan, October 23, 2007. (Goran Tomasevic/ REUTERS)

A wounded Canadian soldier from the NATO-led coalition crawls for cover seconds after his position was hit by a Taliban shell during an ambush in Zhari District of Kandahar Province, southern Afghanistan, October 23, 2007. (Finbarr O'Reilly/REUTERS)

TJ (front center) in late 2004 on his first deployment, in Fallujah, Iraq.
(Courtesy of Thomas Brennan)

TJ sits at the desk in Fallujah, Iraq, where he made his first kill shot,
November 2004. (Courtesy of Thomas Brennan)

Mel and TJ on their wedding day in Lake Lure, North Carolina, April 14, 2007. (Courtesy of Thomas Brennan)

TJ, Mel, and Maddie on the day he deployed to Afghanistan, mid-2010. (Courtesy of Thomas Brennan)

Marines from the First Battalion, Eighth Marines Alpha Company start the day at Outpost (OP) Kunjak in southern Afghanistan's Helmand Province, October 28, 2010. (Finbarr O'Reilly/REUTERS)

TJ "the turd Marine" soaked in his bunk at OP Kunjak, October 29, 2010. (Finbarr O'Reilly/REUTERS)

Finbarr and TJ at OP Kunjak, February, 2011.
(Courtesy of Finbarr O'Reilly/REUTERS)

Private First Class Brandon Voris, 19, of Lebanon, Ohio, from the First
Battalion, Eighth Marines Alpha Company listens to music on his
headphones as a sandstorm hits OP Kunjak, October 28, 2010.
(Finbarr O'Reilly/REUTERS)

Finbarr during his embed with TJ's battalion, Helmand, February 2011.
(Courtesy of Finbarr O'Reilly/REUTERS)

Marines shave at OP Kunjak, 2011. (Finbarr O'Reilly/REUTERS)

The school TJ established near OP Kunjak, February, 2011.
(Finbarr O'Reilly/REUTERS)

Dustin Moon fires a grenade while TJ's squad is pinned down in an alleyway during Finbarr and TJ's first patrol together, October 23, 2010. (Finbarr O'Reilly/REUTERS)

Staff Sergeant Ysidro Gonzalez calls for help as TJ slumps into the safety of a compound after being knocked out by an RPG explosion during a Taliban ambush, November 1, 2010. (Finbarr O'Reilly/REUTERS)

Doc Howard checks Jim Roche's pulse as TJ (left), John Chun (center), and Jamie Orr (far right) sit dazed with concussions. Multiple RPG explosions during a Taliban ambush left all four injured in 2010.
(Finbarr O'Reilly/REUTERS)

An evening storm gathers above the lookout post at OP Kunjak, February 2011. (Finbarr O'Reilly/REUTERS)

TJ and Finbarr
reunited at the
Rock in Randolph,
Massachusetts,
October 2012.
(Taylor Brennan)

An Israeli woman (center) and a Palestinian woman gesture at one
another during a protest by Palestinian women against Jewish visitors
to the compound known to Muslims as the Noble Sanctuary, October 14,
2014. (Finbarr O'Reilly/REUTERS)

A medic helps a Palestinian in the Shejaia neighborhood, which was heavily shelled by Israel during fighting, in Gaza City, July 20, 2014. (Finbarr O'Reilly/REUTERS)

TJ's USMC retirement ceremony in Jacksonville, North Carolina, July 2014. (Courtesy of Thomas Brennan)

TJ, Maddie, and Mel in New York's Central Park, May 2015.
(Finbarr O'Reilly)

Finbarr cycling in Ireland, December 2016.
(Simon Chambers)

The day before Liberia's polls open, protests kick off when the opposition candidate, Winston Tubman, claims fraud during a previous round of voting. He vows not to take part in the next day's runoff against incumbent Ellen Johnson Sirleaf, Africa's first democratically elected female head of state. Johnson Sirleaf has just won the Nobel Peace Prize in the midst of the contested election campaign and is seen by the international community as the country's best hope for recovery after a long-running civil war best known for the feral bands of drugged-up child soldiers who killed and were killed like the expendable pawns they were. Those who survived remain an alienated and traumatized generation raised in a broken country at risk of tumbling back toward violence. Liberian riot police respond to the protests by storming Tubman's headquarters. I'm running beside a police officer when he draws his sidearm and opens fire on the opposition supporters, killing a man in his twenties and injuring others. Nigerian UN peacekeepers intervene and disarm the Liberian riot police, but the familiar electoral act has replayed itself yet again as political leaders toy with the lives of their followers. It's another depressing display of the abuse of power I've so often encountered. I have photographic evidence of what happened, and when I meet President Johnson Sirleaf for an interview a few days later, I tell her what I witnessed. She has heard only the official version, which absolves the police of any wrongdoing. She seems disturbed by my account and asks me to send my pictures to her assistant. I do, thinking for a moment that it might lead to disciplinary action against those responsible. It doesn't. Liberia's brutal police have long enjoyed impunity. The country has known too much violence, too much death. What's another life reduced to a memory?

A few weeks later I'm back in Kinshasa two days before Congolese presidential and parliamentary elections. Police block President Joseph Kabila's main rival from holding a rally. Violence ensues. This time I'm standing between presidential guards with red berets and rolled-up camouflage sleeves when they open fire with AK-47s on unarmed opposition protesters. Their bullets rip through flesh and splinter bones. I take pictures. Bodies and blood on cracked pavement. But are these just another day's titillating images of death, a shooting that barely registers as a blip on the radar of mass violence? I've been covering Congo for a decade, and this is just part of an ongoing pattern since the country became independent from brutal Belgian colonizers who plundered the nation of its vast natural wealth. The death in 1997 of longtime dictator and kleptocrat Mobutu Sese Seko has left the country in the endless grip of an anarchic, self-enrichment free-for-all where various competing factions and warlords use ethnicity to carve murderous spheres of influence and control over resources such as gold, diamonds, silver, cobalt, copper, zinc, timber, uranium, cassiterite (tin), and charcoal. This war for riches has dragged in nine countries and killed more than five million people. (Congo's minerals have long been associated with history's worst conflagrations. During the First World War the brass casings of Allied shells fired at Passchendaele and the Somme were 75 percent Congolese copper. The nuclear bombs dropped on Hiroshima and Nagasaki were made from uranium mined in Congo.)

Reducing Congo—or any of the other African countries I've covered—to a well-worn story of hopelessness and suffering at the hands of greedy despots oversimplifies the narrative and contravenes the very message of nuance and the richness of daily life that I strive to convey through my photography. But the shooting by Congo's presidential guards is the third time in six months I've covered such a scene, the third time I've watched state security forces shoot or clobber ordinary citizens, the third time I've run past that same looping wraparound background of tear gas, broken bodies, and lives lost. It's blending into a continual blood-soaked blur, a circle of misery, and I struggle to see beyond the mounting loss of lives, freedom, and hope. Even Robert Capa, the personification of the swashbuckling war photographer, at times felt overwhelmed by things he'd witnessed.

"It's not easy always to stand aside and be unable to do anything except record the sufferings around one," he said.

When I return home to Dakar, I slide into the postassignment slump, adrenaline spent and energy drained. My antidepressants no longer seem to have much effect. I withdraw socially and return to spending my days watching TV. All I want to do is rest. I feel impotent against the relentless force of violence. Holding it still with a picture seems to change nothing, at least not for the people I've photographed. It didn't help Faustin Mugisa, an eight-year-old Congolese boy who was left for dead in a pile of corpses when ethnic Lendu militiamen hacked his mother and seven siblings to death in 2003. Faustin was found by his father, who carried him into the bush to recover from deep machete wounds and was later hacked to death by the same militia group. Faustin ended up in Beni in northeastern Congo at an orphanage run by nuns, where I photographed the deep scars still slashed across his scalp and small body.

Nor has it helped Cheikh Mukhtar, a Somali elder with a henna-tinted beard who stood blank faced beside me as we watched the tiny rib cage of twenty-month-old Anfac Anwar Mohammed deflate for the last time. She died from starvation on June 5, 2009, at Dagahaley camp in Dadaab, the world's largest and oldest refugee camp, on the Somali border in Kenya's northeastern province.

Or twenty-seven-year-old Abdulaziz Adam Ousman, his nineteen-year-old wife, Gomshea Mohammed Jouma, and their four-month-old son, Moawia Abdulaziz Adam, who together fled genocide in Sudan's western Darfur region and in 2008 and were among 250,000 Sudanese refugees and 180,000 internally displaced Chadians living in a dozen camps scattered along the border in eastern Chad. They offered me a meal even though they didn't have enough to feed themselves.

Or eight-month-old Alexandrine Kabitsebangumi, whose body was lowered in a tiny purple coffin into a gaping, adult-sized grave in a banana grove on the slopes of a smoldering volcano near Goma in eastern Congo. She died from cholera on November 12, 2008. The grove was filled with graves, and reflected light glowed from vibrant green banana leaves sprouting from fertile black earth. As women sang a haunting hymn, the mourners moved aside, allowing me to photograph. There's no joy in getting a good picture from a baby's funeral. Another victim, another memory, another ghost. There are many by now, an army of ghosts dwelling in the shadows of my mind.

The 160 Tutsi refugees in Burundi, most of them women and children, whose names were scrawled in black marker on row after row of rough-hewn wooden coffins in a mass grave, the formaldehyde spray unable to mask the smell of decomposing bodies as a United Nations peacekeeper took notes. The refugees had been hacked, shot, and burned to death during a nighttime massacre by Hutu extremists.

Or Alassa Galisou, the one-year-old boy whose wizened fingers are pressed against the lips of his mother, Fatou Ousseini, in my World Press Photo of the Year, taken in 2005 at an emergency feeding clinic in the town of Tahoua in central Niger. One of the country's worst droughts in living memory had destroyed much of the seasonal crop, leaving an estimated 3.6 million people short of food, including tens of thousands of starving children. A year after my image was taken, a German journalist tracked down Ousseini and her son and found them roaming the desert with nomads. He sent me a photograph of mother and son holding my picture. Ousseini is wearing exactly the same robe and head scarf that she was in my portrait, only now her clothes are faded by the sun and tattered by the wind. Alassa has lived to see his second year but is still emaciated, his eyes hollow and dull, his head too big for his slack-skinned body.

In 1975 the World Press Photo of the Year was taken by Ovie Carter, an American photographer for the *Chicago Tribune*. It was also shot in the Tahoua Region in Niger. It shows a mother's hands resting on the scalp of her starving child, reversing the gesture in my own winning picture. Two images taken three decades apart earn the world's most celebrated photojournalism award by showing the same situation, the same misery, in the same place, in almost exactly the same way. Photographs reflecting history repeated, a hall of mirrors ricocheting images to infinity without going anywhere.

The world appears indifferent to atrocities, abuse, corruption, profound immorality, and hardship, or at least is helpless to address them. Journalists and aid workers respond to each crisis as if it were something new, as if our collective efforts might be more than minuscule gestures in the vast cycle of human history and the merry-go-round of disasters. Yet much of the aid world is self-righteous and inefficient and plays a questionable role in perpetuating conflicts by allowing morally bankrupt leaders to indulge their own worst impulses. Not that the media is much better. I feel more and more like the proverbial vulture swooping in to feed on the carrion of the human condition. The longer I spend covering upheaval—and our collective response to it—the more cynical I become about the motives of the multinational organizations behind our well-meaning band of misfits. The corporations we work for are ultimately driven by profits. Providing a valuable public service and making a buck are not mutually exclusive, but it's increasingly difficult to photograph the pain and suffering of others and then enjoy the rewards that come with success, however that is measured—recognition from bosses, awards, or even just the benefits of a staff job with a good salary that allows me to live in a four-bedroom villa by the sea with a housekeeper who cooks and cleans and a watchman who guards my home. It's this disparity I find hard to reconcile. By some cosmic twist, I've ended up living comfortably on one side of the lens because of misery and want residing on the other. If all my efforts and sacrifices aren't making any difference, what's the point? Is our profession driven more by ego—winning awards and recognition—than by the genuine desire to do good? Should I accept this fact and focus on the job? Or would it make more sense—and be more honest—to leave all this behind and become a wedding or fashion photographer? That would raise some eyebrows. These are my thoughts on a good day. Bad days are another story.

I try to overcome my apathy by exercising. In 2008 I took up surfing. Now the inherent risks offer a thrill that shakes me free of whatever funk I'm in. Out on the water there's no time to think about anything other than that next wave and how to catch it. But one afternoon, after several failed attempts to catch anything while others carve up the surf, I feel utterly defeated. I can't even catch a stupid fucking wave. I give up and swim for shore. Climbing out of the surf and onto the rocks, I step on a sea urchin. Its purple spines dig deep into my flesh. It's a strange moment to realize it, but I know right there and then that I've hit rock bottom. I can find little meaning or purpose in life. I'm in despair again, unengaged, watching the world from a distance. I can see people around me laughing, seemingly carefree and having a good time, but enjoyment and pleasure seem to exist on a frequency imperceptible to me. It's as low as I've ever felt. I need more than medication. Pills are only masking symptoms of some deeper problem.

It's time to address the root causes of my depression. I arrange through Reuters and Dr. Feinstein, my Toronto psychiatrist, to spend three months working in London while undergoing a twelve-week course of psychotherapy. I imagine it won't be much fun, but I'm not going to get better on my own. May as well steer into the skid.

Chapter 11

Forward into the Past

In battle, life would not say goodbye to us.
So what shall we do with the not dead and all of his kind?

—Simon Armitage, *The Not Dead*

TJ, Richlands, North Carolina, July 2011

My alarm clock chimes across a pitch-black room. Slowly I rise. It's late June and Maddie has just turned four. I want to sleep. Standing in the bathroom, I brush my teeth and shave away yesterday's stubble—part of every Marine's mandatory morning routine. The person in the mirror seems somehow less familiar than usual. Downstairs the coffee machine brews. After breakfast I drive along roads flanked by open farmland backlit by a rising sun. Morning dew glinting off the fields gives way to a garish patchwork of neon signs as I reach the strip malls of town. Once I reach the base, I pull into the parking lot, take a deep breath, and step out of my truck.

The morning exercise routine with my men consists of running on dirt pathways alongside a river. Pine trees muffle the sound of our footsteps. After three miles the run ends with sore feet and tired lungs. In the shower I watch the water flowing down the drain. I dread this time of day most. It's when the hours stacked ahead of me seem pointless and unbearable. I dry myself off and dress in my camouflage utilities. Each day this routine gets harder. I keep hoping something will give, that I'll snap out of it and feel like my old self again. Instead I just feel increasingly unworthy, like I can't live up to the standards demanded by the Marine Corps insignia I wear over my heart. A Marine shows no weakness, no pain, especially to his subordinates. I button my shirt and get into costume, into character. Then I'm off to fake the day.

On base the hours are a blur of meaningless tasks at my unit's offices and at the barracks. We need to get ready to train and deploy, but much of this involves tedious paperwork: operational risk management for everything from lightning strikes to gunshot wounds and broken bones to heat stroke. Two months since the end of our vacation and we're still paper pushing. Five more months until redeployment. When I get home in the evening, I park my truck in the driveway. Inside I unbutton my uniform and the facade I've worn all day fades and is replaced by relief. "Daddy, Daddy, you're home!" Maddie yells. I know I should feel a surge of happiness when I see my daughter, but I'm just sad, empty. I give her a hug, but she feels far away. I lie on the couch, feeling lost.

The countdown to returning home started the moment I set foot on that bus that took me away for seven months. But now that I'm home and back in the daily grind, it's going the other way—I'm looking forward to going back. I wonder if it wouldn't have been easier just to stay abroad. I was able, perversely, to cling to a sense of normalcy amid the chaos of deployment. Reconnecting with my family and confronting my new state of forgetfulness and confusion is harder than taking that next step on patrol. At OP Kunjak, looking at a wall of drawings and photographs from home allowed me to simplify life and shape it into an idyllic domestic scene of pretty pictures and bedtime stories for Maddie and hot sex with Mel. Of course the reality is going to be different, but I seem unable to make the mental leap of the reality gap between being home and being away.

I'm not the only one who has changed. I wasn't just a Marine; I was also a father. I shipped out when Maddie was two and returned when she was three. I was scared yet happy, excited yet terrified to meet her again. When I left, she was completely dependent on me. Now it's "I can do it myself, Daddy." That saddens me. I somehow expected time to stand still and for things to be the same when I got home. But of course that didn't happen. Maddie's counting of "ones, twos and, threes" has evolved into "eights, nines, and tens." At bath time she wants to take her own showers. I turn on the water and she tells me to leave the room, then closes the door behind me. The morning rituals have moved on too. At breakfast

Maddie now pours her own Cheerios and milk. She has even started turning on the TV herself. Her days of sitting on my lap watching *Dora the Explorer* are over. I feel bereft. Everywhere I traveled on deployment I brought a collage of Maddie's drawings and paintings. I always kept a picture of her in a pocket over my heart, but by the time I got home it barely resembled her. Of course Maddie still needs me, just not the way she used to. Her life as I knew it no longer exists. The little girl I left behind seems all grown up, and I missed it.

It's not only that I feel distant and unsettled. I'm also scared. I see disturbed patches of dirt alongside the street as potential roadside bombs. I trust there are no explosives buried in Walmart parking lots or community playgrounds, but reminders of Afghanistan still keep me on high alert. Sudden loud noises make me jump. Silence makes me paranoid. It's difficult to switch off after months in a combat zone. So many brushes with death make me feel like I don't deserve to be alive. I feel uncoupled from my relationships. I go through the motions, but hugs and kisses feel hollow. Smiles have no feeling and my tears bear no sadness. I spend hours lying on the couch, staring at the television without actually watching. Every time I look at my legs I think of those who lost theirs and are now struggling through physical therapy or, worse, those who aren't.

I often wonder what Mel's life would be like if I'd died. I become fascinated by this idea and imagine Maddie riding her bike for the first time without me. Or Mel at the altar remarrying. I may be physically present, but I'm preoccupied by thoughts of my own demise.

And yet I don't want anyone to know. The deep sense of pride that keeps Marines from seeking help is instilled in us from day one. At boot camp we are told Marines are Marines, not soldiers (one joke is that "ARMY" stands for "Aren't Ready to be Marines Yet"). We are Marines, not troops. And Marines accept nothing but perfection. Training is full of ditties where the response to the call is "KILL!" One saying is "Trained to fight, born to kill, ready to die, but never will." Death and failure are not options. And if you worry you've failed, you sure as hell don't talk about it.

While there has been some progress in its attitude, the psychological wounds of war are not something the military fully accepts or understands, and I'm in no position to challenge the institutional culture. I'm determined to avoid the fate I've seen thrust upon many Marines who asked for help. Every Marine has issues with the Corps but I love my career. It gives me purpose and makes me happy. I'm part of something and I'm good at what I do. I don't want to jeopardize what I've accomplished. During my second enlistment I saw an infantry Marine at Parris Island ask for help. He drank too much, got into drugs, and tried to kill himself a few times. Instead of getting the help he needed, he became an outcast. Fellow Marines said he was looking for an easy retirement, that he just wanted a VA welfare check. I'm not prepared to give up or give in to therapy. There's too much at stake—my entire career. I still don't know what I would do outside of the Marine Corps, and I need the security it provides. Besides, I don't really know what therapy might do for me. I don't want to ask. I'm afraid of looking stupid. I'm confused about who I am and how to get back to being my old self, but if I admit I need help, I'll have to face my problems head-on. Nothing is scarier than that.

It's a warm summer night. Mel and I are out partying with friends, drinking at bars and local strip clubs. It gets late, and by the time we duck into a greasy spoon called the Kettle for a late-night feed, I've downed plenty of Samuel Adams, Jack Daniel's, Jameson, and buttery nipples—a drink with vodka, Irish cream, and butterscotch and coffee liqueurs. I order water and a hot fudge sundae. I love fat-kid food when I drink.

Then the man walks in. The first thing I notice is his black cane, then his prosthetic leg, which extends well above the knee. I can tell from his high-and-tight haircut and the eagle, globe, and anchor tattoo on his forearm that he's a Marine. My heart sinks. Images of dead friends, crying spouses, and Marines carrying body bags in Iraq flash through my mind. I envision the picture of Staff Sergeant Ortiz-Rivera's oldest son, Andrew, saluting his flag-draped coffin at Arlington a few months ago. He was five. I stand up from the table and head straight for the door, shove it open, and rush outside. I light a cigarette and inhale. Marlboro therapy. Neon signs shoot rays of light through my tears, creating an explosion of colors as I stare into the night. Mel soon comes out looking for me. When she sees my face, she rubs my back as she hugs me and asks what's wrong. I don't want to tell her. I just want to be left alone; if I don't have to discuss what's troubling me, then maybe I'll get over it sooner. I want her to go away, but her embrace makes me feel safe.

Mel deserves an explanation. I tell her I can't shake the scenes from Ortiz's memorial service or the sound of his wife, Veronica, screaming, "Why, God?" as she knelt by the memorial, embracing a framed sketch of her dead husband. The memory gives me goose bumps. What if the Navy chaplain had knocked on *our* door? Would she mourn my death for years, or would she move on? How long would it be before she started dating again? Would she remarry? How long until she forgot about me? If I'd died that day in Helmand, it might have been less painful for her than living like this.

Mel takes my hand, pulls me toward my truck, sits me in the passenger seat, rubs my knees, and tells me to let it all out. I hesitate but then tell her how much Veronica means to me. It feels odd telling Mel about being overcome with emotion because of another woman I hardly know. I only met her at the funeral, but I'm disturbed by her suffering and loss. I tell Mel I'm crying because I too want to die. Life is too painful. I can't take it anymore. I feel like a failure for not being a tough Marine and a strong husband and father, for feeling so weak. I'm exhausted by my nightmares and memories. I wake trembling and sweating, scared from the explosions, the blood, and the cries of the men in my dreams. I haven't slept well in months. I usually get about four hours of restless tossing and turning. I've grown used to my mind racing all night long.

I'm anxious about everything, from the trivial to the life changing. I worry about whether I remembered to buy milk for the morning while also questioning my decisions on the day I got my Marines and myself wounded. The memories from Afghanistan and Iraq are like endless streams of raw video footage that need to be edited down and reorganized to make sense. I'm overwhelmed by fear and shame. I've let Mel down. Again. She deserves better.

I tell her to take me to a pawnshop. Any pawnshop. She's standing by the passenger door of my truck, puzzled. I'm bawling in the leather seat. Mel doesn't understand until I tell her I want to buy a shotgun. It's time to kill myself. I tell her I need to be alone and that I'll do it somewhere far away so she won't find my body. I beg her to leave me be. Take Maddie and go. She refuses.

It's her turn to cry and to ask questions. I don't have the answers. What has she done wrong? Why don't I love her anymore? But it has nothing to do with that. I tell her I love her more than ever, but I'm so lost I need to escape. I can't stand myself any longer.

I lie back in the seat of my truck and stare at the roof. I wonder what heaven will be like. Then I realize I might not end up there, not after the things I've done. My mind is spinning, my heart pounding, my thoughts drifting. At some point I black out. On this night sleep is my savior.

The next morning Mel doesn't have to remind me what has happened. Before I sit up in bed, I already feel guilty. By the time I begin shuffling across our bedroom floor, I'm already in tears. I know I've hurt her. I know I've scared her even more. When I go downstairs, I'm met with a long hug. She wipes my tears. I wipe hers. She begs me to get help. I refuse at first. Then I agree, but in my mind I'm already concocting excuses.

The Navy's medical staff occupies a clinic beneath the commanding officer's wing at the center of our battalion headquarters at Camp Lejeune. People can see when you go to medical. Tight quarters also mean that people can hear you. Marines and their Corpsmen love gossip. Military life can be a bit like *Glee*—the musical sitcom Fin secretly watched in Afghanistan: cliques, gossip, egos. This makes me nervous. I've procrastinated for weeks, and when I finally enter the battalion aid station in mid-October, my knees are weak and my palms are moist. I'm worried about being locked up if anyone finds out I've talked about suicide. When the medical officer asks what I need, I freeze. I've played this scene out in my mind over the previous week. I know this doctor, a Navy lieutenant, from deployment and I've imagined explaining my problems. But now I stumble over my words. I mumble about my anxiety, my nightmares, and being unable to sleep or focus at work or in my personal life. The medical officer, Navy lieutenant George Balazs, reaches out and puts a hand on my shoulder. He says I'm not the only one in the battalion having issues. Many Marines are in treatment, he says. I exhale.

Lieutenant Balazs urges me to enroll in therapy and assures me there will be no repercussions. He books me an appointment at Second Marine Division Psychiatry. Due to a backlog, I'll have to wait two weeks. In the meantime I'm given a prescription for Zoloft, and he warns me that side effects of the antidepressant include dizziness, drowsiness, and a lower libido. I don't care. I'm desperate to feel normal again. If the drugs help, great. I'm required to tell my leaders, but the lieutenant offers to inform my commanders of my decision to get help. I decline. I'd rather tell them myself. I hope they'll respect my decision, not only to get help but also to tell them myself. Besides, I'm reassured by the medical officer's response and wonder whether I'm overestimating the stigma around seeking help.

At company headquarters two of my leaders hear me out. They ask probing questions—whether I'm "good," what I need them to do, and whether I'm going to tell my Marines—to which I answer, "I guess," and "nothing," and "no." They tell me their doors are always open if I want to talk. Afterward I step out of the office and fall into afternoon formation, where my company of some hundred Marines gathers to be counted and to hear the day's orders. One of the men I just spoke with calls the lower-ranking Marines in the company in closer. He has something important to tell us. The men—all enlisted, sergeants and below—huddle in a semicircle as he addresses us. Many of the Marines in the unit are attending military courses required for promotion and fewer than half of the company is present. He then proceeds to tell dozens of us—roughly twenty-five of whom have just graduated from entry-level infantry training recently—that there is a "bitch-ass" sergeant trying to pull the "PTSD punk card." He adds something to the effect of "Any of you fucks who try to pull that shit will get your asses handed to you." I don't remember his exact words. I break formation and walk away before we are dismissed. But the message is clear: I'm toast.

Over a few weeks I attend appointments on base at the Concussion Recovery Center and at Second Marine Division Psychiatry for mental health evaluations. My leader made my future very clear. I might as well give this recovery thing a try. It might be my only chance of getting my career back. At my first mental health appointment, my Navy forensic psychiatrist, Dr. Rebecca Webster, discusses how I could benefit from taking a low-dose sleeping pill every few days in addition to my antidepressants. She explains the medications Zoloft and Lunesta and their possible side effects—dizziness, decreased sex drive, aggression, loss of coordination, and death—and what I should do if I have trouble with the drugs. She makes me repeat my regimen. I write down instructions so I don't forget. Antidepressant in the morning, hypnotic in the evening.

She assures me that I've taken the most difficult step and that I've been through worse. She explains prolonged exposure therapy and cognitive behavioral therapy—the two most common regimens in the military for post-traumatic stress—and warns me I won't enjoy them. "It's like peeling a scab off," she says. "It hurts, but not like the initial injury." I'm relieved by her concern and thank her repeatedly for not trying to put me on countless pills. She explains it's not her style. She's matter-of-fact and curses like a Marine. She isn't what I envisioned in a psychiatrist. This reassures me. At the end of my appointment, she explains that she's placing me on light duty. This means I'm stripped of permission to handle weapons. I can no longer train in the field with my fellow Marines—something I've always enjoyed. It's not because I can't be trusted with a weapon, she explains; it's so my mind can relax. It also means I won't be going back to Afghanistan with my battalion in four months.

As we walk from her office into the lobby, she reminds me to call or e-mail her if my leaders "don't like" her medical recommendation. I'll see her in four weeks. I'm not upset about that but dread being around my unit. I don't want to be singled out again in front of my peers, leaders, or subordinates. I hide in my truck and sleep with the air-conditioning on. I'm ashamed by my choice to pursue therapy and already feel the repercussions. I don't want to stir the embers.

On October 29, 2011, seven months after returning from Afghanistan, I officially begin therapy. I arrive fifteen minutes early for my first consultation. (In the Marine Corps, the saying goes, if you're early, you're on time. If you're on time, you're late. If you're late, you're fucked.) I sit watching Fox

News on the waiting room TV. I consider walking out, but I don't. A guy opens his door and beckons me. He's a lanky Caucasian with graying hair. His handshake is firm and his button-down shirt is tucked neatly into his pressed slacks. He introduces himself as Frank. As I sit down, my palms grow moist. Frank sits just a few feet away. The room is cramped. Maybe five feet wide and ten feet long. A small pressed-board desk, three chairs, cabinets full of diagnostic manuals and trauma books. He sits in a rolling office chair leaned back against a small window. I sit in the chair closest to his desk. My voice wavers and I begin to shiver despite the dry heat of his office. I give curt answers to Frank's initial questions. He seems all right, but I'm still skeptical. Frank warns me the first sessions will be difficult but says just showing up is the hardest step. Over the following weeks we slowly build a rapport. Frank is blunt with his advice. He isn't afraid to tell me if I'm the one to blame when I talk about stress with Mel or Maddie. Our conversations don't feel clinical. He doesn't make snap judgments—at least I don't think so. He gets me talking and just lets me go—no matter how little sense I might make. He doesn't get visibly frustrated that I'm having difficulty finding words for how I feel or what I'm going through. He explains that the kind of therapy he'll be using is called prolonged exposure therapy—the repetitious storytelling of traumatic events as a means to desensitize the patient. When it's time to begin, Frank asks me to think of my most traumatic event from Iraq and Afghanistan. I have plenty to choose from, but I know which one to focus on.

Frank assures me that I'll be safe and that if things get out of control he'll bring me right back to the calm environment of his office. This scares me. I'm afraid to begin, but I know I have to do it. It's the only way to get my old self back. Frank then instructs me to close my eyes, lean back in the chair, and tell my story in the present tense. So I start.

Fallujah, Iraq, November 10, 2004

It's early in the morning and I'm sitting in a dilapidated brown leather chair, re-cessed in the shadows of a second-story room in a government administrative building. It's the height of Operation Phantom Fury, a large-scale U.S. attack on

Fallujah involving day after day of relentless firefights. I'm separated by about two hundred yards from an Iraqi insurgent carrying an AK-47. The sights of my M-16 are perfectly aligned as I prop my elbows on the desk in front of me. The clear tip traces the center of the insurgent's chest as he creeps around the corner of a mud wall and moves toward our position. It's the first time my training has been so deeply tested. I feel a wobble of fear. I hesitate, then pull the trigger. The weapon's recoil nudges my shoulder as the insurgent crumples to the ground. The scent of burning gunpowder fills the room. I fire two more rounds into the motionless torso, then stare in amazement as the insurgent lies lifeless, his black and red scarf undone. The sun rises across the city's skyline. It's my first kill. I'm nineteen.

Pulling the trigger for that first kill is beyond difficult. But the more I do it, the easier it becomes. As the operation progresses, I grow accustomed to "slaying bodies." It's what Marines are trained and paid to do. It gives me a high I've never felt before. And as my comrades fall, the killing becomes a sweet revenge. It doesn't feel bad. Killing the enemy feels good. After a few days I feel like a seasoned warrior. We've been inside the city for more than a week with no showers and barely any food, but there's plenty of ammo and we make sure to use it. The rules of engagement are simple: If it moves, kill it. Only one person I know has been killed so far. Blowing stuff up and shooting the enemy is a thrill. Getting shot at is the biggest rush I've ever felt. We laugh and joke while under fire. Running back and forth, doing our jobs, having fun. It's an infantryman's dream.

Word comes down that there's an insurgent stronghold a few hundred meters from the compound we've occupied for the night. We move out into the cool morning darkness, boots crunching on the stony ground, gear clinking in the day's early silence. We are spread out along a narrow street and I feel safe moving alongside these men trained to fight, trained to kill. When we storm a compound supposedly housing insurgents, we instead find an abandoned basement with a cage and what appears to be a torture room and execution site with bloodstains and claw marks on the mud walls. The scene is unnerving.

When we get back outside, an eerie quiet falls on the streets. For the first time in more than a week, an entire morning passes without a firefight. We feel a sense of disappointment. Have the insurgents fled the city? Has all the fun ended? We're still keyed up and itching for a fight, craving the noise and excitement of battle to break the monotony.

Then machine guns open fire on us and rounds ricochet off walls as we dive for cover. From behind a collapsed wall, I can see the muzzle flash in the window of a mud hut up ahead. Our squad leader calls in a contact report as we bump and bound down the street toward the enemy guns, clearing buildings as we move to be sure we don't get surrounded. I take a position with a clear shot seventy-five meters to the target building. As I perch on a rooftop and load my SMAW rocket launcher, enemy fire chips away the chunks of wall around me. Our team leader clears the back-blast area. Boom. I fire the rocket straight through the window. Perfect shot. Half the building collapses and rubble flies upward. The incoming fire has stopped and we maneuver to the building to check the aftermath of the blast. We've had our combat fix for the day. Now it's time to collect our reward. I'm curious to walk through a blast site for the first time. I want to see the destruction my weapon has caused. I need to see the assholes who were shooting at us to make sure those fuckers are dead. Inside the remains of the house, rebar and two dead insurgents lie on the floor, their torsos and limbs at odd angles. Pools of blood surround their dust-covered bodies. Their machine guns are mangled from the blast. It's the first time I've seen brain matter. As I look across the room, I see two more bodies lying in the corner—smaller bodies. Much smaller bodies. Kids' bodies. The first child is a little boy who can't be more than seven or eight years old. He's dressed in blood-stained tan clothing. His head is caved in. I nearly vomit, but I manage to choke it back. The second child is a little girl of maybe four or five. She's torn in half, her entrails strewn about the room. I stare at the bodies, fighting back tears. Kids. Accident or not—I killed two kids. Other Marines pat me on the back, saying, "Good shot," but I can't take my eyes off the two small bodies. I killed them. Nobody else. Just me. I pulled the trigger. I'm at fault. I wanted to see dead bodies, and here they are, but I'm not ready for this. Why were they here? Those kids weren't shooting the machine guns. They aren't the enemy. They don't deserve this. I walk away from the building in silence, my head hanging low, filled with shame. We move on to clear the next building.

The first time I try to tell Frank the story, I barely make it past the initial machine-gun fire before succumbing to flashback. The feeling of being back on patrol again is visceral—first the room grows cold, then I can feel the warmth of the desert, the grittiness of the sand against my skin, the smooth metal of my weapon, and the weight of my gear. And then, like the voice of God, I hear Frank's from across the desert dunes. The voice tells me to count to ten and come back to the room. On the count of ten, like magic, I snap back to the present. Frank tells me to stare at a picture on his wall and to focus on its vibrant colors. It is a lively painting of a Parisian café, and I have to pay attention to the trees, especially the leaves. As I focus, Frank walks me through my breathing, slowing my heart rate. Once I stop sweating and my body stops shaking, Frank tells me to start again from the beginning. No break. No time to relax. Again Frank tells me I'm safe.

It takes about eight more sessions before I can tell the entire story. Eight sessions of reliving the deaths of two innocent Iraqi children. Eight sessions of pain and suffering. Eight sessions of trying to move beyond the repeating loop of images trapping me in the past and preventing me from moving forward with my life.

Each session is a step in the right direction, but in addition to my psychological wounds, there's a physical one too, hidden beneath my skull. When I undergo a brain scan in the spring of 2012, a year after returning from Afghanistan, doctors will discover a golf ball–size section of damaged matter in my right frontal lobe, an area that affects mood, balance, memory, speech, and behavior, including impulse control. As I'm learning, the intertwined nature of traumatic brain injury and post-traumatic stress means it's almost impossible to know where the bruised brain ends and the wounded mind begins. My medical records show that I was diagnosed with "Grade III Concussion with Loss of Consciousness" on November 1, 2010, the day of the Taliban ambush, but the scan is the first clear evidence of my traumatic brain injury.

For now though, in the fall of 2011, my sessions with Frank mean I'm finally getting the treatment I need, but it comes at a cost, just as I'd feared. By my second appointment with my psychiatrist, I've been removed from my position as section leader with my old unit and transferred from Alpha Company to a makeshift company for Marines being phased out of the Corps for offenses such as drug abuse and domestic assault, or upon completion of their contracts. I'm treated on a par with junior Marines, stripped of my responsibilities, and made to stand in formation behind them. A Marine senior to me belittles me daily, calling me "weak" and "the sorriest excuse for a Marine sergeant." Despite the fact that he's on medical hold for noncombat injuries, he acts as if he's better than the rest of us. When I confront him in his office, away from the group, I tell him I'm seeking help so I can return to full duty—to get my mind right so I can deploy again—the Marine says I just need to "suck it up" and stop being "such a bitch." He laughs and says he's helping by being tough on me and that I just don't know it. I've been in the Corps for nearly eight years by now, and I've known other Marines like this one. We call them shit bags, wasted uniforms, misappropriated tax dollars. Such Marines should be discharged after their first enlistment, lest they become a tumor that spreads. There's no doubt this "leader" is doing more harm than good.

The new company within my unit that I'm assigned to is mostly Marine Corps deadwood—men willingly leaving active duty and others who have broken laws. Some Marines in my old company stop talking to me. I find out they've been threatened with punishment if they get in touch with me. My psychiatrist downgrades me even further from "light duty" to "limited duty," which means my status has gone from being a suggestion that can be ignored by commanders to being a doctor's order that must be obeyed. And then they deal me one more big surprise. When I go to deliver my papers with these new orders to the office of the senior Marine who has been giving me a hard time, he greets me with a grin.

"I've got a gift for you, stud," he says. "You're going back to Alpha Company and you're heading to Afghanistan in a few months. Better cancel those medical appointments and pack your gear."

I'm shocked. I've been assigned to this new group for nearly a month, and I'm desperate to return to full duty and to deploy with my men. For years I ran from the idea of being a career Marine—twenty years is a long time—but I just reenlisted a few months ago, on September 11, 2011. Now that my career is in jeopardy, I want nothing more than to continue wearing a uniform. But the chit in my pocket means that's impossible. I say nothing, pull it out, unfold it, and hand it across the desk. His grin fades as he reads the paper. His face pales. He explodes with a stream of expletives and orders me out of his office. I walk back along the corridor and down the stairs. I can still hear his voice. "Little bitch!" There isn't anything he can do. My chit is a medical order and my chain of command must follow it.

The attitude I encounter has long been ingrained within the military. Aggression wins wars. The Corps telling its Marines to get help feels like lip service. Fear is contagious. If unsure men appear to be getting off lightly, malingering is likely to become a problem. This concern was typified in a memo from General George S. Patton to all commanders in the Seventh Army, then stationed in Italy, on August 5, 1943.

"It has come to my attention that a very small number of soldiers are going to the hospital on the pretext that they are nervously incapable of combat," Patton wrote. "Such men are cowards, and bring discredit on the Army and disgrace to their comrades who they heartlessly leave to endure the danger of a battle which they themselves use the hospital as a means of escaping."

Patton's memo was uncovered by Eric Jaffe, author of *A Curious Madness*, a book about an American combat psychiatrist and a Japanese war crimes suspect. The order, Jaffe writes, came two days after Patton slapped a private named Charles Kuhl, who was being treated for "moderately severe" anxiety at an evacuation hospital in Sicily. A week later, at another hospital, Patton slapped another private, Paul Bennett, who was also recovering from a breakdown. Patton demanded that Bennett return to the front lines and drew his sidearm to show he meant it.

By the middle of 1943 mental breakdowns made up 15 to 25 percent of all battle casualties, Jaffe writes. At the time of Patton's order, the Army was discharging 115,000 soldiers a year for psychiatric reasons. Numbers went down later that year, when the military ordered psychiatrists to join infantry divisions in combat and treat mental casualties at the front lines.

The controversy delayed Patton's promotion to major general and earned him censure from General Eisenhower. Patton did issue a formal apology but still felt the best medicine for "mental anguish" was tough love. In the seventy years since Patton's outbursts, our understanding of PTSD, as well as its causes and possible treatments, has increased dramatically. There are supportive doctors, and maybe even officers. Attitudes in the ranks, however, have yet to catch up.

After my run-in with my leader—who, I later discover, was himself enrolled in mental health treatment at the time of his attacks on me— the medical officer helps me transfer to another unit that falls under the Second Marine Expeditionary Force, still at Camp Lejeune. My new tasks involve inspecting barracks, doing paperwork, and supervising work orders. The medical officer warns me that after the infantry, everything will seem dull. But I'm told that if my condition improves I will be allowed to return to my old infantry unit.

My new commanders welcome me, know my history, and say they're glad I'm seeking help. If I work hard and keep out of trouble, they say, I'll be respected. The medical officer is present for the introductions and I feel reassured this unit will be better. Still, I'm no longer in the infantry. My life has changed. A new course has been set.

Chapter 12

The Voice

There's not a drug on earth can make life meaningful.

—Sarah Kane, *4.48 Psychosis*

Finbarr, London, December 2011

London in winter probably isn't the best place to spend three months when clinically depressed, but it's a familiar place. My uncle Michael and aunt Trish live here and we've always been close. Mike, himself a photographer, piqued my interest in photography when I was a boy and has shaped the way I see the world. I often visit him, Trish, and their two grown children in southeast London after my Afghan embeds to decompress in a place that feels like home. This time they've made up a spare room for me to use while I spend the next three months working on the Reuters London news desk. The plan makes sense—an extended family visit, work in a new and safe environment, with weekly visits to a psychologist for cognitive behavioral therapy—but I'm quickly reminded that newswire photographers in cities like London usually work a very different beat from those in war zones.

I've braced myself for mundane work. I even welcome it, assuming it will be a relief not to have to deal daily with complex logistics and security concerns, to come home to family at the end of the day, and switch off in the evenings, and sleep in my own bed. I'll be able to go to museums and plays, see movies, and enjoy cafés and restaurants in one of the world's most vibrant cities. In other words, I'll get a taste of normal life.

I tell my editors I'll cover anything, no matter how insignificant or boring. They make sure I do. I'm sent to cover art gallery openings, news conferences, film premieres, and court cases. The work of a big-city news

photographer is an unglamorous daily grind. I'm a
creativity of those who do it well, day in and day
tures at dull events where I see nothing to ph
mind-set isn't helping. Aside from "feeding the be
pelling reason to stand freezing outside a cour'
dozen or more photographers all waiting to take the same p.
someone walking through a doorway, or to photograph a politician entering or exiting the prime minister's office. Or to snap a white-gloved
gallery worker holding a painting worth millions of dollars before it goes
to auction, or Mark Wahlberg strolling into a ballroom at Claridge's to
promote a new movie. Yes, these things matter. Just not to me.

One Sunday afternoon I'm sent to cover the sixty-sixth annual clown
service at Holy Trinity Church in East London. The church holds an annual service in memory of Britain's best-loved clown, Joseph Grimaldi,
who lived from 1778 to 1837. A church full of grown men, including the
priest, wearing colored makeup, baggy trousers, and oversized shoes. I
hate clowns.

London's gray winter bleeds life from my days. I awake every morning dreading the day ahead. I linger in the shower and drink my coffee
slowly, steeling myself for the morning commute. The crowded trains
clatter and screech, and a communal hush of resignation amplifies tinny
headphone music. Pallid faces, blank stares. Runny noses, dry coughs,
and bulky clothes. My rides home are worse, especially after pubs exhale
their lubricated customers into the night.

The London routine feels alien and absurd. Britain's boozing culture
doesn't make sense to me. Is everyone just as unsatisfied with life as I
am? My mind drifts and my spirits sink. This is the seductive nature of
war. Paradoxically, life-threatening situations are life affirming to the
survivors, deluding us into feeling more powerful, invincible even, and
we become ever more drawn to that highest of highs. Some call it the
wargasm. The climax of combat. After such an intense experience, all
else seems banal.

I know it's pitiful to whine. I have my physical health and am employed at a well-paid job for a major news agency. I travel the world on an

account and have attained a degree of professional success,
ch services with clowns notwithstanding. I have a relatively secure
iddle-class life of freedom, comfort, and privilege. I'm not faced with
the kind of desperation and distress I've forged a career documenting. I
don't have to worry about where my next meal will come from, nor
whether my family will survive the next militia attack or outbreak of disease in some desperate corner of the world. I'm not being crushed by the
slow grind of poverty. But the thing that has driven me—my passion for
my work—has let me down, and my perspective on life has been distorted, the link between reality and my perception of it has come undone,
and I'm stuck wallowing in self-pity.

Going to see a shrink must focus the mind and senses. The sunny December air is crisp and cold. I feel hyperalert, sensitive to every quiver of
sunlight, to the growling of a black cab and the hiss of tires against pavement. My psyche is about to be turned inside out by a stranger, probed
and analyzed. No wonder I feel vigilant.

Inside the offices of Positive Health, I meet Dr. Brian Marien. Dr. Feinstein, my Toronto psychiatrist, has referred me to him. His corner room
on the second floor is bright and welcoming. Dr. Marien has a warm
presence and a distracting resemblance to my photographer friend Marcus. We talk for a bit and then he wants to show me some slides on his
computer. I put my coffee on his desk, and when he turns his laptop to
show me the screen, it knocks over my cup, spilling the contents onto his
new carpet. Great start.

If Dr. Marien is annoyed, he doesn't show it. After we've cleaned up
the mess, Dr. Marien starts by showing me a series of slides outlining
some basics about how the brain works. He explains the disconnect between the rational brain—the crowning glory of human evolution—and
the emotional brain. The rational brain, located in the prefrontal lobes
close to our foreheads, helps us to engage with the world and to organize
feelings and impulses. Toward the back of our heads is the limbic system,
the reptilian part of our brain, also known as the lizard or monkey brain.
This is where emotions are generated and memories stored. There are no

neurological pathways between the two areas. In other words, we cannot control how we feel. This is one of the difficulties in treating anxiety disorders, phobias, depression, and PTSD. No matter how hard we try, we can't think our way out of the problem or, more accurately, the feeling. It's like telling someone who is blushing to stop feeling embarrassed or instructing someone to stop being in love (or, conversely, instructing someone who is not in love to fall in love). It can't be done.

Then there's the watchtower—the medial prefrontal cortex (MPFC), the middle part of those lobes behind our foreheads. The MPFC, when working properly, keeps the emotional brain from spinning out of control, allowing us to choose how we react to upsetting news, disturbing events, or tantalizing prospects. When that ability to control our responses breaks down, as it does in those suffering from PTSD, we revert to our true animal state: The moment we detect danger, we're plunged into the fight, freeze, or flight survival reflex. Dr. Marien's lesson offers some rudimentary insight into how my visceral physical reactions—the out-of-body experiences, flashes of anger, and even depression—are controlled by neurons firing inside my brain.

My course of cognitive behavioral therapy with Dr. Marien consists of twelve weekly one-hour sessions. The talking therapy is aimed at breaking down negative thought patterns and behavior to allow me to escape the grip of rumination and self-abnegation. CBT focuses less on the past than on existing problems and aims to improve a patient's general outlook and sense of optimism by breaking problems into smaller, more manageable parts.

During one of our early sessions, Dr. Marien pulls a piece of dried fruit from his pocket. We're going to do the "raisin exercise," he says. He hands me the raisin. There's pocket lint stuck to it. He tells me to take the raisin between my fingers, to roll it back and forth and feel its texture and consistency. He tells me not to answer out loud but to describe to myself what it looks like, as if this were a Rorschach test. When I look at the dried piece of fruit between my fingers, it reminds me of the parched and wizened skin I've seen stretched over corpses. Human jerky. I'm then told to smell the raisin, to put it to my ear and listen to the sound of it rolling back and forth against my fingertips. Then Marien tells me to put the raisin in my mouth—not to eat it but to feel it against my tongue, to experience the texture—then to bite it and compare the taste with the smell.

"How does the raisin feel in your mouth? Describe the experience of the raisin."

"Okay," I tell him, and mutter something. What I think is, *What the fuck is this nonsense?*

Dr. Marien explains that the exercise is about building awareness and learning to focus on the here and now. It's about being in the present moment and not missing out on it. Much of our anxiety—whether related to PTSD or depression—is due to being trapped by memories of the past, he says, or is the result of fears about what might happen in future. And with that, I'm introduced, via a piece of dried fruit, to the concept of mindfulness. The Eastern concept of mindfulness is rooted in Buddhism but has in recent years gained mainstream popularity in the West. It mostly involves being consciously aware and constantly noticing new things, even in familiar environments. It's about engaging with and being curious about the world around you. Mindfulness, Dr. Marien tells me, can change brain chemistry and is a powerful buffer against anxiety disorders, including depression. Okay.

It seems way too simplistic. As if chewing a raisin and stopping to look at flowers or cracks in the sidewalk can make life seem better. Good joke. I'm even less receptive to the idea of meditation, which aspires to much the same thing. I'm skeptical. I'm also desperate. I agree to listen to a few guided meditations on audio recordings. I put it off for a while, but to my surprise, once I try them, I find them relaxing. Still, I'm not convinced they'll offer a magical cure.

During other sessions we discuss my war experiences, but also my family history and, of course, my parents. There's my mother, an indomitable extrovert who emerged from humble origins on a tiny Welsh dairy farm to become an internationally respected medical oncologist in charge of running one of the world's best cancer-care programs, in Canada. And there's my wayward father, the introverted eldest son of poor Irish immigrants to England who worked as a tree planter so we could make ends meet when we first moved from Ireland to Vancouver when I was nine. He held a number of administrative jobs until he left our family during my first year at university after a string of affairs finally exhausted my mother's patience and eventually ended their marriage. He'd been an attentive and loving father until then but was pretty much absent after that. His departure was hurtful to my mother, my younger brother, and me, and, for various reasons, I've dodged his efforts to reconcile since. And so I shaped myself in the image of my formidable mother. It was inevitable, but she's a tough act to follow. Not only has she had a successful career as a doctor, but she's also an avid outdoorswoman who skis in the Rockies, hikes in Patagonia, ventures to places like Nepal and Antarctica, and solo skippers her own small sailboat for weeks-long journeys along Canada's western coast. She is proud, doting, and supportive, but also demanding. She never hid the high expectations she held for my brother and me. Those expectations have guided most of the major decisions I've made as an adult. And they may be behind my unremitting feeling of inadequacy.

"There you are." Dr. Marien nods and smiles when I articulate this. "Your mum sounds like an impressive woman. So it's worth thinking about how her influence has shaped the way you view things."

It makes a certain amount of sense. It's not as if my life as a photographer were the sole factor affecting my mood. It's never that simple. My father struggled with depression, and his mother, my grandmother, alluded in some of our conversations to having felt "low" for long stretches during her life. And her mother, my great-grandmother, spent the later years of her life in an asylum, committed for hysteria, which was likely a form of depression. So there's a history of mental health issues dating back generations. The first memory I have of feeling the grip of depression—although I didn't recognize it then—was in high school, after my best friend from my teenage years, Acron Eger, went on a holiday Christmas trip to the Caribbean with his family and never returned. On New Year's Day in 1989, the twenty-nine-foot powerboat transporting Acron, his sister, Vija, his mother, Frances, and their two boyfriends between Mayreau Island in the Grenadines and Kingstown, the capital of

St. Vincent, vanished without a trace. A ten-day search turned up nothing, other than rumors of a shady boat captain involved in drugs and gunrunning and speculation about pirates and kidnapping. Acron and I had been the closest of a tight-knit group of friends that formed our school basketball team from sixth to tenth grades. Acron was our star player, a straight-A student, and the driving force who inspired everyone else to excel athletically and academically. We were all devastated by such a strange turn of events, but the mystery of his disappearance was especially difficult for me. Acron and I had fallen out when I transferred schools and joined a rival basketball team the year before—a betrayal he could not abide. He never spoke to me again, and the rest of our friends on my old team followed his lead. I didn't have the comfort of their friendship when Acron disappeared. For years afterward I had dreams of Acron and his family stranded on an island somewhere or being held as slaves in some kind of concentration camp, or of his returning and our reconciling. His other friends had similar tortured dreams.

"I wasn't sleeping at all—terrible nightmares for months," one of my former teammates, Jesse Katz, told a reporter who wrote a story about Acron and our team twenty years after his disappearance. "Just of him dying, how he dies. Pirates, being shot, being killed, being drowned, being eaten by sharks, being stranded on an island, starving—just everything, every single night."

Aside from a grandparent, it was the first time I'd experienced death, and with it the sudden realization that people could be there one day and gone the next. That realization left a mark. I'd always been a bit of a withdrawn kid, but Acron's disappearance turned me even further inward.

"When something like that happens," another one of my high school teammates, Peter Rubin, told the reporter, "I'm not sure it ever goes away."

One of the things Dr. Marien wants to know about is my "self-talk," my internal monologue, the way I interpret and explain things to myself. His example involves locking a set of keys inside a car. Most people would feel annoyed with themselves for committing such an error. But most people accept that this can happen to anyone and then get on with resolving the problem. Someone with negative self-talk will berate themselves and believe that they're responsible for always doing stupid things that make life difficult. They feel responsible for their problems or for being unable to cope with life's barbs. Sounds familiar.

I will come to know this internal monologue as the Voice, a shadow version of my self, some nefarious part of my consciousness, always there, whispering and taunting, threatening to grow louder. The Voice twists and distorts my outlook, creating a warped lens on life. It's like that little cartoon devil who sits on a movie character's shoulder, only the Voice doesn't urge me to do bad things; it convinces me that they're already bad, that they'll only get worse, and that it's my own damned fault. Unlike in the movies, there's no little cartoon angel on the other shoulder to challenge the Voice. That's where mindfulness and CBT come in—they are counterbalances and help reverse the cycle of negative thinking driven by the Voice.

Battling the Voice, I learn, requires a kind of practice and discipline similar to regular exercise. The mindfulness tasks I'm given—meditation, breathing, and reflection—force me to step outside myself to see things from another angle. In this sense they're like photography. The mind, like the eye, offers a given perspective, but we can develop how it views things and learn how to process the world anew. I came late to photography, starting professionally only at thirty-four. I had to learn quickly how to tell a story with a camera instead of using my pen and notebook. It took time and effort, but I got there, bit by bit. I try to apply the same approach to the practice of mindfulness. I'm not yet convinced of how effective it really is, but I give it a try.

If nothing else, it prompts me to look differently inside my own family. Unlike me, my uncle Mike makes photographs mostly for his own enjoyment. He spent years kayaking in and walking along the river Thames, scavenging odd bits and pieces washed up along the sandbanks. The waterway has long been a transit route, and the tide's ebb and flow churns up shards of history dating back centuries: carved clay tobacco pipes, worn yellow construction bricks, red roof tiles, bottle necks, bottle stoppers, bits of fishing tackle, lead or plastic toy soldiers, rubber gloves, ironwork, Roman coins, Roman figures, medieval jug handles, crockery chips and pottery shards with Tudor, Stuart, Georgian, or Victorian markings, hooks and hammerheads, ax handles and wooden clothes pegs, buttons, leather shoe soles, cattle-bone and boar-bristle toothbrushes, pieces of World War II antiaircraft shells, German Bellarmine jars, copper boat nails, porcelain dolls' legs, a 1950s hot-water bottle, worn pieces of French and British china bearing royal crowns and coats of arms. The list goes on. More than four thousand fragments gathered over fifteen years, artfully arranged and beautifully photographed to create a remarkable body of work he titled "Fragments from the Foreshore, a Liquid History of the River Thames." The pictures provide vivid and unexpected glimpses into everyday life along the Thames, ancient beliefs, and the river's historical role as a transit artery and dumping ground.

Mike's visceral attachment to the real world is infectious and always brightens my mood, but until now I'd never understood why. When I describe Mike to Dr. Marien, he looks thrilled.

"You see, your uncle Michael is a very mindful guy," he says.

On December 29 I receive an e-mail from the *New York Times* editor who runs the paper's photography blog, *Lens*, telling me to check out the site. I go to the *Lens* home page and see the headline FROM A MARINE'S SIDE OF THE CAMERA. The byline is Thomas James Brennan, accompanied by the picture I took of TJ looking miserable in his bunk at Kunjak. I wrote a piece for *Lens* when TJ was injured, and I've been in touch with him sporadically during the previous months, and over the Christmas holidays, but unbeknownst to me, he has conspired with *Lens* editors to write an article that offers a rare insight into what happens on the other side of my lens. The story tells of how we met, TJ's initial suspicions about journalists, and some of the experiences we shared, including his bewilderment at my obsession with photographing Afghan doors.

"Finbarr O'Reilly told my story and the stories of my Marines," TJ writes in the article. "By doing so, he helped me find my door. For this, I will forever be grateful. Sadly, it may take years of trying for our schedules to match up, but eventually I'll be able to tell him in person. Not over coffee, though. This time, I'm buying him a beer."

The story provides a jolt. For the past few months I've been wallowing in my own misery and uselessness. Reading TJ's story, I discover I've had a lasting impact on at least one person. I shoot him a quick message.

"Hey TJ, is that some kind of Marine ambush in print? You got me good."

For me, no award could match the plain and honest words of gratitude from a grunt who got blown up in Afghanistan. His article allows me to take a first step toward regaining my sense of purpose. And it sparks something in TJ, seeing his byline in print and knowing he has reached me through his writing. And he has more to say. Much more.

Chapter 13

Media Boot Camp

We tell ourselves stories in order to live.

—Joan Didion, *The White Album*

Finbarr, London and Dakar, March–August 2012

The online comments from *NYT* readers get TJ thinking about how the public is detached from the reality of America's wars, the military, and the kinds of experiences that make up his life and the lives of so many others. He wants to write a monthly blog or column about military issues to make that connection.

I'm not so sure. It's an interesting concept, but I doubt TJ can write well enough or that he can identify the aspects of military life that might resonate with civilian readers. And I'm skeptical there will be much appetite for such a thing. One piece does not a career make, even in the *New York Times*. Still, he's finding solace in writing—it's therapeutic—so I encourage him to keep going.

"I find it helps me not only get things off my chest but it helps me organize things in my head," he writes a few weeks later. He's been working on something he wants to show me. "It's not as eloquent as what I wrote about you because it's still in the brainstorming stage so be gentle please. I'm a sensitive young man with feelings. Don't break my heart."

Spoken like a proud Marine. I open the file and read the short essay he has titled "Something Gets Left Behind." It's five paragraphs long and includes the following:

Coming home to your family after a deployment is a very bittersweet feeling that is nearly impossible to put into words. I'd been a war fighter for 7 months and the Corps expected me to turn that side of myself off immediately and turn the civilian side of me back on just as quickly. It wasn't working like that. My work began to suffer. My wife and daughter began to suffer. I became sluggish. I was depressed, lethargic and antisocial. The events of my past had finally caught up with me and I could no longer handle them on my own. It took me almost seven months after I came home from my deployment but on October 29 2011 I began treatment. Since beginning my treatment I have realized that I'm not alone.

The last line hits home. The loneliness and sense of isolation afflicting those who suffer from depression or PTSD can be debilitating. Here we are, both back home, both struggling, and both working our way through therapy. We now have more than just war in common. And we can understand each other in a certain way. Once you realize you're not alone, the cloud begins to lift.

The worlds of traumatized people are fundamentally at odds with those of others, causing a deep chasm of estrangement and solitude, which leads to a desire for "twinship," according to the psychoanalyst Robert D. Stolorow. "When I have been traumatized," he writes in *Trauma and Human Existence*, "my only hope for being deeply understood is to form a connection with a brother or sister who knows the same darkness."

I figure if TJ can develop his writing and tell his story, it can serve a real purpose beyond what it does just for him. Others struggling through similar emotional pain might draw strength from a Marine with the courage to speak out. It's worth a shot.

His first drafts are rough, but over the next few weeks, with work, his story slowly emerges. With additional research and some interviews, the piece balloons to three thousand words. I want to help, but I also want TJ to struggle and to learn to find his own voice. And struggle he does. He doesn't know how to set up and conduct interviews, or when to follow up on phone calls, or even how to introduce himself when calling subjects for quotes.

It's journalism boot camp, with me as drill instructor. After nearly a decade in the Marine Corps, TJ is used to suffering, and his frustration is often palpable but good-humored.

"I just wanted to take this opportunity to tell you how much I dislike you," he writes at one point. "I still cannot for the life of me figure out how to rework those few sentences."

TJ often sends me a draft and, while I'm working on edits, an updated version lands in my in-box, and then another, and another, along with text and messages asking for feedback. The barrage of stories and his queries are demanding, but there's no doubting his enthusiasm. Eventually, after more than four months of back-and-forth, the story has the necessary elements, but it's far too long for publication. After all the work he's done, TJ is dismayed when I tell him he'll need to cut it in half. But the next day, there it is, stripped down to 1,100 words.

"So this is mental health awareness month. What do you think the chances of getting this thing done this month are?"

"Perfect news peg," I answer. "See? You're thinking like a journalist already! You've been converted!"

"Ha-ha, I didn't tell you what I was thinking about for my career," TJ says. "I had a dream about being a journalist."

"Sure it wasn't a nightmare?" I ask.

Whereas TJ is dreaming of getting into journalism, I'm trying to get out of it, or at least take a break. My sessions with Dr. Marien are nearly complete and my time in London seems to have improved my outlook, but I'm still wary of returning to high-stress work in conflict zones. I need more time away from that kind of environment. I apply for a Nieman Fellowship at Harvard, which would require a sabbatical from Reuters. The university's Nieman Foundation each year invites twenty-four journalists—twelve foreigners and twelve Americans—to spend an academic year researching a topic of their choosing. The foundation prepares journalists for the next stages of their careers. My application includes a proposal to study psychology with a focus on exploring how conflict-induced trauma affects the mind and body and how that in turn affects mood and behavior. The idea is to direct my research in a way that can help me understand in an intellectual capacity some of the things I've experienced on an emotional level. My friendship with TJ—and my growing concern for his welfare—makes this an obvious topic of study.

On February 22, 2012, I'm scheduled to have a thirty-minute Skype interview with the selection committee. That morning, as I'm prepping for the interview, news breaks that the American war correspondent Marie Colvin and the French photographer Rémi Ochlik have been killed in Syria. Shelling by government forces hit the media center where they were staying in the rebel enclave of Baba Amr. They were killed instantly. Several other journalists are wounded and trapped in the city. I don't know Colvin, but I spent some time in Tunisia and Libya with Rémi. He was freelancing in Libya and I offered him a ride in my car from Benghazi back to Egypt. We chatted a bit on the long drive but were both so exhausted from weeks on the front line that we slept for most of the ride. News of their deaths is only the latest shock wave to hit the journalism community. A week ago Anthony Shadid, the two-time Pulitzer Prize–winning correspondent for the *New York Times*, died from a severe allergy attack while being smuggled out of Syria by rebels. I didn't know Shadid well either— we only had breakfast together a few times in Libya, including the morning of his capture by Gadhafi's troops—but this most recent round of deaths heightens my anxiety about returning to work in war zones.

In March I get the phone call saying I've been granted the Nieman. It won't start for six months, but the news comes as a relief. It feels like a window has opened. One of the biggest problems with major depression is feeling like there's no purpose to life, no greater meaning. Any sense of possibility evaporates. The combination of my therapy, TJ's article, and now the news of the fellowship lifts my spirits. There's other good news too. In early 2011 I agreed to be filmed for a documentary, *Under Fire: Journalists in Combat*, produced by Dr. Feinstein, my Toronto therapist, and based on his research into the psychological costs of covering war. In addition to being interviewed in London and Dakar by the director, Martyn Burke, I filmed frontline footage while embedded with TJ at Kunjak and while working in Libya and Ivory Coast. *Under Fire* is one of fifteen films long-listed for a 2012 Academy Award. The film doesn't make it to the final list of five nominees, but my participation in the project has reinforced my desire to delve deeper into an exploration of trauma psychology. Also, the fellowship will put me on the same continent as TJ, whose parents live just outside Boston, close to Harvard. I plan to collect on that beer.

Meanwhile, TJ's story is ready. I suggest he try the *New York Times*'s *At War* blog. *At War* is described as "a reported blog from Afghanistan, Pakistan, Iraq and other conflicts in the post-9/11 era" created by the paper to provide "insight—and answer questions—about combatants on the faultlines, and civilians caught in the middle." The editors already know his name from his *Lens* piece, which gives him an advantage and a little extra confidence, but he'll have to learn how to pitch a story.

"This may sound dumb, but what do you put in the subject line for an official e-mail to the *NYT*?" he asks.

After a few weeks of exchanges with *Times* editors and some maneuvering past Marine Corps public affairs, which has to approve anything submitted for publication, TJ sends me a message.

"It's accepted by the *At War* blog!!!"

Two days later, on June 22, 2012, the *Times* publishes TJ's two-thousand-word story, "Living with PTSD and Allowing Myself to Get Help." The piece reveals his struggles navigating his return home from war, his feelings of emptiness and of guilt, and his sense of being lost. He writes openly about his PTSD and the stigma attached to asking for help.

"PTSD is something that some in the military do not accept or understand," he writes. "Unlike physical wounds, it is invisible, intangible. I once heard a senior Marine say PTSD was 'fake.' In a way this makes sense for a military institution that prides itself on toughness and resilience in the face of adversity. But the time has come to realize that all battlefield wounds must be healed.

"My change started slowly," he continues. "Some wounds have healed. Others still have scabs. In order to fully heal I need to peel back those scabs to reveal what lies beneath."

The rawness and honesty I saw in that first draft he sent months ago is now on public display. More than a dozen comments are soon posted, applauding him for speaking out with such grace.

"Thomas, Thank you for your courage and honesty in sharing part of your story with the world. In doing this, you serve your fellow veterans in a whole new way," writes Peggy Spencer, MD, from Albuquerque, New Mexico.

"The VA and the 'system' is really not doing a very good job at helping out Vets," writes another. "How many more must die before everyone realizes that the 'system' is broken?"

TJ is ecstatic. Sharing his story and taking control of his own narrative gives him a sense of empowerment. Public approval from strangers doesn't hurt either. For someone who has lived—and has seen others die—by the gun, wielding the power of the pen is a revelation.

"It feels unreal," he says. "The response from my friends has been great. Especially the ones that have PTSD. They say it explains how they feel too, which is what I was after. I'm glad I could be their voice."

The piece also allows TJ to explain things to Mel in ways he has otherwise been unable to articulate. In the wake of his brain injury, he often has difficulty expressing himself through the spoken word. Writing, however, allows him to reveal his thoughts more clearly. He's on a high, and the rush of seeing his byline attached to an article he struggled over for so long fills him with pride.

"Learning has occurred," he says, and it's clear the experience has only deepened his desire to further explore journalism. Jim Dao, the *At War* editor, encourages him to submit more work, boosting his enthusiasm.

Three days later, TJ tells me about an encounter he had in the waiting room at the brain injury clinic, where another Marine had come for his first postcombat checkup. The Marine feared what the doctors might find. TJ noticed his speech problems. When the Marine got up to go to the bathroom, TJ noted his awkward gait. When he returned, TJ asked the Marine how long it had been since he got back from Afghanistan. February 9, 2011, the Marine answered. It was now June 25, 2012, almost a year and a half later.

TJ is outraged. "How it took him so long to be referred for care is appalling and an insult to the sacrifice he made for his country!" he vents. "Semper fi my ass!"

Without either of us realizing it, TJ has found his calling. His experience confronting postwar emotional turmoil puts him in a unique position to write about a military system that is failing combat veterans after a decade of wars in Iraq and Afghanistan. And he's determined to do it, constantly shooting me questions about how to approach an idea, or asking whether a newspaper might be interested in his thoughts on some topic or other.

Mentoring TJ is satisfying to me as well. His commitment to learning and the progress he's making are inspiring. It feels good to support someone else who is struggling. Through his writing TJ is doing more than healing himself and giving a voice to other service members. He is also pulling me along with him, drawing me out of my own funk of despair.

It turns out that one of the best ways to help a depressed person is not to do something for him but rather to ask him to do something for you. Give him a task. Make him feel useful. Make him realize he *is* useful. Over time this can create what's known as a "helper's high." The mesolimbic pathway, or the reward center of the brain, is stimulated, releasing endorphins and decreasing depression by creating a greater sense of purpose and of happiness. Studies have shown it also lowers stress levels and increases self-esteem. And like other highs, it's addictive. The helper's high becomes an uplifting foil to the downward cycle of negative thoughts and rumination that can make depression such a deep and difficult hole to escape.

Over the next six months I work with TJ as he writes a series of pieces for *At War* that underscore the challenges faced by members of the military seeking help for mental health problems. He writes about flaws in the Department of Defense's Post Deployment Health Assessment and the difficulty of negotiating the Physical Disability Board of Review and the Integrated Disability Evaluation System, which rates a service member's fitness for duty. He explains "the brotherhood of combat" and publishes a piece on how writing can "calm and compose the injured brain." In addition to his personal stories, he reports objective pieces about military issues such as alcohol abuse, the repeal of the "don't ask, don't tell" law on homosexuality, and the role of women in the Marine Corps. With each piece his writing improves. Eventually he is submitting stories without my help. In addition to appearing in the *Times*'s At War blog, his work is published in the *Huffington Post* and *Stars and Stripes*. Broadcast media outlets such as CBS, Fox News, and the BBC call him for comments on military issues related to his stories. His most powerful writing, however, comes in a piece for *At War* titled "Ending a Life, and a Part of Yourself, for the First Time." It addresses the question so often asked of combat veterans—"Did you kill anyone?"—and provides a far more comprehensive answer than most people really want.

Finbarr, Cambridge, Massachusetts, August–December 2012

The first Harvard class I attend is Professor Thomas Kelly's "First Nights," which teaches the stories surrounding opening-night performances of five seminal works of classical music: Monteverdi's opera *L'Orfeo*, Handel's *Messiah*, Beethoven's Ninth Symphony, Berlioz's *Symphonie fantastique*, and Stravinsky's *Le Sacre du printemps*. Professor Kelly's lecture is held in Sanders Theatre at Memorial Hall, a towering High Gothic building erected in honor of the Harvard men who died in defense of the Union during the Civil War. The wooden 1,166-seat theater, completed in 1875 and renowned for superb acoustics, has hosted speakers such as Winston Churchill, Theodore Roosevelt, Martin Luther King Jr., and Mikhail Gorbachev. I'm a long way from OP Kunjak, and the collegiate atmosphere transports me back twenty-four years to my own days as a wide-eyed student on the first day of term. For the past year or so, I've been worn out and feeling hopeless, but sitting in Sanders Theatre, I enjoy a surge of excitement about a future that has for so long seemed gloomy. I'm basking in this rare flush of optimism when a freshman sits down in the pew beside me.

"Oh, excuse me, sir," he says, "Is this row reserved for faculty?"

Thanks, kid. Way to spoil the moment.

My biggest challenge now is navigating my way across campus by bike and figuring out how to sign out a library book for the first time in twenty-three years. I take pleasure in simple luxuries such as being able to drink tap water, use a vacuum cleaner, shop at overstocked supermarkets, call friends on clear phone lines, and walk along sidewalks that aren't cracked on streets that aren't flooded or laced with IEDs. The electricity never cuts out and the Internet always works, even when it rains. I've rented an apartment in a leafy neighborhood beside the Charles River. I guess I'm going soft, or reverting to my roots of white, middle-class privilege. I should feel more uncomfortable about this than I do. In truth, it feels pretty fucking great.

After my initial introduction to mindfulness during my therapy in London, I'm intrigued to find several courses on the subject offered at Harvard. I drop in on a few of the classes, including one in the psychology department on mindfulness and decision making, taught by Professor Ellen Langer. I get to the seminar room a few minutes early and Langer is already seated at the front of the doughnut-shaped arrangement of desks. I sit down nearby and mention that because it's shopping week, when students drop in and out of classes to sample and decide which professors and courses they like, I might have to duck out early to check out another class on decision making.

"Which one?" she asks. I give her the name of the course and the professor. "Oh, don't go to that class," she says. "You'll be much better off here."

I have to chuckle. I sat in on another mindfulness seminar in the theology department this morning and it was painfully flaky and full of intolerable show-off students. I'm steeling myself for more of the same in Langer's class, but it couldn't be more different. As the classroom fills, Langer launches into an entertaining monologue explaining all the ways we are mindless, from the way we think and the assumptions we make to the way we behave. In one example she asks the class to add one plus one together. The answer, of course, is two. But is it always? Uh, yeah.

"So, if I have one piece of chewing gum in this hand and another piece of gum in this hand, and then I stick them together, how many pieces of gum do I have?"

The class groans. Langer's point is that we constantly make mindless assumptions because we believe things to be a certain way. They don't have to be. She explains that mindfulness is all about being in the moment and constantly noticing new things and challenging norms. Langer acknowledges that meditation could be an effective path to mindfulness but believes meditation is unnecessary and possibly even limiting. To her, it makes more sense to live mindfully all the time. Her idea is that if people—and society as a whole—could become more engaged with the present instead of consumed by the past or concerned about the future, then we would live much healthier, fuller lives. Her belief is that wherever you put the mind, the body follows. And her years of research support the idea that changing our minds can shape our physical health.

Back in 1979, when she was a young scholar at Yale, Langer took a group of elderly men and quarantined them for a week in an old New Hampshire monastery that had been retrofitted to look like a home from 1959: vintage furniture, floors, carpets, and decorations, 1950s issues of *Life* magazine and the *Saturday Evening Post*, a black-and-white TV running news and shows from that year. The men were made to carry their own luggage, do chores, and manage their own household without assistance while speaking in the present tense as though it were 1959—basically to live as independently as they had two decades earlier, when they were still young, without regard to the many infirmities that afflicted them in later life. What happened by the end of the week would quickly pass into legend, at least among psychologists: The men seemed to grow younger. Height, weight, gait, posture, hearing, and vision all improved. So did performance on intelligence and memory tests. Joints were more flexible, shoulders wider, fingers more agile, arthritis retreating. On the last day of the experiment, Langer was kicking a soccer ball around the garden with the same men who on the first day could barely walk without support.

The results of Langer's "counterclockwise study," as it is known, secured her status in the field of psychology, and she's been running variations of it ever since. She became the first tenured woman in Harvard's psychology department and her early findings gave rise to a question that has consumed her career ever since: If purposeful attention to our immediate surroundings can turn back the clock of biology, what else can it do? She has written more than two hundred research articles and eleven books, including an international bestseller, looking at things like control, success, aging, illness, and decision making, all through the prism of mindfulness.

Langer's seminars are entertaining, and joining her psychology lab takes me on a yearlong exploration of mindfulness and the practice of living in the moment. A few months into my fellowship, though, I meet Bessel van der Kolk, a Boston-based psychiatrist who has spent his career researching trauma and treating its victims. His work is even more closely related to what I've come to study. Van der Kolk first became involved with trauma when he joined the VA in 1978. At the time, PTSD had not yet been recognized as a formal diagnosis, but he soon discovered an emerging phenomenon of traumatized war veterans. Tens of thousands of men who'd served in Vietnam were suddenly coming out of the woodwork nationwide, suffering from flashbacks, beating their wives, drinking and drugging themselves to suppress their feelings, and closing down emotionally. In the years since, Van der Kolk has written more than a hundred peer-reviewed papers on subjects such as self-mutilation, dissociation, and traumatic memory, and he is the author of *The Body Keeps the Score*, a book detailing his life's work. His patients range from abused children and incest survivors to combat veterans and torture victims from around the world. Van der Kolk is a controversial figure, with ideas that challenge some of the long-held beliefs of the psychiatric mainstream, but he remains hugely influential and his followers regard him as a pioneering hero in the field of trauma research and treatment. Van der Kolk believes that trauma has to do with the body being reset to interpret the world as a dangerous place. That reset begins in the deep recesses of the brain in regions that, he says, no cognitive therapy can access. He's a harsh critic of the traditional trauma treatments still used by the VA, including CBT, and especially of overmedication and prolonged exposure therapy—the kind of therapy TJ has undertaken with Frank. Van der Kolk argues that prolonged exposure therapy is the worst possible treatment for traumatized vets because rather than healing them, it desensitizes them to suffering.

There's plenty of evidence to indicate that such therapies are ineffective. Thirty-six major clinical trials of therapy for PTSD among active-duty troops and veterans, conducted between 1980 and 2015, concluded that the most widely used therapies for PTSD—cognitive processing therapy

(CPT) and prolonged exposure (PE)—were only marginally effective, Pulitzer Prize–winning author David Wood writes in his book, *What Have We Done: The Moral Injury of Our Longest Wars*. Between one third and one half of patients receiving CPT or PE did not demonstrate meaningful symptom change, and two thirds of those receiving therapy still had PTSD symptoms afterward, adds Wood, citing a paper published in the *Journal of the American Medical Association*.

"I found this outrageous," Wood writes. "The only therapies widely available from the United States government for combat veterans were ineffective. We sent people to war, and when they came home (emotionally damaged), either they were ignored, or they were diagnosed with PTSD and given therapy that didn't help. How did this happen?"

Wood's explanation is that the government relied on studies of traumatized civilians when it endorsed the use of CPT and PE in 2008, but that war trauma is inherently different from civilian trauma in that it recurs over repeated deployments and not only involves threat to life and limb but also entails deeper emotional wounds related to devastating losses and morally compromising experiences. Van der Kolk goes a step further, suggesting that such therapies are worse than just ineffective and can actually be damaging. The massive backlog of active duty service members and veterans awaiting mental health care has created a political backlash in Washington, but Van der Kolk tells me in conversation one day that he sees this as a kind of blessing.

"Thank God they're not getting treated," he says. "These forms of therapy, they don't work. They only retraumatize the patients. Yes, it numbs them to their traumatic experience, but it numbs them to everything else in life too—relationships and the ability to feel connected to the world."

Van der Kolk argues there are many more effective ways of treating PTSD that should be used, but the VA isn't using them or is too bureaucratic to deliver those treatments effectively. In order to heal, he says, trauma victims need to process and release their traumatic memories through their bodies. Van der Kolk himself uses a variety of treatments, including yoga, theater therapy (where trauma victims act out Shakespeare plays), and eye-movement desensitization and reprocessing (EMDR), a form of therapy used to treat everything from trauma to anxiety.

I meet Van der Kolk during a joint presentation organized by the Nieman Foundation as part of my fellowship. Our talk is held in a crowded seminar room, where I've been invited to discuss my work in conflict zones and the impact of witnessing violence and where he explains how trauma affects the brain and body. After I show the audience of about forty people my photographs and videos from Congo, Libya, Afghanistan, and elsewhere and describe some of the impact that work has had on me, Van der Kolk begins his part of the presentation by saying, "I don't really want to talk after seeing this presentation. And I think that most of us don't really want to talk because it's just too horrendous. When you see these kinds of images, the speech part of your brain actually shuts down, so it's virtually impossible for people to give voice to these experiences. Images linger rather than the words. And the tension between images and words has always been central to my work in traumatized people."

He goes on.

"What always strikes me about pictures like this is that—and," he says, turning to me, "maybe you've been struck by this also—is how little impact they have. These pictures are being seen, but they're not being processed. And that's what makes your work so painful."

His comments perfectly capture my moral conundrum. Invoking the pretense of serving a cause larger than my own, I intrude upon the lives of others at their most vulnerable. Yet change is incremental, often imperceptible, and not always for the best. This has contributed to my disillusionment and despair.

Van der Kolk also points out that whereas people may be horrified by the kinds of images I've shown, those images also energize them, a phenomenon akin to the buzz of excitement accompanying a crowd exiting the theater after an especially violent action movie. His approach to treating trauma also involves mindful activities. The big issue with trauma, Van der Kolk says, is not so much what happened in the past but how it interferes with people living in the present, how it gets in the way of being fully alive in the here and now.

Our physiological reactions to trauma deaden our ability to feel emotionally alive, he says, and being mindful helps bring back our ability to appreciate the small everyday details—such as breathing and movement—that make up our lives. Van der Kolk cites three decades of research showing how, when exposed to danger, our bodies increase stress hormone levels that help us to cope and fight and to be alert and alive. Over time, however, as our brains keep being bombarded by stress hormones, the brain regulates itself in order to cope with the onslaught. Before long, and once the danger has passed, we no longer feel anything. We feel numb.

"Maybe a bit how we all felt after seeing Finbarr's pictures," he says.

So those who are traumatized risk going through life not feeling much. This often drives traumatized people toward risky or exciting behavior in order to elevate their stress hormone levels.

"Paradoxically, reexposing yourself to danger makes you feel alive while safety gives you a feeling of discomfort," Van der Kolk says. "What you see with combat soldiers is they enlist, they hate it the first time around, and the next time they go, they come home—and the best depiction is in the movie *The Hurt Locker*, where these guys are very competent in combat, very loving with each other—and they come home and they are playing with their kid and they feel nothing. You see this in policemen, prostitutes, and people who are involved in chronically high-stress situations. Once they're taken away from that high-stress situation, they start collapsing, they become ill and drink themselves to death, and that kind of thing. So the whole issue is how can you continue to feel something?"

He's a strong advocate of yoga and meditation. I've been trying meditation from time to time since London. It seems to help, but two new activities I engage in during my fellowship support ideas espoused by both Langer and Van der Kolk about the mind-body connection, and I enjoy them more than meditation. Every week I join a dozen other people for a three-hour life drawing class taught by Anne McGhee, a retired artist, and featuring a naked model striking a series of poses ranging in duration from a few seconds to more than half an hour. I have never drawn before, but, with gentle encouragement from Anne and others in the room, I scratch away with my charcoal sticks on the rough newsprint, struggling to translate the human form in front of me onto paper. I have varying degrees of success, but the experience is profound. I float out after each class as if in a dream, having spent the previous hours entirely focused only on what was in front of me—the model, the paper—and my body moving to connect the two. I'm so concentrated that, upon leaving class, I sometimes have to look around at the street outside to remind myself where I am. Rarely do I feel as relaxed and centered as I do after one of Anne's classes. And I'm pretty sure drawing helps me in other ways too.

"Learning to draw . . . is certainly not about Art with a capital A. The true subject is *perception*." Betty Edwards writes in her book *Drawing on the Right Side of the Brain*. "The larger purpose was always to bring right brain hemisphere functions into focus and to teach [students] how to *see* in new ways, with hopes that they would discover how to transfer perceptual skills to thinking and problem solving."

This "transfer of learning" seems especially relevant to someone whose perception of the world has shifted and become negative and defeatist. In addition to lifting my mood in the moment, learning to draw, however poorly, almost certainly stimulates my mind and revives some of the problem-solving abilities that have allowed me to thrive in challenging environments.

I also start training in martial arts and attending regular exercise boot camps. I begin working out intensely for two or three hours daily, sometimes more. In addition to thrusting me into a different social and mental space beyond Harvard's academic setting, the sustained level of physical activity forces my mind to live in the moment. Learning hand-to-hand combat and sparring with opponents makes it impossible to worry about the future or ruminate on the past. My mind becomes entirely focused while training, as if aware of every muscle and fiber in my body. It no doubt also increases the level of stress hormones flowing through my body, giving me a small, safe dose of the rush and excitement usually provided by working in risky environments. I return home battered, bruised, and physically exhausted but mentally alert. It's well documented that exercise helps battle depression and, just like the drawing classes, the training nudges both my body and my mind into a much healthier place. Van der Kolk suggests that regularly engaging in such "mindful" activities has an effect on the brain similar to that of meditation, helping to rewire neurological circuits. For me, at least, it lowers the volume of the Voice. And it's certainly a better way than constant, intimate exposure to death as a way to inhabit the present.

Chapter 14

Coming Undone

We look the same. We talk the same. . . . But inside, without really comprehending why, we are hugely changed. The person we have always known is strangely missing. . . . The only way back is after first passing through the gates of death.

—Clark Elliott, Ph.D., *The Ghost in My Brain: How a Concussion Stole My Life and How the New Science of Brain Plasticity Helped Me Get It Back*

TJ, North Carolina, October–December 2012

By late 2012 the common thread between me and Fin is journalism rather than war. I'm working on occasional articles for the *At War* blog while he's enjoying his Harvard sabbatical. We're both adapting to the quiet life stateside. I'm debating whether to grow a beard while Fin is posting pretty pictures of autumn leaves changing colors in New England. Compared with OP Kunjak, this is the land of comfort and plenty. But looming over me is the knowledge that by the end of the year my career in the Marine Corps will be finished. I completed two enlistments and reenlisted for another four years in the fall of 2011, after deciding that I wanted to keep building my career in the Marine Corps. But right after making that decision, I learned that because of my injuries I had no future as a Marine.

I've known for twelve months that I'll be medically retired on December 31, 2012—twelve weeks from now—and I've taken the necessary steps to financially protect my family by submitting to months of medical and psychological evaluations to determine the level of disability compensation I'll receive upon retirement. The military has rated me 100 percent disabled, meaning I'll be entitled to lifelong health and education benefits, as well as a monthly pension. Not bad. Still, it's not enough to live an extravagant life or even to provide the kind of life I want to for me,

Mel, and Maddie. I've got about three months to figure out what the hell I'm going to do with my life as a civilian.

In October Fin invites me to join him in Cambridge for a special event. His Nieman Fellowship requires him to do a one-hour presentation to the twenty-three other fellows and faculty, outlining his life and career. The presentation is called a "sounding" and the theme is "Why I Do What I Do." He explains that the weekly soundings by each fellow are the most intimate and revealing part of an academic year spent on personal exploration. They require a level of reflection and self-analysis these high-achieving journos rarely have time for during their busy work lives. The soundings are open only to Niemans, their partners, staff, and guests invited by the speaker. Fin wants me there.

I'm excited to go but also anxious. The connection we first made in Afghanistan and then revisited during months of online conversations might not translate into real life. Keeping Fin safe in Helmand came more naturally to me than visiting him at some hallowed ivory tower. Fin's career seems to consist of an impossibly glamorous lifestyle where he jets around the world stepping onto history's stage whenever the call comes, allowing him to brush shoulders with world leaders, celebrities, and now Ivy League academics. I still don't know much about his family, his love life, or his aspirations. I know him only in the narrow role of a conflict photographer. My perception is a limited view of Fin's life, but even the reality is far beyond my own experience. I've earned an associate degree in business management online while in the Marine Corps. I'm now working to earn a B.A. from the University of Massachusetts at Amherst via online correspondence, but I've not been in a classroom since high school. Before setting my sights on journalism, my loftiest ambition was to open a coffee shop. Any university is intimidating, as is any crowd of professional journalists. But this is Harvard, and despite my *NYT* bylines, I'm still Sergeant Brennan, a Marine with a two-year college degree. I'll be way out of my element.

More worrying than my perceived academic shortcomings is the lingering impact of my brain injury. During conversations I still have trouble articulating ideas; I sometimes struggle to find the right words and my Marine vernacular slips out. What if I come off like some dumb grunt, some stereotypical foulmouthed Marine? I take a few days off to travel to Boston for a long weekend, knowing my trip will also give me the chance to introduce Fin to my family in Randolph, a thirty-minute drive south of Boston.

I text Fin as I park my sister's car in front of his Cambridge apartment. It's on a street of three-story multifamily homes. Cyclists zip past and joggers wearing headphones trot along the sidewalks. Fin and I are both smiling as he walks down his front steps to meet me. We're both heavier than we were at Kunjak. I extend my hand. Fin gives me a hug instead. The cocktail social before Fin's sounding isn't like the barracks parties I'm used to. Nobody throws a mini fridge out of a window, the wine isn't in a box, and the food isn't Domino's pizza. Nobody is funneling hard liquor from the second or third story and nobody is fighting or bleeding.

When Fin steps to the podium, he starts by explaining his childhood, his transition from the written word to photography, and how he has grown to question the profession of photojournalism—or at least his place in it. Fin has told some of his Nieman colleagues about me and my *New York Times* stories, but it isn't until the end of his presentation, after he's traced the arc of his own life and career, that he answers the sounding's underlying question of why he does what he does. He shows clips of my work projected onto a screen and describes the evolution of our working relationship.

Then, in his closing remarks, Fin says: "It's a very rare photograph or story that changes the world, but it is possible to have an impact on individual lives. The often brief but intense encounters I've had on assignment can be far more satisfying than having a picture on the front page of a newspaper or magazine (although that's nice too). Of all the stories I've told tonight, I'm proudest of my relationship with Sergeant Brennan, working with him over the past year, mentoring him, and seeing him grow as a journalist. Alongside his war tattoos of lost comrades, he now has a tattoo of a quill and inkpot. By now you should have some idea of why I do what I do. But in case you need a flesh-and-blood example, he's sitting right over there."

I'm stunned. Hearing Fin tell a roomful of journalists that my first story about him was more valuable than any award he's ever won catches me off guard. I assumed my visit to Harvard was a chance for us to meet up, not that there was any greater reason behind Fin's invitation, or that I might have had the kind of impact on his life that he's had on mine. Maybe this is his way of getting me back for the article I wrote on *Lens*—his idea of a journalistic ambush.

All eyes turn toward me. Most of the fifty or so people crowded into the room didn't know I was present. If Fin is trying to deflect attention, he's just pulled off a masterstroke. During the dinner and drinks that follow his presentation, I become the center of attention. Fin's colleagues ask me questions and listen to my stories. One after another, they encourage me to keep writing. It's a rush. For the first time I'm surrounded not by Marines who question my pursuit of journalism but by other journalists who treat me as a colleague. It's a curious role reversal; just as my Marines accepted Fin into our closed circle, his fellows have welcomed me into their tribe.

The weekend after Fin's sounding, I pick him up for dinner at my parents'— the first time he'll meet them in person. We eat Cap'n Crunch chicken, and Fin apologizes to my mom for the photos that nearly made her faint. Our dinner conversation is cheery and full of laughter and revolves around Fin's work, his family, and his Harvard studies. Afterward I drive him home. We agree to meet again before too long. When I get home, my mom is making coffee and putting out more dessert. As I walk past her, she pulls me aside, embraces me, and tells me she's glad I've found a friend outside the Marine Corps, someone who can expose me to a world beyond the military. I agree, but I'm actually troubled by my deepening friendship with Fin. I know his friends and colleagues have been killed and that more journalists are dying or being abducted at alarming rates. I'm beginning to understand and work through my trauma. I live with the constant fear that my veteran friends might kill themselves, or that friends still on active duty might get killed in a combat zone a world away. Now I have another person to worry about. I wish Fin didn't live such a dangerous life, even though it's how we first met. When most people tell someone, "See you tomorrow," they believe that they will. I no longer take such things for granted. I try to shrug off such negative thoughts. But for hours I lie awake envisioning dead friends and missed funerals. I worry that Fin's could be held in the not-so-distant future.

I wonder what the fuck America's wars are really about, whether there was ever any chance they could have instilled democracy in places like Iraq and Afghanistan, where citizens seem to be of little concern to their own governments. I wonder how many Iraqi civilians and Afghan villagers just want the same things I want now: to be left alone, to be happy, to have a healthy family. How many times did I make that impossible for them? My job wasn't to figure these things out. My job in Iraq was to fight and kill on command, and in Afghanistan it was to get my men in and out alive. In that sense I accomplished my mission. At the time, that's all that mattered. But the longer I sit with it, the less I can accept the claim of "mission accomplished."

I'm not against war. And I'm not naive about what happens in war. Some people deserve to die. When our leaders send us to war to kill our enemies, civilians die too. Some causes are worth fighting for. But having seen that happen—having killed civilians myself, and living with the emotional fallout—I'm less gung ho on war than I once was. Our stated goal was to help people and to make our country, and the world, a safer place. I can cling to the belief that individually we were well intentioned, for the most part. But we fucked up. So many times.

On one occasion, outside Hadithah in 2004, a white sedan with yellow doors sped toward my platoon's checkpoint on a remote desert highway. The checkpoint was tucked behind the downward slope of a ridgeline to conceal it from view. This limited a driver's ability to turn away unnoticed. We put out Arabic road signs telling drivers to slow down and then stop, but the approaching car wasn't slowing down. The driver ignored a single warning shot to the engine block and a pen flare fired at the vehicle. Our rules of engagement allowed our machine gunner to open fire with the Pig, a four-foot-long M240 that weighs more than twenty-five pounds and fires 950 rounds per minute. The Marine flipped the weapon off of safe and fired burst after burst through the fire wall and windshield of the car. The driver slammed on the brakes and stopped. Then, shaken, he staggered from the car with his hands up. The passenger, a woman cradling a baby, followed him. The hood, windshield, and seats were riddled with dozens of bullet holes. The man, his wife, and their newborn child somehow emerged without a scratch. The husband had been texting on his phone while driving and did not notice our warnings. The mother had been sleeping with the child in her arms. They were lucky to have survived. Other families during my deployment didn't. The children of men we questioned during foot patrols in Iraq were sometimes kidnapped and killed by members of Al Qaeda. Many of those men had told us nothing. That didn't matter. Their children were dismembered and their body parts left in their homes as a warning.

How does handing out soccer balls, coloring books, and pens, or even building a small school, make up for anything like that? Is it any wonder I can't sleep? If those people hated us afterward, or wanted revenge, I can't blame them.

I try to convince myself that maybe some of those kids who survived will remember laughing at me that time I fell on my ass trying to kick them a soccer ball while overloaded with gear. I hope they remember the tiny outdoor school we built for them near OP Kunjak and that they keep striving to continue their education. Or that they know my squad found an IED outside their home in Afghanistan before their mother or father found it the hard way.

The night of Fin's visit, I lie in my childhood bed, my stomach full of my mom's food, but I can't settle. I'm trapped inside the distorted mind-set of a warrior. Our universe is unpredictable, random, and unsafe. We are confronted with a world that constantly threatens our very existence. My idea of a safe and just world has been shattered. At least that's one thing I share with the Iraqi and Afghan civilians we were sent to help.

I fly home to North Carolina the next day.

My medical retirement has been set for the end of the year. The Marine Corps has deemed me unfit for continued military service. I could stay on, but only on permanent limited duty, meaning I can't deploy and would basically become an office flunky. I joined to be a grunt, and if I can't do that, then what's the point?

As part of my exit, I'm required to attend a week of transition seminars that encourage veterans to milk the VA for as much disability money as possible and offers lackluster classes on résumé writing. Almost every speaker tells us it's important to own a tie, as if they think we'd turn up for a job interview in sweatpants and a tank top. All of the instructors and speakers are in their midforties and older—not exactly my demographic. The seminars are uninspiring.

Part of me wants to go to nursing school and pursue emergency medicine like Mel. Maybe become a paramedic. I apply for government contract jobs as a weapons and explosives instructor. I've already switched my major to journalism at the University of Massachusetts, but I'm not sure it will pay the bills. I think about owning a coffee shop—a long-standing dream. I even toy with the idea of becoming a psychologist, but then think better of it. Too much studying required, plus I no longer trust my memory when lives are on the line. How do people figure this stuff out? I know stories make me happy. Mel and I have been talking on our front porch during the warm summer nights.

"Just do whatever will make you happy," she says night after night. "You've got a second chance in life to do absolutely anything you want to do. Not many people get that opportunity. Do what makes you happy."

Then I come to a decision. I really do want to be a journalist—despite the shitty pay.

One of the stories I write for *At War* toward the end of 2012 addresses the question so often asked of combat veterans—"Did you kill anyone?" I write that taking someone's life brought me face to face with the darkest side of myself, that there are nights when I see the faces of people I killed, that there are days when I get lost in vivid memories of violent combat for minutes at a time, and that killing has left me emotionally numb.

"In the last eight years, I have not been able to cry unless I'm reminiscing about Fallujah," I write in the article. "It is as if my brain created a space where feelings were lost or delayed. And when I did feel emotions after killing, it was often the sense of relief that I was not on the receiving end—an emotion that might readily, but incorrectly, be interpreted as satisfaction.

"I wonder what life will be like without the thrill of combat or the agony of taking a human life. I'm sure I will become nostalgic watching videos and reminiscing over old photos. But more than anything, I worry about the part of me that I lost and whether I will find it somewhere down the line."

I'm breaking taboos by being open about my struggles, and over the past year I've become one of *At War*'s most prolific contributors. My piece on what it feels like to kill is selected by editors as one of the blog's top ten pieces of the year and is included in an e-book. When that story first appeared online, a Marine veteran of Iraq called me up and told me he'd been planning to commit suicide until he read my piece. That's good enough validation for me to keep going.

These small successes give me temporary boosts, but even as my writing career is taking off, the reality of my military career coming crashing to an end overshadows everything else. I'm about to have my identity as a Marine stripped. Frank and Dr. Webster continue to tell me that healing takes time—there's no magic pill. If I'm ever to find that part of myself I lost in Iraq, it isn't going to happen in the military. The brotherhood of men that swears to be "ever loyal, ever faithful" is about to cut me loose.

I've got two months of vacation days owing, so I use them up by taking leave for November and December, the last two months of my Marine Corps service. I'll be leaving the service with a whimper instead of a bang. Not great for an explosives guy like me. On the bright side, I've been offered a job as a reporter at a small daily newspaper in Lumberton, North Carolina. It isn't much, but it is a start, and I'm keen to have something lined up for when my Marine Corps career officially ends. I'm afraid I'll be an embarrassment to Mel if I end up unemployed or stuck in a meaningless career. I'm determined not to become another veteran left by the wayside, another sad statistic. The drawback is that Lumberton is a two-hour drive from Jacksonville. Taking the job means living in a rented apartment during the week and coming home to see Mel and

Maddie on weekends. It also means breaking even: The rent and gas to travel back and forth claim most of my salary.

During my first few weeks on the job, I speak with Fin often by phone as I make the transition from writing personal pieces without time constraints to dealing with daily deadlines on breaking news. I'm excited to be officially working as a staff reporter for a newspaper, and I become friendly with some of my newsroom colleagues. The ones I confide in about my brain injury nickname me "Golf Ball," a playful reference to the size of the damaged tissue inside my skull. As a newcomer, I don't mind the friendly joke—at least it's better than being called a "boot."

And besides, I still have a lot to learn.

I'm afflicted by the young reporter's misplaced belief that I'm ready to take on more than the ribbon cuttings and the parades that the *Robesonian* has to offer. I'm too impatient to understand that I'm getting the foundation I urgently need. All I know is that the daily newsroom grind is uninspiring. I cover city council meeting after city council meeting. I return from hours-long meetings to my editor asking whether anything exciting happened. It rarely did. His response is usually the same: "Better make it sound exciting. I need it within the hour." It doesn't help that my editor is an old-school newsman who harangues and belittles me as he tries to fit me into his mold. I find his pomposity and arrogance grating. None of the reporters ever file a lede that isn't rewritten. His edits strip away personal writing styles to make articles formulaic. My frustration is rooted more deeply than my growing disdain for the grind of a daily newsroom. I'm miserable. The stories offer me little escape. It's not the kind of writing I enjoy, and I start to question my decision to pursue journalism.

My editor is always getting on my nerves, but on the evening of the Newtown, Connecticut, shooting at Sandy Hook Elementary School on December 12, 2012, he pokes his head out of his office. "Hey, Thomas, you better not come in here with a trench coat trying to go all PTSD on the place." *That's it*, I think. I stand up from my desk and slam my rolling chair underneath before storming into his office. He keeps a dumbbell in front of his door to symbolize that it's always open. I kick the iron weight into the Sheetrock beside his desk and slam the door shut. "If you ever say anything like that to me again, I'll beat your fuckin' ass," I tell him while leaning over onto his desk, looking down on him seated in his chair. Not exactly the most diplomatic approach, and I'm only proving his misguided point about the correlation of PTSD and violence, but he crossed a line. I lift my hands from his desk after glaring at him, then swing open the door and storm out. I'm still on deadline for the day and hope that any kind of writing, no matter how mundane and uneventful, will help quell my anger. My coworkers avert their gazes. My editor never apologizes and neither of us speak about it to anyone. I turn in my story, clock out, and call my girls. Mel and Maddie bring me solace, and it took moving away from them again to understand this. I don't want to stay in Lumberton, but I can't quit until I find something else. I'm not ready to risk being seen as a failure. My retirement from the Corps already feels like a monumental defeat. I wasn't good enough to make it. I treat being a reporter at the *Robesonian* the same way. I can't disappoint my girls more than I already have. I start looking for other jobs online when I get home.

The distance from home and regular clashes with my editor soon take a toll. I argue with Mel, who, despite encouraging me to pursue my new career, feels I've once again abandoned her and Maddie, this time choosing journalism over our marriage. She supports me and wants me to be happy, but she works full time as a nurse at the hospital emergency room while also looking after Maddie. My weekend trips home grow fraught and lack intimacy. Each Monday I return to work drained of happiness and hope.

As the holidays approach, things get worse. Two days before Christmas I tell Mel over the phone that I want to resolve our issues and reclaim our marriage. But Mel says she's no longer in love with me. My decision to move away for the job has changed her feelings for me. She's just been too afraid to tell me. "I'm done. I can't do it anymore," she tells me over the phone. "We're over."

It comes crashing down on me: For the past eighteen months I've taken Mel for granted. I've distanced myself from her, not because she

couldn't understand me but because I couldn't explain what I've been going through. I've drifted so far from who I once was that our connection
has been severed. And now I need her close again. I ask for one more
chance, but Mel says she's given all she can.

When I walk in the door on Christmas Eve, Maddie leaps into my
arms shouting, "Daddy, Daddy!" and flailing her legs as she dangles from
my neck. Mel remains rooted to the couch. No greeting. No kiss. I go into
the bathroom and cry. I don't know what to do. I'm lost in my own home.
I don't know where I should sit. I don't know what to say. And I don't feel
welcome. I imagine divorce proceedings, moving out, and losing my
family. I cry again imagining not being around for my Goober. Mel and I
hardly speak the rest of the night and end up on opposite sides of the bed.
I can't take it anymore. I'm gripped by paranoia.

I ask Mel how we can salvage our marriage. Her answers chill me.
I've put my career ahead of family, she says. Twice. And I've become
unbearably introverted and removed. Over the past year of therapy I've
become physically and emotionally numb, except when I'm verbally
lashing out at her or berating her with accusations of infidelity. I've ignored her. I've verbally abused her. I've become a stranger. And I've stopped
being a good husband.

"I don't know who you are anymore," she says, "and it's impossible to
be in love with someone you don't know."

Her words crush me. Even worse is the way she says them. There are no
tears, no anger, no fear. It is as if she's given up, as though she no longer
cares. And that scares me. So does being alone.

I then do something I've never done during our five years of marriage.
I go downstairs to sleep on the couch. I've always made a point of telling
Mel I love her and of giving her a kiss and a hug before going to sleep,
even when we've been arguing. Even during our worst times, tucking
Mel into bed when she comes home from a long night at the hospital is
something I look forward to. The kisses sometimes feel hollow, but I need
her to know I love her before she falls asleep. I dread ending the day on a
bad note and I fear the guilt of never being able to say I'm sorry. I still
have a warrior's ingrained belief that another day is never certain: I don't

want anger to be a final memory should something happen during the night.

On Christmas morning Maddie is puzzled to find me sleeping on the couch. I tell her I was trying to catch Santa. Then I bring over her gifts. As we read together on the couch, I smile for the first time in weeks. I'm not bothered by my mistakes. The day passes without incident and Mel seems pleased with her presents—a diamond necklace, a pair of Nike runners, a new Littmann stethoscope. Keeping with tradition, I've wrapped pairs of Old Navy socks, chewing gum, and thong underwear and addressed the tags with sexually suggestive hints, like "To: Here's New Socks, From: The Guy Who Knocks Them Off." Her smile gives me hope. That evening I ask Mel if we can talk things over before going to bed. As we speak, I break down. The thought of losing Mel and Maddie scares me more than combat ever did. I can't live without them. Mel doesn't promise anything but says she'll try. I'm relieved, especially when Mel kisses me back before we sleep.

The next day I take Mel and Maddie ice-skating, hoping it will be a family activity we can all enjoy. But in the car Mel suggests I'm trying too hard. She thinks I'm forcing things. Maybe I am. I'm desperate to make things better, but we end up fighting again as Maddie wails in the back-seat. We scream so much that I pull over the car three miles from our house, step out, and slam the door shut. I begin walking home. No words are spoken. Mel runs around the car to the driver's seat, puts the car in gear, and drives away. When I get home, I retreat to my upstairs office, close the door, and stare at the wall adorned with my military citations, photographs from my deployment, and framed copies of my favorite articles. Among the memorabilia is my Purple Heart citation. I read the words on the embossed paper through watery eyes. I punch the glass cover, cutting my hand, and tear the citation from the frame. I rummage through my desk drawer and pull out the Purple Heart medal I was given on Christmas Day in Afghanistan two years ago. I run my thumb over the smooth purple and golden brass. If I hadn't been wounded, I wouldn't be having these troubles. I would still be in the Marine Corps with my brothers. I wouldn't have had to submit to the humiliating ordeal of therapy. I wouldn't be losing my wife and daughter to a medical condition I can't control.

I tear the citation to pieces and watch as the shreds flutter to the floor. It doesn't help. It changes nothing. It makes things worse. I've just destroyed something for which many have paid dearly. I think about Staff Sergeant Ortiz-Rivera and how his widow, Veronica, cherishes his Purple Heart. I feel ashamed and nauseated. What would she think? How could I have disgraced the oldest medal in the military? I decide I don't care who is hurt. Nobody knows what I'm going through. They don't understand my pain. I pick up the pieces of my citation, stack them on top of one another, and clip my Purple Heart to the bundle. I walk downstairs, open the trash can, and drop everything into the bin. I hesitate before closing the lid. I promise myself that this will be the beginning of a new chapter. No more living in the past. No more feeling defeated. It's time to preserve what matters most—my family.

My resolve doesn't last long. Back in my apartment in Lumberton two days later, I write my suicide note.

"To the woman I love with my whole heart and soul: You are finally free of the terror I have caused in your life," I write. "I'm sorry for everything I have done to you. I deserve every bit of sorrow I feel. Never forget how much I love you and cherish the times we spent together. I'll hopefully see you on the other side."

Then I swallow an entire bottle of my prescription sleeping pills and wait for the darkness to come. Checking out is easier than I expected.

I lie on my bed. This whole apartment is the same size as my kitchen back home. The walls are yellowed, and my only decorations are piles of clothing, takeout containers, plastic bottles, and litter strewn across my desk, floor, and kitchen. I stare at the eagle, globe, and anchor debossed on the outside of the grease-stained Marine Corps–issued boots tossed on the bedroom carpet.

I close my eyes and wait. Tears slide from the corners of my eyes and drip from my ears onto my pillow. I've gone from being a strong and supportive father and husband to this. To nothing. How have I fallen so far? Then I imagine my daughter's tears and her shame once she understands her father quit when life proved too difficult. The thought shakes me. I can't be a failure to my daughter. I can't leave her to a life without me. I can't have her think I'm a failure. My Goober needs me. And I need her.

My eyes flick open at the thought of her crying before my flag-draped coffin. I recall the pain in Veronica Ortiz's wails of mourning during the memorial service for her husband. I feel the stomach acid inching up the back of my throat with each imagined crack of a final twenty-one-gun funeral salute. Veronica's sobs transform into Maddie's. As I rush to the bathroom, my mouth fills with vomit. Dozens of little white pills float in the toilet bowl. I can hear taps playing in the back of my mind. Have I puked up all the pills? I ram my fingers down my throat, vomiting more. I fall back onto the bathroom floor and wonder what I have done. Staring up at the ceiling, I want to hear Mel's and Maddie's voices.

I begin dialing Mel's number. Three digits. Delete. Stare at my phone. Dial again. Delete. Over and over. I dial. I delete. I don't know what to say. I hate what I've done. Death isn't what I want. I don't want Mel to take Maddie away. Ashamed. Embarrassed. My mind races. Divorce. Loneliness. More sadness. Ten digits. The phone rings.

Mel answers and I tell her what I've done. I'm hysterical. My sentences don't make sense. They're fast and jumbled. I shout. Then whisper. Cry. Then yell. I'm erratic, irrational, and clouded. Iraq. Afghanistan. Childhood. Suicide. Life. Death. I'm pacing around my apartment. Kitchen. Bedroom. Balcony. Then bathroom. Repeat. I'm sweating. Still crying. She tries to calm me down. I can't. Breathe. Slow down. "Tell me what happened. How much did you take? Did you puke them all out?" She cries. I cry. I stammer and stutter. I just want someone to talk to. I don't want to be alone. My apartment feels smaller than usual. The world larger. I'm afraid to open my door. I don't want to go outside. I feel guilty for calling her. I apologize. Over and over. For insults old and new. For being hurt. For asking her to marry me. For being insane. Three hours ago we hung the phone up after screaming at each other. About how I wasn't the man she fell in love with. I'm not. I tell her every reason why. How I've abandoned her. How I've given up on us. And myself. On Maddie. That I'm just going through the motions. Not being a husband. Nor a father. I apologize for letting her down. She offers to come and see me, but I want to hang up. I'm afraid she thinks it's just a ploy to win her back—to keep her from leaving. I want her. But I don't. Nothing makes sense. I pace even more, pick up my bottle of Lunesta from the counter. The bottle now empty, the pills in my toilet, swirling with bile and bits of food. A mess just like my mind.

I call my local psychiatrist's office, but it's closed. I call Fort Bragg, a local Army base. After being transferred half a dozen times to various offices across the base, I'm told to call my local Veterans Affairs hospital since I'm two days from retirement. They don't provide a number. I don't think to ask. But they do tell me to enjoy my weekend. The woman who answers the phone at the VA hospital in Fayetteville, North Carolina, is "sad to inform" me that because I'm still on active duty, the Department of Veterans Affairs cannot assist me. "I'm sorry," she says. The phone clicks as she hangs up.

I just want a release, an escape from my emotions and the medicated blur. I just want to talk, to get things off my chest, to remove some of the weight. I can't call my friends, family, or fellow Marines. I'm ashamed, too afraid of what they will think. If they cared, someone would have noticed. A stranger seems more approachable. Sitting in an office with Frank or Dr. Webster—my social worker and psychiatrist while I was in the military—felt safe, but admitting my problems to those I'm closest with is frightening. What if they can't help? What if they don't care?

I jump in my truck and speed along a country road. The crisp December wind blowing against my face feels good—so good that I can't remember afterward how I get to the Southeastern Regional Medical Center parking lot in Lumberton. I walk toward the red letters of the hospital's entrance. They mesmerize me as I take a last drag from my cigarette, flick the butt to the ground, and walk through the revolving doors to the front desk. I tell the triage nurse the reason for my visit: attempted suicide. As he checks my vital signs and goes through a slew of insurance and intake questions—What happened? Do I have insurance? What's my medical history? How do I feel now?—I assure him I no longer have any desire to harm myself or others. I just want someone to talk to. They tell me I will. Soon.

For more than three hours I sit in a dimly lit corner of an emergency room hallway wearing a drafty hospital gown. The only doctor I see spends roughly one minute with me and tells me they will keep an eye on me for a while "because veteran suicide is a big deal and we want to make sure you're okay." Then he walks away. I'm offended yet at ease with his saying this. I know it's a problem. I've lost fellow Marines to suicide. But I know I've learned my lesson. I just want to talk to someone. I still haven't. Letting out a sigh, I rest my elbows on my knees, lay my head in my hands, and stare at the wall. I'm alone again.

I doze off. I don't know how long I sleep, but I'm startled awake when two police officers nudge my shoulders. They give me a choice between following them voluntarily and being handcuffed. It takes me a moment to understand what's happening. I'm being involuntarily committed to the psychiatric ward. I go with them, too stunned to resist. Everyone in the emergency room seems to stare as I walk down the hallway, flanked by the officers. On the elevator I break down and cry. I'm being escorted through the hospital like a criminal—a prisoner. All because I asked for help.

The elevator jolts to a halt. The doors slide open and I'm ushered past a guard and told to stand next to the nurse's station. The wing is cold with stark walls. It smells of body odor, bleach, and piss. With inch-thick glass and solid metal doors, it looks like a prison. Staff members file paperwork at their desks and tap away on keyboards as I shuffle in. A worker pushes a plastic meal cart down the hallway. I stand in awe at the array of people inside. Some wander the hallways aimlessly; others sit in rubber chairs scattered about a large room. With their glassy eyes, they all look doped up.

A nurse asks about my current daily medications: 150 milligrams of Zoloft for depression, 25 milligrams of Abilify to stabilize my mood, 200 milligrams of Topamax and 100 milligrams of tramadol for migraines, 1,600 milligrams of Motrin for my aching joints, 10 milligrams of clonazepam for anxiety, and 3 milligrams of Lunesta for sleep. The nurse warns that if I refuse new medication, I could be forced to comply. I'm allowed to call Mel. I'm not able to tell her that the hospital involuntarily committed me. She wants to visit. I beg her not to. I tell her I won't let her see me like this. It's too embarrassing. It's selfish, but I need to get through the hospital stay on my own. To be better for her. To begin working through more of my problems so we can work toward our future. In the back of my mind I worry she thinks this was a bid for attention—that I did it only to keep her in my life. She says she knows it's not, but maybe she's just humoring me. She cries. I cry. A few hours ago I wanted to be by her side. Now I'm too embarrassed to let her visit. By the end of the first day I learn to ignore time. I try to ignore life beyond the walls of the psych ward. I tell myself that being here is all a bad dream and that it will soon be over. Bedtime comes after I receive more medication than I'm used to. I'm told it will help me sleep. It does.

By the afternoon of my second day in the hospital, I still haven't spoken with any senior staff about what I'm doing here. I ask to see one of the nurses. I want to know what medications I'm being fed and when I'll see a psychiatrist. My head feels blurred and foggy, like trying to see underwater. All I want to do is sit down or sleep. I'm told the medication is what the hospital psychiatrist has ordered. I have yet to meet him. I vaguely remember watching television and making small talk with my fellow patients. We laugh at the schizophrenics and crack jokes about other patients drooling on themselves. At least they don't realize how shitty this place is or how little they're actually being helped. We poke fun at the "window lickers" and the guy having a conversation with Jesus. It is a cynical way to pass the time, but it works. Then I'm lying in bed. Two days down, two to go.

Morning comes sooner than expected. It's Monday. I need to call my boss. One of the nurses gives me the number for the *Robesonian*. I tell my editor I'm in the hospital with kidney stones, and I walk back to the dining area. As I'm forcing down chalky eggs and slurping decaffeinated black coffee, a nurse tells me it's my turn to see the psychiatrist. I expect a cordial handshake or at least a hello but get nothing. The psychiatrist asks mundane questions as a nurse grabs my wrist and reads from my hospital bracelet. He asks if I know why I'm here. Am I still suicidal? I resist sarcasm and tell them what they need to hear to discharge me. I made a very rash and regrettable decision. I've learned my lesson and have a support network I know to use in case this happens again. I'm irritated when they talk about me as though I'm not in the room. *Thomas Brennan, twenty-seven, married, one child, military veteran, history of post-traumatic stress and brain injury. Deliberate suicide attempt two days ago. Psychiatric history of post-traumatic stress disorder. Anxiety disorder. Depression.* The impersonal medical jargon goes on and on. They say I've been calm and cooperative. I'm holding back my anger. It's the bedside manner Mel always complains about. Dry. Clinical. Dehumanizing. The doctor suggests changes to my psychotropic regimen. I object. This failure was my own, not the fault of any medication. Besides, I'm tired of feeling like a lab rat. Our meeting lasts less than five minutes. The doctor doesn't answer any of my questions. He makes no eye contact. Then he motions toward the door and says I'll be discharged the next day. Our conversation is over. I have wasted three days—three days that make me swear I will never again ask for help from someone I don't know. One night left.

Blood pressure. Lunch. Blood pressure. Dinner. Medication. Bed.

If it weren't for the medication, I would never have slept through my last night in the hospital. I'm too angry at how little is being done to help me or ensure follow-up treatment. When I wake, my discharge papers are beside my bed. At the nurse's station I thread my laces back through my shoes. I grin. And then, sliding my belt through the loops, I begin to chuckle. I can't dwell on how I nearly killed myself. The whole hospital episode has been too absurd, and I'm relieved to be out, acting again of my own free will. The nurses look at me awkwardly as they lead me through the door and into the elevator.

With my suicide attempt I've hit rock bottom. Things can't get much worse. But a week later one of my squad members from OP Kunjak, twenty-nine-year-old Corporal Nicholas Austin, is out on an evening motorbike ride near Washington DC when he swerves to avoid a deer. He's going too fast and loses control. His funeral is held eight days later.

Austin did two tours of duty, one in Iraq and the other in Afghanistan. At OP Kunjak he kept to himself. He never complained and was always ready to do whatever was necessary. All he wanted was to get the job done and get back home. In Afghanistan he reminded me of myself in

Iraq. He listened to music, played cards, and read books. He was a wiseass who always tried to find an excuse not to do something, but he was reliable. It's more than six months since we last spoke. We lost touch as we went our separate ways outside of the Corps. His death brings back that familiar twinge of guilt for being unable to protect one of my men. I felt a fleeting taste of success when I was being published by the *Times*, but now I feel like a failure again. I'm no longer in a position to look out for my Marines, I'm unable to hack it at a small-time newspaper, and my marriage is falling apart. Since I returned from Afghanistan, it's as if the ground keeps shifting under my feet as the aftershocks of my deployments upturn my life. I wonder whether I will ever escape war's grip. But my self-inflicted brush with death provides some clarity. I know I can't survive on my own. And I refuse to give up on Maddie and Mel. They need me as much as I need them. I know I have to go home.

Luck, it turns out, is on my side. Two weeks after I am released from the hospital, my hometown paper, the *Jacksonville Daily News*, gets in touch. Their military reporter is leaving and a replacement is needed to cover the many local bases and the tens of thousands of veterans outside the gates. Am I interested?

PART THREE

After War

Chapter 15

Home, Again

Whether recovery occurs spontaneously or in a defined treatment setting, recovery only happens in community.

—Psychiatrist Jonathan Shay, *Odysseus in America: Combat Trauma and the Trials of Homecoming*

TJ, North Carolina, January 2013

The drive to move home from Lumberton takes two hours. I'm by myself and there's plenty of time to think. The phone calls from my parents, Mel, and Fin are supportive. They offer hope and promise, but it feels like a trap. Like it's only a matter of time before they confront me about my suicide attempt. I park my truck in our driveway and I'm met with a flurry of kisses and long embraces. My parents have come from Massachusetts. Mel is off from work. Maddie is ecstatic to see me and doesn't know the real reason I'm back. Mel hugs me first. Her tears dampen my shirt. My mother does the same. My father doesn't say much. He offers to listen. He hugs me the tightest. I'm instantly depressed. The relief I felt when I packed my few belongings into my truck for the move back home evaporates. I feel guilty for hurting so many people who love me.

Our mood is somber and we're mostly silent. Small talk is forced as we all sit across from one another in our living room, yet everyone keeps asking if they can get me something or do something for me. Their pity irks me. Three hours later my mother and I are screaming at each other in the hallway outside Maddie's bedroom. She blames herself and asks why I would do this to her, says that I should have called her and that I'm selfish. She says Mel is to blame. I cry. She cries. We both slam doors as we storm off to bed at opposite ends of the hallway. My parents drive home the next day. The crack in my relationship with my mother will be hard to repair. It hurts. But it's the first time I understand how Mel must have felt when I screamed many of those same insults and accusations at her.

My first days back from Lumberton are awkward, but things gradually start to improve at home. I can tell she's watching her words, not wanting to upset me or cause an argument. I'm doing the same. It's different from the passionate reunion we enjoyed upon my return from Afghanistan. The separation this time has been emotional, not physical. And yet it's the bodily space each of us occupies that has to adapt to the presence of the other. At first, falling asleep in each other's arms is impossible. Sex feels hollow, unfulfilling. But we soon fall back into old habits. I tap her on the butt as she walks upstairs, or she tries to tickle me, only to end up on the receiving end instead. I love how she giggles when tickled. We hold a pizza-making competition punctuated by playful teasing. We trash-talk each other's efforts, pointing out that dough is too flaky or too moist. We mock the size and shape of the other's diced vegetables. And we laugh.

On my first day at the *Daily News*, a small-town newspaper with half a dozen reporters and two editors, I pull into the parking lot, climb out of my truck, grab my notebook from the passenger seat, and tuck in my button-down shirt. My sleeves are rolled up, revealing my forearms sheathed in tattoos. After my experience in Lumberton, I feel like a student at a new school on the first day of class—will I fit in or will I be the strange outcast, mocked behind my back and avoided in the cafeteria?

I brace myself, step through the front door, and make my way to the office of Cyndi Brown, the paper's managing editor. She greets me with a look of surprise. I wore a suit for my job interview and she's clearly alarmed by my tattoos. I asked Brown during the interview about the company tattoo policy, but now, looking at my bare forearms with the inked words "kafir" and "carpe diem," as well as green, red, purple, and orange images of a voodoo zombie, an angel, four-leaf clovers, a cartoon Teddy Ruxpin holding blocks of TNT, and likenesses of Mel and Maddie, Brown says she hadn't realized the extent of my bodily decorations.

"I've got a lot more than you can see," I say, pulling my sleeves up above my elbows. "I never like to hide my tattoos. They tell my story."

Brown urges me to be discreet when covering assignments and not to wear short sleeves in conservative settings. I know I need to dress the part. Even the Marine Corps frowns on body art and bans Marines from getting new tattoos—an order that is largely ignored and that ended the careers of many of my friends. These were stellar Marines, the kind of men you want beside you in a firefight. One, a valorous award recipient, was denied reenlistment for getting a massive eagle, globe, and anchor— the Corps' own emblem—tattooed too prominently on his forearm.

After introductions to fellow newsroom staff, I'm issued an old laptop, then told the paper has been without a military reporter for nearly a month. There's a backlog of stories to cover. When I sign into my new office e-mail, a stream of messages with potential news items downloads onto my screen. The computer chimes with each new e-mail. I watch as the list grows longer. And longer. One award for valor. Then another. An event at the local Veterans of Foreign Wars post. A citywide initiative for homeless veterans. The Military Spouse of the Year Award. Unveilings of military monuments and memorials. One after another. I know I'm not expected to cover everything immediately, but the avalanche of messages is daunting. I read through them, ranking each by priority, then begin hunting down the relevant contacts. The next thing I know it's late afternoon. My first day of work is done. When I enter the kitchen, Mel and Maddie call out, "Surprise!" On the counter is an ice cream cake— my favorite dessert—with a single candle burning in the center. Maddie rushes forward, wrapping her arms around my thigh, and wishes me a happy first day at work. Mel walks over and joins us for a family hug. She gives me a quick kiss.

"You better blow out that candle before it burns the house down," she says.

After dinner we tuck Maddie into bed and read her a book.

Later that night I feel more hopeful than I have in years. Sure, I'm anxious about fitting in at work, but I've been making a conscious effort to reengage at home. It seems to be working. For too long I've allowed myself to drift emotionally. When I first returned from deployment, I suppressed my emotions and tried to mask my pain. I believed Afghanistan was my war, not Mel's. I couldn't have been more wrong. I ignored that

Mel had also gone to war. Her battle was wondering if I'd ever come home and whether she'd have to raise Maddie without me.

Over the next few weeks I start to rebuild my relationship with Maddie. I share pictures of her on Facebook and spoil her with treats and toys. On one occasion she gives me an unexpected treat in return. I'm walking her into school after we both oversleep. I forgot to set the alarm and she's late for class. As we move through the school corridors, the Pledge of Allegiance comes over the public address system. Other students continue on their way. Some chat and say hello. Teachers say their "good mornings." People carry on with their duties. Maddie, however, stops and stands with her little hand over her heart and recites the pledge, ignoring everyone who talks to her. I'm overcome by emotion and almost start crying right there in the hallway. I'm so proud of my little monstah. At age five she has more respect for the pledge than many of the adults at her school. But it's not even about the pledge or what the words or flag represent. What gets me is her respect, and her poise. Maddie is proud to tell people I'm a veteran and happily informs them that "Daddy has a brain injury and forgets stuff." When we're shopping, she always looks for copies of the *Daily News* and tries to find my stories. Seeing how proud she is encourages me to keep trying to get better.

Mel and I enjoy rescuing dogs, and our family soon grows to include a fifth dog, Mr. Luke, who will be trained as my service dog—the classy pup who gets to leave the house. I don't know whether this will actually help, but I'm ready to try anything. Mel brought up service dogs to me after she had treated a few veterans in the emergency room who came in with service animals. They told her the dogs often comforted veterans. I had also spoken with many veterans who find four-legged companions therapeutic. I hope it will help ease my anxiety and curb my feeling of being outnumbered in crowds. Mel and I decide it's worth a try. I drop Mr. Luke off at a facility where he will spend months training to become certified under the Americans with Disabilities Act's criteria—obedience, etiquette in crowds and public spaces, and silence. He's returned to me certified, his fluffy yellow tail wagging and his tongue sticking out over his under bite. He's ready to work. Mr. Luke becomes a calming presence, providing a foil to the aggravations and irritants that can set me off. At home he's part of the pack—Mr. Luke, two pit bulls, a Great Dane, and a Chihuahua—all rescued as runaways or from a pound or puppy mill. Maddie feeds them together. In the mornings before work I put on his vest marked "Service Dog, Do Not Pet" and bearing Purple Heart, Iraq, and Afghanistan patches. Maddie asked to decorate his vest and I'm glad she's excited about something that could've been embarrassing for her—a broken dad who needs a crutch. Her enthusiasm makes having Mr. Luke by my side less shameful. His vest also marks working hours for him. Once it's on, he's trained to flip the switch from his usual hyper and disobedient self to restrained and calm. Mr. Luke comes with me to the newsroom and on interviews, and it helps me cope with being around strangers. Mr. Luke might be a walking advertisement for something being "wrong" with me, but a degree of comfort creeps back into my life. Having him around means I've always got someone to talk to, and his under bite makes me laugh. Some nights he sleeps in or at the foot of our bed, but most nights he sleeps with Maddie and one of our pit bulls, Damien. When Mel works nights, he sleeps in the bed with me. He's not my favorite warm body, but he's a welcome new piece in the puzzle of my life I'm putting back together.

My first assignment for the *Daily News* involves covering the opening of a new building site for local government offices (part of my role at the paper is general-assignment reporting when needed). I watch as overweight middle-aged white men in dark suits and dress shoes scratch the muddy earth with golden shovels and grin for a photo op. I soon move to more interesting military issues, but there are still challenges. I cover a Marine infantry battalion returning home from a combat-heavy tour in Afghanistan. I wander through the crowd of lean, battle-hardened Marines. I recall the bewilderment I felt at my own homecoming, that knot of excitement and trepidation, the anticipation mixed with the fear of not yet knowing what changes had occurred within me or at home. I want to capture the essence of the moment, to do it justice, to convey to readers the relief washing over the waiting family members who have long feared a phone call in the middle of the night or, worse, the dreaded knock on the door from two military officials in full ceremonial dress. I want to show the darkness and sadness I know the Marines are trying to leave behind as they grapple with the almost blinding brightness of coming home. And I want to probe the troubling space between the two worlds of home and away. In other words, I want to explore the realities most people avoid.

But when I return to my desk to write, I don't have the material I need. I asked the wrong questions or was unable to prompt my interview subjects to say anything beyond the usual clichés. I file the story, but I feel shitty, yet again, for letting Marines down.

I fumble my way through my early assignments until a seasoned crime reporter named Lindell Kay, a balding, bespectacled, and rotund Navy veteran who occupies a nearby cubicle, takes me under his wing. Lindell is not the most physically appealing figure—his body odor announces his presence and his fingers are often greasy with fast-food residue. But he always commends me on a good story and offers constructive criticism as needed. He makes me promise to ask him any questions, even stupid ones, and I often do. My rookie queries prompt Lindell to lick his lips and stare off into space before answering in a thick southern drawl. Lindell is a blunt talker. His advice is often mixed with friendly condescension. When I ask him whether I need to attribute every sentence when paraphrasing, Lindell does his lip-licking thing and, after a brief pause, answers: "Late Monday evening a man died, he said. Bob Jones found his son face-first in the toilet with blood smeared on the floor, he said. After checking his son for a pulse and removing his head from the water, he said that he next called 9-1-1. He was frantic, he said. Would you want to read that?"

I chuckle. At least I'm not being mocked behind my back.

In April Finbarr asks me to participate in a lecture series aimed at connecting undergraduates with academics, journalists, and authors. The ninety-minute panel discussion will cover how Fin and I have worked together, first in Afghanistan, then as I turned to writing. I've just finished speech therapy and my brain is still unpredictable. I've taken a break from psychotherapy. My stint in the psych ward in Lumberton made me distrust civilian mental health providers. Being involuntarily committed to the hospital for four days confirmed my fear: Civilians don't know shit about people like me. The first time I came to Harvard, I was just in the audience. Now I'm on a podium inside a redbrick building in an Ivy League lecture hall that features carved busts on pedestals, a towering fireplace, and painted portraits of old white men adorning wood-paneled walls. I still haven't set foot inside a classroom since high school, when I used to do everything possible to avoid public speaking. I look out at the audience and see dozens of people with three-piece suits, backpacks, notebooks, pantsuits, and ripped jeans. I see few tattoos, and very few people who look like they've ever strayed off campus, other than family members who've come to see me. How can these people comprehend what I've been through in Iraq and Afghanistan? Will my blunt approach translate? Will I even be able to articulate my thoughts? My injured brain is better at expressing ideas through writing. Words still elude me when I'm speaking, or shift into unformed shapes in my mind. Letters become scrambled and sentences become unhitched from their meaning. It's an everyday fear for me. The idea of becoming incoherent scares me. It scares many of us with "invisible" injuries. I don't want to humiliate myself or embarrass Fin. Worse, will I shame the Marine Corps? Despite feeling betrayed by the military, I constantly dread making the "brotherhood" look bad.

After introductory remarks and half an hour of moderated discussion, I walk to the podium. I start by reading part of my *New York Times* story about what it feels like to kill. My mouth is dry. The paper trembles in my hands. It's the same story I've struggled so hard to tell Frank in the privacy of therapy. Now I face an audience made up mostly of strangers. I begin.

I explain how taking another person's life transported me to the darkest side of myself, how there are nights I can still visualize the faces of those I've killed, how there are days when I become lost in vivid memories of combat for minutes at a time, how my experiences have left me emotionally numb. It was easy then to fall back on the powerful logic that it was either me or them, or worse yet, one of my fellow Marines. But that logic leaves questions with no easy answers. Did I in some ways come to enjoy killing? Was the loss of a life, and my innocence, worth it?

"Looking back on it now, I feel bad that I did not feel bad," I conclude. "Taking someone's life changes you, whether you like to admit it or not. It took me a long time to notice and admit the changes within me. It is something most people will never have to do. And I'm envious of those people. I look back on taking an insurgent's life and can't help but think I went a little crazy from doing so. I wonder from time to time what I was like before that day many years ago. But I also realize I will never be that person again."

When I return to my seat, the moderator asks why I chose to challenge the taboo of writing about the psychological impact of killing—one of the most fundamental but least discussed acts of war.

I explain that it seems as though everyone says, "Thank you for your service," but anybody who has served knows that the next question is usually "Have you ever killed somebody?" That question, I explain, is the hardest part of dealing with hapless civilians, even if they mean well. But I understand why they ask. I'm just as curious when I meet other veterans. I want to know whether we'll understand each other on a level deeper than words can convey. The issue is that whereas I carry guilt for killing, other veterans may feel inadequate for not having killed. They may feel they didn't "do their part." They may feel they carry less of a moral burden, which imposes another kind of emotional weight. The casual question about having killed is superficial, but it taps deep into private traumas. And every experience of trauma is unique. Thanking us is fine. Let us bring up the things we've done.

I wrote about killing because I wanted to discuss the moral complexities involved and to show how killing toys with our conscience to create an emotional turmoil that can consume us. Some of us feel like murderers. Some of us feel like we did the wrong thing. Some of us feel like we did the right thing. Whatever the case, we're not just imperial storm troopers mindlessly zapping people without consequence.

Sitting in the audience, at the back of the lecture hall, is Kevin Cullen, a Pulitzer Prize–winning *Boston Globe* columnist. Cullen was one of the judges who acknowledged the pieces I'd written in a recent citation from the Dart Center at Columbia. During the Q&A session toward the end of our talk, Cullen stands, takes the microphone, and addresses me. He says the articles I wrote helped other veterans, including his own nephew, Tim, who was a soldier with the Tenth Mountain Division. Tim was injured in several IED blasts while serving in Afghanistan. He wanted to join the police force when he returned from duty, Cullen explains, but no police department would touch him. Not after he was diagnosed with PTSD and TBI. He was another piece of broken gear, discarded.

"Our family struggled mightily to try and show him the love and support he needed, but it was hard," Cullen says. "He eventually stuck with the [VA] program and he got better. Part of his healing and part of his therapy was [reading] what you write. You should know that, and you should be proud of it. Last month [Tim] became a member of the Charlotte Fire Department as an EMT. So for him, I thank you."

Afterward people approach me with more comments, questions, and anecdotes. Yet Tim's story sticks with me. Writing, I'm discovering, is painful. Not only the writing itself but grappling with my own experiences and emotions and self-doubt. At times I wonder whether the struggle is worth it, whether it makes any difference at all. But the feedback from veterans and civilians alike encourages me to keep going. Cullen's story about Tim is further proof I'm on the right track. After the Harvard panel, Cullen writes about me in his column for the *Globe*.

"His words are more than one Marine's attempt to reconcile the scrambling of his brain and his slow, wobbly return to ordinary life. They are a lifeline for other vets struggling in quiet desolation," Cullen's story says. "He's traded his M-4 rifle for a keyboard. He's learning the business from the ground up, as military affairs reporter for the *Daily News* in Jacksonville, N.C. He is in the middle of an extraordinary transition, from warrior to journalist, from soldier to civilian. And, like a good Marine, he's making the best of it."

When I return to the newsroom in Jacksonville, I pin the article onto the corkboard at my desk, where it hangs beside Maddie's drawings.

During my first three months at the *Daily News*, I put my therapy sessions on hold. Mel is worried, but I've promised I'll resume them if things start to slip and that I won't lie or try to hide my difficulties. I mean it. I know I'm not fixed, but don't think I can be. I feel somewhat better and believe I'm good enough for now. She makes me promise that if she thinks I need it, I won't argue and will go. I agree. Therapy seems beneficial—it helped me in the past—but sometimes it also seems pointless. Therapy wasn't there for me when I called the hotline from my apartment in Lumberton, and I never gave it a second chance. All trust was gone. And I have too much else to do. Keeping my mind occupied allows it less time to stray. In addition to reconnecting with my family and working a full-time job, I'm studying evenings and weekends for my B.A. in journalism. And I'm still writing occasional articles for the *Times*'s *At War* blog.

The flow of responses I continue to receive for my work on military mental health inspires me to start my own charity organization, called Fog of War Inc. I launch a Web site and Facebook page to raise awareness about veteran mental health and to provide a forum for open discussion among veterans and family members. The organization's slogan is "Making Invisible Wounds Visible."

On the Facebook page I post comic strips and inspirational quotes, including one by an anonymous source: "When something bad happens you have three choices. You can either let it define you, let it destroy you, or you can let it strengthen you." To prompt discussion, I post pictures with questions such as "What do you miss most about combat?" One comment that echoes others is "The adrenaline rush of the bullet snaps, the communication between boys, the F-16 show of force after being pinned down for an hour, but the camaraderie with all you mother fuckers the most."

I work alongside David A. Blea II, another medically retired, combat-wounded grunt. We served together at Parris Island as marksmanship instructors and ended up moving into the same subdivision years later.

at Yale after writing two books. Both have also graduated from Columbia's Journalism School. *At War* was also the starting ground for a fellow
Marine grunt and my favorite post-9/11 military writer, T. M. Gibbons-
Neff, who has become a staff reporter for the *Washington Post*. *At War* has
also hosted stories from physical therapists at Walter Reed, widows, military spouses, and countless ranks from each military branch.

Jim Dao arrives late for the award ceremony, explaining he's been
working to deadline. I'm honored he's even made it. He's the deputy
national editor of the *New York Times*, he's on deadline, and he's taken
the time out of his busy day to be here. He could easily have canceled,
but here he is, meeting my parents and talking with my grandfather
about how they live ten minutes away from each other in New Jersey.
Jim's commitment and my being here are further encouragement that I
may be able to carve out a space for myself in the world of journalism.
They're also reminders of how far I still have to go—careers don't develop overnight.

As the ceremony begins, Bruce Shapiro, the director of the Dart Center, stands behind the podium and welcomes everyone to the event. He
describes the Dart Center as a global resource for journalists who cover
violence, conflict, and tragedy ranging from family violence and street
crime to war and human rights abuses. Bruce is passionate and devoted
to responsible trauma reporting. He is an award-winning journalist and
professor at Yale and Columbia. He is also a trauma survivor. He was
once stabbed and seriously injured during a random knife attack at a
café in New Haven, Connecticut.

The Dart Award is the oldest project at the Dart Center, focusing its
mission on demonstrating why language, descriptions, and their impact
matter within trauma reporting. Bruce looks across the crowd. "The
real story begins when the cameras leave the room, when the sound
trucks leave a town, when the suspect is hauled off in handcuffs—it's
weeks, months, years later until the real story begins." The Dart Awards,
he says, are for the news "nobody wants to hear."

This year there were more than a hundred submissions by major
news outlets from around the world. The final judging, Bruce explains,

was done by not only journalists, but clinicians, leading academics, and advocacy groups looking for not just accuracy but dignified accuracy. He adjusts his thick-framed glasses and purple tie, looks across the audience, and begins describing the winning entries.

Bruce calls my work wide-ranging and far-reaching. He says it has had an impact on my generation of service members and our families. I walk to the podium not knowing what I should say. Riding the subway here earlier—the first time I'd seen anyone urinate into a Dunkin' Donuts coffee cup on public transportation—and then pacing the grass in front of Pulitzer Hall before the ceremony, I tried to drill talking points into my head so I wouldn't forget. Now I have a dumb-assed smile on my face as I begin to address the crowd. I've forgotten what I wanted to say. I'm standing underneath a stained-glass window that once made its home at the *World*, the newspaper launched by Joseph Pulitzer himself. I'm speaking at an event with some of the most accomplished journalists in the world, who have published stories exposing government corruption or exploring the gruesome aftermath of genocides. No pressure. I begin with the obligatory thank-yous and stare at the framed citation in my hands.

2013 Honorable Mention Dart Award
for Excellence in Coverage of Trauma

The powerful and profound series of pieces by
Thomas J. Brennan
offer a uniquely personal and clear-eyed account
of military culture and life as a veteran.

Then I look up and remember this isn't just about me.

"This is for the twenty-two veterans a day who commit suicide, and this is for the one active-duty service member a day who commits suicide," I say, before asking those gathered to listen to the millions of veterans and families from the wars in Iraq and Afghanistan. "They all have stories worth hearing."

I start to get choked up as I turn from the podium. Then it's Jim's turn to speak.

"When Thomas's work came to me, he had very little experience writing," he says. "This kind of writing makes a difference to veterans, who have been through these experiences and who really gain strength from reading the types of things that Thomas has written. Thank you for recognizing that."

Jim and I make our way back to our seats. As I sit down, I don't feel courageous, as he described me. But I do feel proud. My work has had some impact.

Then I realize that I forgot to thank Mel, Maddie, and Fin. During the panel discussion after the remainder of the awards are presented, I right my wrong. Still, as I walk down the stairs from the journalism school at the end of the event, I call Fin to jokingly apologize. He says something to the effect of *Now that you're a big shot, you don't need me, huh?* He's disappointed he missed the ceremony. He had planned to be here, but he was at Mount Auburn Hospital in Cambridge, having just had surgery that day to repair a ruptured Achilles tendon. I can't be upset, but I wish he were here. Not one to extend elaborate compliments, Fin ends our call with something he has said to me only a few times before. This time it holds even more weight.

"Congrats, man," he says. "You deserve it."

Chapter 16

Echoes of Iraq

War exposes the capacity for evil that lurks not far below the surface within all of us. And this is why for many war is so hard to discuss once it is over.

—Chris Hedges, *War Is a Force That Gives Us Meaning*

Finbarr, Cambridge, Massachusetts, and Jacksonville, North Carolina, April–August 2013

On the afternoon of April 15, 2013, two bombs explode close to the finish line of the Boston Marathon. Three people are killed, more than 260 injured. The bombings plunge the city—and the country—into a panic. Three days later, on April 18, when the FBI releases surveillance footage of two suspects, the brothers Dzhokhar and Tamerlan Tsarnaev, the pair react by killing a Cambridge policeman and carjacking a vehicle at the gas station around the corner from my apartment.

That evening I'm at home, reading, with my friend and fellow Nieman, Jeneen. Our fellowship year is winding down. What seemed like an elastic amount of time ten months ago now feels like a rubber band snapping back into place, and I'm a bit on edge. After months of reading, writing, and mental and physical rehabilitation, I feel better than I have in ages, and I don't want that sense of contentment and stability to slip. The marathon bombing is a reminder of the kind of places I usually work. I worry that returning to them will upset a delicate internal balance.

We're sitting in my living room when I hear an explosion. Then another.

"Weird," I say. "That kinda sounds like grenades."

Then the police sirens wail and our mobile phones vibrate and ping with emergency alerts sent out by campus security. "Stay indoors."

A massive days-long manhunt has turned into a violent car chase to nearby Watertown, where a late-night firefight on a suburban street kills the elder brother, Tamerlan Tsarnaev. Dzhokhar Tsarnaev manages to escape by driving a stolen SUV at police, running over his brother's body before speeding away. He then abandons the vehicle and flees on foot. For the next twenty-four hours, Boston and Cambridge are on lockdown. Schools are closed, public transit is suspended, and people are told to stay indoors as thousands of security forces—police, state troopers, the National Guard, SWAT teams, and FBI agents—scour deserted streets on foot and in military-style vehicles while helicopters buzz and swoop overhead, until they eventually apprehend a skinny and bewildered-looking nineteen-year-old wearing jeans and an Adidas hoodie. TV networks show him bloodied in the glare of a spotlight with the word "captured." A citywide celebration follows.

The bombings are the worst attacks on American soil since 9/11 and stir traumatic memories for friends in New York and elsewhere. Boston area residents grapple with the emotional fallout and anger. One of my Nieman colleagues, David Abel, a *Boston Globe* reporter who happened to be at the marathon finish line at the time of the bombings, gets drawn into covering the story. He is clearly shaken by having been so close to the explosions himself, and perhaps it's just fatigue from being emotionally involved with intense coverage on a major news story, but he appears to age years in a matter of weeks.

For a few days, maybe really only a few hours, civilians in a major American city have experienced what civilians in war zones experience every day and what service members also face on deployment: not knowing who or where the threat is, and the fear that an invisible attacker can strike anywhere, anytime. Six months after the bombings, when David Abel goes to interview David Henneberry, the Watertown resident who discovered the bloodied Dzhokhar Tsarnaev hiding in his backyard, in his twenty-four-foot dry-docked boat called the *Slip Away II*, Henneberry and his neighbors are still twitchy. One woman two doors down refuses to sleep in her old bedroom overlooking her backyard. She's also afraid to walk her dog at night. Others say that they're more vigilant and that they become anxious whenever they hear helicopters or sirens nearby.

"There's a greater sense of insecurity," one neighbor, Dumitru Ciuc, tells David while showing him bullet holes in the back of his house, in his fence, in his grill. "You just don't know what's going to happen; you don't know who's a friend and who's an enemy."

The memory of the Boston trauma and the fear and uncertainty it evoked are forever etched into the minds of those who experienced it. Now multiply that by a hundred, a thousand: Imagine having to confront such experiences daily for weeks, months, and sometimes years. It's what TJ and other members of the armed forces endure. Even without the moral burden that comes with killing, or feeling like you've failed those who depend on you, is it any wonder some soldiers and Marines crack?

Two weeks after the Boston bombings, in the last month of my Nieman Fellowship, I'm jumping to intercept a half-court pass during a pickup game of basketball in Cambridge when there's a sudden, sharp shock below my left calf. It feels like I've been shot in the back of the leg. I played high school and college basketball, I played regularly in Congo and Senegal and joined Rwanda's top club team. Now, sitting lame on the hardwood, my foot hangs, loose and floppy, from my ankle. I know straightaway I'll probably never play again.

A surgically repaired Achilles has an expected recovery time of nine to twelve months, and the injury is a major blow. The past ten months of the fellowship have been restorative. I've been in a safe and intellectually engaging environment, surrounded by friends and colleagues, many of whom have become friends for life. My mood and feeling of resilience have improved, which I also attribute to my focus on fitness. For the past five months I've been doing intense martial arts training and boot camps, sometimes up to twelve hours a week. It's well documented that exercise helps battle depression and, with my injury, I'm concerned that being couchbound and restricted to moving on crutches for the next few months could mean more than just a physical setback. I'm due back at work in two months. There's no way I'll be physically ready.

And yet I feel an encouraging shift. Before my sabbatical year, this sort of injury would have derailed me. Now I conceive of the injury as a challenge to overcome. I'm frustrated, yes, but determined not to wallow in self-pity.

When I turn up at my martial arts studio less than a week after my injury, my trainers aren't too surprised to see me. Those who have committed as fully as I have to training are a hard-core bunch, though not in an aggressive sense. The studio promotes a healthy atmosphere for friendly, like-minded people of all ages to learn Krav Maga, a form of self-protection developed in Israel and used by the country's military. The philosophy as we learn it revolves around avoiding physical confrontation but knowing how to manage and end it quickly and brutally if there's no alternative. With my injury I'm unable to train on the mats, but the instructors amend boot camp workouts so I can perform the exercise circuits one-legged, then watch the rest of the class.

Before long I'm back on the mats at my martial arts studio doing light, noncontact work. Continuing my training, even in a limited capacity, is critical to keeping my spirits up. But at this point there's no way I can return to the rigors of working in Africa. I need months of physical rehab before I'll be able to walk properly, let alone run or work in hostile environments. Reuters agrees to put me on three months' paid medical leave and I spend the summer in Cambridge focused on recovery.

By August I'm able to walk gingerly, but before I leave the United States to resume work in Senegal, I make a trip down to North Carolina to see TJ. He picks me up at the Jacksonville airport in a red Chevrolet truck fitted with outsized, knobby tires that whir over the tarmac and rub against the wheel well on sharp corners. The August air in North Carolina is thick and humid. It makes my leg stiff and swollen. TJ drives with the windows wide open and the air-conditioning on full blast. The wind blows his cigarette smoke around inside the truck, along with a mini blizzard of white ash that settles on the dashboard and on my clothes. We drive past fields of tobacco and neat rows of cornstalks. TJ says the towering stalks remind him of patrolling through Helmand's cornfields during the first weeks of his Afghan deployment.

"You'd get all wrapped up in ten-foot-high corn with all the rustling leaves, and it sounded like people were all around you," he says. "It was freaky as hell."

There's another strange echo. After decades of war, many Afghan villages have graveyards or gravestones scattered by roadsides or in gardens and behind houses. The paved roads curving through farmland outside Jacksonville also have small pockets of gravestones scattered here and there, leftovers from family plots long since lost to the march of suburban sprawl.

"Weird, huh?" TJ says. "I never really noticed them until I came back from Afghanistan."

We pull into the cul-de-sac where TJ bought a home after returning from his last deployment. It's a street of cookie-cutter clapboard houses with unfenced front lawns and black mailboxes perched at the end of each driveway. Families of active-duty or retired Marines occupy nearly every home. TJ's house sits at the end of the row. His truck is too jacked up to fit into his garage. We park in the driveway.

Inside the house, air-conditioning filters through a central system, and the beige and olive walls are adorned with wooden plaques with the words "peace," "love," and "tranquility." TJ's dogs bark and jump all over us as we enter. Maddie is bouncing too, excited to meet me for the first time. She immediately wants to play the memory game, which involves a deck of cards with pairs of matching images placed facedown on a table. Whoever matches the most pairs wins. It's one of Maddie's favorite games, but TJ isn't so keen.

"I can never remember anything," he says. "It's like a blank slate as soon as you turn them over. She always kicks my ass."

Still, he doesn't do too badly. Allowing for a little cheating, Maddie wins with ten pairs to his seven (I get nine).

I don't meet Mel until the next day. She works an overnight shift at the hospital and is bleary-eyed and wearing sweatpants when she comes downstairs that afternoon. For me, Mel and Maddie have long existed only in pictures hanging above TJ's bunk at Kunjak or as characters in his writing.

"Hey," she says by way of greeting. "What are you guys doing?"

I'd expected a hug or a handshake, but perhaps she's still too groggy and, as it turns out, is "not a huggy person," as TJ later tells me. Maddie pulls on TJ's hand, begging him to play, and Mel asks him about shopping and social engagements for the weekend.

TJ wants to show me around Jacksonville and Camp Lejeune, the sprawling military base carved up by wide tree-lined boulevards, which serves as a nerve center for the USMC. The base and its environs are home to a mix of 170,000 service members on active duty, their dependents, retirees, and civilian employees. It includes eleven miles of beach capable of supporting amphibious operations, thirty-two gun positions, forty-eight tactical landing zones, three state-of-the-art training facilities for military operations in urban terrain, and eighty live-fire ranges. I've never seen anything like it. This mighty Marine Corps engine, geared for war, would dwarf even the giant multinational base at Kandahar Airfield.

When TJ points out the VA office that processes disability claims like his, I see that it's housed in a single small bungalow, a tiny appendage out of proportion to the whole. There are a few other VA facilities scattered across the base, but it seems telling that this one is smaller than the post office building across the street.

Outside the base the city of Jacksonville is an extended collection of strip malls, with franchised restaurants and car dealerships lining the main roads. Jacked-up trucks and Ford Mustangs roar along the streets. Fox News is broadcast on televisions at the airport, where a café whiteboard with a Coca-Cola ad features a handwritten message that reads *BORED? Pass the time with a Video Game and a beer!*

I can understand why TJ was apprehensive before his first visit to Harvard. Jacksonville is a land of bland conformity, a place where the Marine Corps mentality rules and friction between military culture and civilian life is greased by a collective mind-set. For TJ, venturing alone beyond the safety of such an institutional bubble is no small thing.

We drive to a strip mall for brunch and huddle together in the crowded foyer at the International House of Pancakes while waiting forty-five minutes for a table. Screaming kids and hungry, impatient parents swarm around us. Amid this noise hangs an awkward silence. The intimacy we established in the remote intensity of OP Kunjak feels distant. I've just spent the past year in academia, enjoying a life of privilege while sipping lattes in bohemian coffee shops or drinking expensive wines at Ivy League dinner parties hosted by Nobel laureates. It was a weird turn for me, but still within my comfort zone. TJ's life here—strip malls and monster trucks, tired wives, barking dogs, and giddy kids—is a world apart. I wonder whether the differences in our daily existences away from war will erode the bond we forged in Afghanistan. But over the weekend I realize our connection extends beyond the incongruous details of our lives.

We spend Saturday at a motorcycle show and drag race, where TJ has bought a vendor space for his Fog of War booth. I'm of two minds about his Fog of War initiative. TJ says he launched it to help other vets, but I wonder whether it risks keeping him stuck in a loop, reliving things that keep him from moving forward. Still, he seems to enjoy doing it, and I'm impressed that he seems prepared to take on such challenges. It sure beats languishing in front of the TV. We set up the tables and the small marquee tent on the hot tarmac of the parking lot beside other booths selling all-terrain vehicles, stencils for jackets and gas tanks, leather clothing, and other biker paraphernalia. The roar of Harley-Davidsons and the smell of burning rubber drift from the track. TJ's booth has a donation box, and I'm struck by the generosity of passersby, many of them bikers or families connected to the military. Everyone has time—and a few dollars—for a veteran. At one point a retired Marine with a service dog stops by with his wife and two daughters. He's quiet and keeps his dog between himself and the gathering crowd. He and TJ strike up a conversation. I leave them and set off in search of an oversized hot dog and fries.

I sit on the bleachers eating my lunch as stunt riders zip back and forth doing handstands on handlebars and sending clouds of acrid smoke billowing from spinning tires. A man standing against the fence in front of me with his wife and two children is wearing a leather biker vest with a patch that reads "Combat Vets Association" and "Vets Helping Vets." This, it seems, is the right place for TJ, at least for now. He finally has the family and community support he needs and has found a new direction to pursue. Things are never going to be easy, but he's moving forward.

By contrast, I'm on my way back to Africa.

TJ, Jacksonville, North Carolina, August 2013

Each evening during our visit, Fin and I sit outside on the front porch, insects buzzing around the lightbulbs, my cigarette smoke curling upward in the muggy air. We talk into the night, just as we'd done at Kunjak, only now we sit on comfy armchairs instead of dusty camp cots. One evening after midnight, almost three years after we first met, I decide to tell Fin a story from Iraq, one he's not yet heard. It takes place in November 2004 during the battle of Fallujah, the deadliest combat of either the Iraq or the Afghan war. The offensive is considered by many to be the Corps' most iconic urban battle since Vietnam. During six weeks of fighting, 95 Americans were killed and 560 wounded.

The battle was in full swing and we'd long ago run out of clean socks, body powder, and tobacco. The initial enthusiasm for the offensive had waned. A sniper round through the heart had killed an officer for whom I'd been a driver during the first half of our deployment. More friends fell as we pushed farther into Fallujah's warren of streets. Lance Corporal Matthew Brown and Lance Corporal Gary Koehler were wounded. Then another and another. Lance Corporal Bradley Faircloth, one of the guys in my battalion, was clearing a building when he saw an insurgent lying asleep inside a room.

"As soon as I shot him, a frag [grenade] was thrown at us," Faircloth told a BBC journalist who was embedded with us. "And then it just exploded. I was back about ten meters so I only got a little bit in my face and my leg."

Two days later Faircloth was hit again, once more in the leg. He was patched up and continued fighting. The twenty-year-old from Mobile, Alabama, was known for his toughness—he'd been a defensive lineman in high school—always going first through the door when storming buildings, earning himself the nickname "The Barbarian." At night he sometimes slept inside a body bag to keep warm. Some Marines did that, but most of us were too superstitious.

On Thanksgiving Day I lubricated my weapon and checked my rocket launcher and projectiles, making sure they were ready to fire. Surrounded by violence, I was feeling increasingly seduced by the power of destruction. For a demolitions man there was nothing better than watching a house crumple after firing a rocket through an entryway. The streets were quiet as our patrol headed out. We moved between houses and narrow alleyways, expecting to come under attack. Nothing. As we were turning back to base, a single shot rang out. Then another. Sniper. A heavy volley of machine-gun fire burst from a nearby window. I wanted to fire a rocket into the building, but one of my superiors ordered us to storm the compound instead. As the first Marine kicked in the door, there was a burst of enemy fire. I knew that whoever was on point must have been hit, but there was no gunfire as the rest of our Marines cleared the house, just screaming. *Room clear! Corpsman up! Room clear! Corpsman!* Then I saw two insurgents escaping from behind the compound and sprinting into a nearby building. Squirters. I shouldered my rocket launcher and fired in their direction. Three walls of the building collapsed and the house folded outward. I ran with three other Marines toward the collapsed structure and found two bodies lying outside, blown clear by the blast. I stared at the figures. One was mangled and missing both legs. Blood pooled beside his torso. The other figure was still moving. At that moment someone called out saying that Faircloth had been killed storming the compound.

My eyes stung from sweat and tears of frustration. Weeks of heavy combat had put me on edge. Friends had died; others were wounded. I'd fired a rocket that killed two children. Now Faircloth was gone and his killers lay dead and dying on the ground in front of me. If I had fired my rocket into the building, I thought, Faircloth would still be alive. We hadn't been great friends, but I felt closer to Faircloth in death than I had in life. I couldn't imagine him dead. The guy seemed invincible, but now he was being zipped into a body bag. Should I have acted faster? Been more aggressive?

I walked toward one of the insurgents, who was barely alive. I stared down into the eyes staring back at me. A blank stare. I thought of all my friends who had been killed and wounded and of the blood and the pain and the suffering we had been through. A bullet would be too kind. This vile thing deserved worse. I picked up a cinder block from the rubble, dropped to my knee, stared into the dull blackness of his eyes. I watched as his brain matter continued to ooze from his shattered skull. My knuckles turned white as I clenched the brick in my fists. Ready to crush his skull. Bury his flesh and bone into the earth beneath him. Someone pulled me away and I stood, looking at what I'd done. It didn't feel real. The insurgent was dead, finally. And I watched him die. Face to face. Staring into his eyes as they turned opaque. I was elated. I even smiled. In my world—spinning into madness—I'd reclaimed control, if only for an instant. In my rage I felt raw power. No remorse. Not now.

This was justice, I thought at the time. Now I know, though, that this brand of justice has a cost.

Maddie is going to be late for school. "Daddy, Daddy, let's go!" It's Monday morning and Fin's visit to Jacksonville is nearly over. I have to drop him off at the airport and get myself to work. But Maddie comes first.

Maddie was born between my deployments to Iraq and Afghanistan, and it was not an easy birth. Mel had two miscarriages during our first two years of marriage, with one requiring emergency surgery. As Maddie's head crowned, the doctor asked me if I wanted to help on the final push. I wrapped my hands around my daughter's tiny rib cage and tugged, terrified of hurting her as her legs emerged. I handed her to the doctor and cut the umbilical cord. The nurse cleared Maddie's mouth and nose and handed her to Mel, who wept. But Maddie's skin had a worrying yellow tint. Tests revealed she had jaundice, and while it was a common and treatable ailment, Mel and I were distraught. Maddie spent most of the next two days beneath a blue light wearing protective sunglasses. For the first time in years, I prayed. I was raised a Catholic, but the two miscarriages and my experiences in Iraq had placed a barrier between me and the idea of a just God. It felt selfish turning to religion now, but my daughter's birth that morning felt like a miracle. As I prayed for her recovery, I realized there must be a God—or at least something that made childbirth possible. Not a man in the clouds or an almighty being. More like a spark that makes each of us unique. For the first time I apologized for things that had happened in Iraq. I begged forgiveness for the people I had killed there, especially the children. Then it dawned on me. Maybe the two miscarriages were penance for the two children I had killed. I suddenly felt an inner peace I had not experienced in a long time. As I stared into the nursery at my daughter, I felt sure she would be okay. After two sleep-deprived days it was time to take Maddie home. On the drive I looked at her in the rearview mirror every few seconds. Pulling into the driveway, I braked as lightly as I could, rolling the car to a stop. Maddie was fast asleep. I undid her car seat, carried her inside to her pink bedroom, and put her to bed. I stared at her swaddled in her blanket. I kissed my fingers and pressed them against her forehead. As I closed the bedroom door, everything felt right.

Finbarr, Cambridge, Massachusetts, August 2013

After my visit to Jacksonville, I better understand the complexity of TJ's trauma. It runs much deeper than the effects of his injury in Afghanistan; in fact, that incident only added weight to his experiences in Iraq. Multiple tours of duty layered one set of problems upon others. In his book *On Killing: The Psychological Cost of Learning to Kill in War and Society*, Lieutenant Colonel David Grossman explains that most warriors are reluctant to kill but that the military has developed sophisticated ways of overcoming this instinctive aversion. Part of that training involves seeing the enemy as "other." Killing is difficult enough to begin with, but if we believe an enemy is anything like us, it's virtually impossible. To kill an enemy, he has to be subhuman. Bessel van der Kolk, the Boston trauma expert, touched on this during our seminar session at Harvard.

"The Marine Corps understands this very well," he said at the time. "When you're under danger, you bond very strongly to the people who you are in danger with. And you need that cohesion to your unit in order to be able kill other people because it becomes a world of Us versus Them. Ordinarily we are not all that good at killing people at random, but the more scared you are, the more you see the world divided into Us versus Them, and the more you feel loyal to your troop, the more you feel the other people are going to put you in danger. That works pretty well until your best friend gets killed. Because at that point you feel personally unbelievably injured, and then you start taking revenge and you start doing things to other people that break all moral codes. Then you really start feeling like a freak because you have done terrible things in the name of love and country. And you cannot go home. Bonding makes it possible for people to do it [kill other people], but at the same time it kills you inside. It all has to do with love and hate. It's a very tough thing."

When TJ sends me a written description detailing the death of the Iraqi insurgent, he at no point refers to the insurgent as a person. Instead the enemy is an inanimate object or possibly an animal. This distinction provides the psychological shield required to kill. These are some of the words he uses in that description: "Just as it stopped moving and rolled onto its back. . . . I stared intently at its face, its eyelids flickering as it looked up at me. . . . It should have been easy to pull the trigger, so easy, but I couldn't. This vile thing deserved much, much worse." And then, "I don't remember how long the four of us stared at it lying on the ground inches from death. Its face had been mangled and its skull had been crushed. The life left its eyes."

Chronicles of trauma-induced behavior date back to Greek mythology. After his friend Patroklos was killed in battle, Homer's great warrior Achilles flies into a blind rage and attacks Patroklos's killer, the Trojan hero Hektor. Achilles' rage is fueled by guilt—it's his own inaction in battle that led to Patroklos's death. After slaying Hektor, Achilles ties his body to a chariot and drags it around the city, brutalizing it for twelve days and preventing the Trojans from reclaiming the corpse. Achilles' desecration of Hektor's body flouts a tradition of allowing dead warriors to be collected from the battlefield and given proper burial. Achilles also weeps, tears out his hair, experiences intrusive memories of the dead, is unable to eat, proclaims his guilt for not covering Patroklos in battle, then prays for his own death. Some twenty-seven centuries after *The Iliad* was written, such reactions would today be recognized as classic symptoms of post-traumatic stress.

Jonathan Shay devotes an entire chapter of *Achilles in Vietnam* to what he calls that "ambiguous borderline between heroism and a blood-crazed, berserk state in which abuse after abuse is committed." This often occurs, Shay says, after the death of a warrior's special comrade.

Countless warriors since Achilles have entered into the berserk state, sometimes resulting in acts of heroism, sometimes in atrocities. Other times it thrusts men into that moral gray area found on the battlefield. Shay tells the story of one Marine who stumbled upon a North Vietnamese soldier hiding in the bush. The soldier opened fire but only grazed the Marine, who emptied the magazine of his M16 into his enemy.

"Then I saw blood dripping on the back of my hand and I just went crazy," the Marine told Shay. "I pulled him out into the paddy and carved him up with my knife. When I was done with him, he looked like a rag doll that a dog had been playing with. Even then I wasn't satisfied. I was fighting with the Corpsman trying to take care of me. I was trying to get at him for more."

In the context of battle, and in the throes of a berserk state, TJ's wish to inflict harm upon the enemy beyond the violence required to kill him is disturbing, yes, but also deeply ingrained. He was trained to kill and he did it. By stripping him of the moral boundaries imposed by society, the military prepared him to do what he did. It did not prepare him—or any other soldier—for the emotional recoil of killing. Fear, exhaustion, hate, disgust, and the irreconcilable task of balancing these emotions with the need to kill eventually drives the soldier so deeply into a mire of guilt and horror that he tips over the brink into the realm of insanity, writes Grossman. Fear isn't even the strongest factor steering the mind toward madness. Witnesses to war are often exposed to the same brutal conditions that instill fear of death or injury in war, but most cases do not become psychiatric casualties, according to Grossman, whose research dates back to the Civil War. During World War I, for instance, the probability of becoming a psychiatric casualty was greater than that of being killed by enemy fire. This drove the logic behind carpet bombing cities during World War II, by both the Germans and the Allies. The idea was to try to inflict mass psychological casualties among the civilian population. Military strategists envisioned vast numbers of gibbering lunatics being driven from cities by a rain of bombs. It didn't work. Fear of death and injury alone cannot cause the level of trauma that comes with the moral crisis associated with killing.

TJ committed the most intimate act possible. He killed a fellow human being and knelt over him in a murderous rage, watching the man die from the wounds he had inflicted. We are socially programmed not to kill, and there are few things more damaging to the human psyche than betraying one's own moral code. The result is "moral injury," an increasingly popular term among veterans and psychologists. This is different from the brain injury TJ later sustained when I was with him in Afghanistan. TBI is a physical, albeit invisible, injury where the brain is damaged, causing changes in cognitive function, mood, and behavior. The official VA definition of moral injury involves "an act of transgression that creates dissonance and conflict because it violates assumptions and beliefs about right and wrong and personal goodness." In other words, it's an emotional wound, a bruise on the soul. For many veterans moral injury is the deep philosophical anguish and the sense of betrayal over being led into battle and killing for a country whose reasons for waging war unraveled, destroying any belief that the mission served some concept of a greater good. Part of TJ's problem is that he knows he did something terrible, something for which society will judge him—even though he was doing what he was trained and paid to do. Killing stole his innocence, but war does that. TJ's sense of guilt will always remain, but that's what differentiates him from a psychopath. His actions that day in Iraq were not those of a demented individual. They were a window into the darkest corners of the human psyche.

This is a place most people prefer not to look, but TJ grapples with it every day, as do countless other veterans who were sent to war on dubious pretenses—to avenge the 9/11 attacks, to make America safer, and, later, to bring stability and peace to Iraq and Afghanistan—and as security at home and abroad has grown only worse, and as the motivations behind America's longest wars dissolved one by one, so did the moral justification for killing. Yet in that critical moment when a decision must be made whether or not to kill in combat, it is not politicians, generals, or society that is held to account; it's the lowly grunt left standing in the line of fire.

"To place someone in that circumstance, in which a momentous moral choice demands to be made," writes David Wood in his book *What Have We Done: The Moral Injury of Our Longest Wars*, "is to expose them to a lasting sense of betrayal by higher authorities who didn't have to make the decision. To a lifetime of having to keep a secret—or of bitterness at being judged. Guilt, perhaps for having violated the rules. Shame for taking a life in an act that could be murder. In short, a deep moral injury."

Violence perpetrated in war is an uncomfortable reminder of what we are all capable of doing. It's an ugly reflection of something we'd rather ignore. Yet I've seen echoes of TJ's behavior in the celebratory reaction I witnessed at Ground Zero on the night Osama bin Laden was killed. (I'd been in New York at the time attending the memorial for Chris and Tim.) Crowds reveled at the site where so many other violent deaths had traumatized a nation and shocked the world. After the Boston Marathon bombers were killed and caught, the city streets erupted in the kind of public celebration usually reserved for major sporting victories. Islam requires the dead to be buried within twenty-four hours, but residents blocked Tamerlan Tsarnaev's body from being buried in Massachusetts. Both bin Laden and Tsarnaev were seen by many as the enemy, as "other." Those who celebrate the capture and killing of terrorists, and what TJ did in Iraq seem like points on a continuum. The fine line separating the two may be only the levels of stress and threat to which each was exposed. Yet the immediate reaction to the deaths was identical: elation.

Trying to reconcile in peacetime what happens in war can tear a man apart. War reflects that side of human nature we prefer to disregard.

"If human beings were shown what they're really like, they'd either kill one another as vermin, or hang themselves," wrote Aldous Huxley.

Or both. The suicide epidemic afflicting the military has many causes, but the moral weight of killing may be the greatest burden to bear. Who is responsible for all those lives lost, individual soldiers and Marines or those who sent them overseas to kill and to die?

On the day we met, TJ showed me the tattoo traced across his chest with the words "Only God Can Judge." As an atheist, I hadn't grasped its significance. Now I get it. For TJ, those who have never experienced the fear and confusion and messiness of war have no right to condemn him for the things he's done. He'll leave that reckoning to a higher power. If there is one.

Chapter 17

Marching Back Through Time

*Think you're escaping and run into yourself. Longest way round is
the shortest way home.*

—James Joyce, *Ulysses*

TJ, North Carolina, summer 2013

"Korea—now, that's where all my problems come from, not from World
War II or Vietnam," says Max Cribelar, a three-war veteran. "That
doesn't mean we didn't get our asses knocked around over there, but Korea was just terrible."

Cribelar is what some vets would call a "hard charger." He served enthu-
siastically as a field radio operator in all of America's major wars of the past
half century, including frontline combat in both Korea and Vietnam.
Cribelar even wrote to the Department of Defense during Operation Desert
Storm in 1995 offering to come out of retirement in his midsixties. His proposal was declined in writing and the letter hangs framed on the wall in
his home.

I've started working on a series of articles on veterans for the *Daily
News*. The stories are framed as brief profiles or biographical sketches,
but I want to explore the challenges each veteran faces in the aftermath
of conflicts ranging from World War II and Vietnam through to Korea,
Iraq, and Afghanistan.

I tell them that I too am a vet, and I'm careful not to press my interview subjects too hard. Sharing wartime experiences with strangers is
difficult. I don't want them to feel exploited. But I soon find that the
men— especially the World War II veterans—are eager to talk. Some
even tell me things they haven't shared with family. It's the first time in
my reporting that I've allowed myself to open up to my subjects by

revealing my own stories and bridging generations. Even though I've always tried to reach other vets through my writing, this is different, more intimate. I'm sitting face to face with other men familiar with the snap of a bullet. Men who know the fear and euphoria of combat. They've felt the pain of seeing friends and comrades maimed and killed. They're men who know what it's like to put other men to death. Men who know that mistakes are made in war. And that guilt will drive you mad.

On the day I ring the bell of Cribelar's Jacksonville home, the eighty-five-year-old answers the door himself and ushers me inside. Cribelar is bent by age and the waistline of his trousers is hiked up to his rib cage—old-man style—but he walks and talks faster than I do. He's wearing a red-and-black checked flannel shirt and his glasses look big despite a prominent forehead. Light wisps of gray hair are combed over the back of his head. As we sit in the kitchen, Cribelar's dog, Sandy—his "little buddy," as he calls her—a small white thing, yaps away in the backyard. Cribelar's wife and granddaughter occasionally drift by and run an arm across his shoulder as he recounts his past. For most of the interview, though, the only sound in the room with me and Cribelar is the ticking pendulum of a wall-mounted clock marching the seconds back through time, across decades, from B-25 bomber flight missions over islands of the South Pacific in 1945 to the frostbitten winters of Korea's Chosin Reservoir in 1950 to the sweltering heat of Vietnam during the battle for Da Nang and the Tet Offensive in 1968.

Cribelar, who served in the Air Corps in the Pacific as an eighteen-year-old during the dying days of World War II, joined the Marines in 1950. Shortly after finishing recruit training, he deployed in July of that year from Camp Pendleton as a radio operator with the Fifth Marine Regiment. By mid-September he was part of the famous Inchon landing, in which, under a counterintuitive plan devised by General MacArthur, an amphibious landing surprised North Korean forces by coming ashore at a dangerous location well behind enemy lines.

"Inchon had the look of a place created by some evil genius who hated the Navy," wrote David Halberstam in *The Coldest Winter: America and the Korean War*. "It had no beaches, only seawalls and piers. The small Wolmi-do (Moon Tip) Island, presumed to be well garrisoned, sat smack in the middle of the harbour, effectively guarding the port and splitting the landing zone in two. The currents inside were notoriously fast and tricky—and none of these factors was the worst of Inchon's perils; the real danger was the tides."

Those tides were some of the highest in the world and risked leaving the landing ground a vast and exposed mudflat. In other words, a defending machine gunner's wet dream—stacking bodies while you hold back the trigger. General MacArthur himself spoke of Inchon being a five-thousand-to-one shot. Yet Cribelar and the rest of the Fifth Marine Regiment landed and executed one of MacArthur's legendary masterstrokes. Things didn't always go as smoothly for Cribelar. A series of later miscalculations led to the debacle at Chosin Reservoir. There Cribelar's unit was stretched too thin across inhospitable terrain. Roads were icy. Supply routes were often impassable. Medicines and rations froze. Batteries for vehicles and radios malfunctioned. Lubricants turned thick and gooey and jammed weapons.

"We still had summer uniforms as we fought them during the winter," Cribelar says, describing his summer herringbone uniform and a light field jacket. "We didn't get our winter uniforms until halfway through the reservoir in November."

Fighting was intense. Conditions were desperate. When I ask Cribelar whether he ever killed, the old Marine blinks hard, his voice rises a pitch, and he turns up his chin. "Yep," he says, without revealing anything more. I ask whether he knows how many people he killed, but he says he doesn't.

Cribelar grew hardened to carnage. Arms blown off by artillery. Corpsmen removing Marines' boots, tearing frozen skin from their feet. Fingers breaking off from frostbite. Watching others kill. Doing the killing.

"Maybe you'd call me cold natured, but I was fighting to keep myself alive, I was fighting to help my buddy. You looked out for the one beside you and the one behind you looked out for you. That's why they call it a band of brothers—you looked out for each other. It didn't dawn on me to think I was fighting to help the Koreans. We were fighting just to stay alive."

His comments make sense to me. We had an American flag on Kunjak but it wasn't why we fought. We had pictures of our families but they weren't our reason either. It seems clichéd, and maybe it is, but I fought for Big Nig and Scary Spice. For Demon and Jimbo. Baby Huey and Carlton Banks. I fought to bring them all home alive. Everything else was secondary.

Chosin Reservoir claimed the lives of 4,385 Marines. Thousands more suffered noncombat injuries, wounded by cold weather and facing a lifetime of reliving the war in their dreams.

Although captivated by Cribelar's battlefield exploits, I'm just as curious about his adaptation to life back home. Things were different back then, he says. The American public was weary of war. Veterans didn't receive the kind of support and welcome home that veterans of Iraq and Afghanistan mostly enjoy today. Nonprofits didn't build veterans homes. There weren't free vacations. Veterans went back to work. It was all they could do. During the Vietnam War veterans were spit upon, something today's veterans are unlikely to encounter. When Cribelar's ship returned from Korea, he and his fellow Marines were given hot coffee, processed off active duty, and sent home. Thank you for your service.

With each veteran I interview, my historical context for framing my own experiences grows. I'm beginning to understand how war transcends generations. I can relate to these men despite the age difference—nearly six decades in Cribelar's case. There is never any suggestion that veterans of one war have it worse than those of another. Every person's experience is different. Each has been changed by their role in America's wars. Many of the veterans have not discussed those roles in twenty years or more. On one occasion I interview Nic Swinson, an Army medic with the Eighth Infantry Division. Swinson landed on Normandy's Omaha Beach on June 6, 1944, armed only with a five-inch pocket knife, and spent a year in combat as he moved with the Allied forces advancing across France and Belgium into Germany. He earned two Purple Hearts and two Bronze Stars for valor. Despite the horrors of combat and the agony of getting shot, one of the worst moments for Swinson was when his unit broke down the wall of a Nazi concentration camp.

"We saw those Jews getting thrown into the burning pit," Swinson tells me. "I'll never forget that sight. We had to take them and give them a bath and give them clothes. That don't leave your head. That don't leave your heart."

Our three-hour conversation is interrupted by one of Swinson's three middle-aged daughters. She enters the living room to suggest her father take a break. As I follow her toward the back door to go for a smoke, I find Swinson's two other daughters in the kitchen, crying. They want to speak to me outside. Before the interview they had asked me to go easy on their father, as he was old and frail. Now I'm worried they are going to berate me for pushing the old man too far. Instead they thank me. Their father has never told them much about life during the war or what his mind was like upon returning home. They had no idea what had happened to him on D-day or that he had helped liberate a concentration camp. He kept his medals and ribbons pinned to a corkboard, they say. He never explained them. They never asked. The pain their father has kept hidden for so long moves them. Swinson has confided in me as a fellow veteran.

I leave each interview with mixed emotions. Meeting men who have survived the traumas of war and gone on to lead full and productive lives is uplifting for me. They've all coped by keeping themselves busy. Idle minds are evil playgrounds, they say. I know what they mean—it's why I've been keeping busy too. And while these older veterans have managed to cope and build lives from the wreckage of war, they're still grappling with the mental scars decades later. It's little comfort to imagine I could end up the same. I'm trying to be optimistic, but sometimes I still worry that I've got a life sentence of feeling like shit.

The veterans I'm speaking with don't dwell on the horrors of war but instead focus on the good parts of life. They've all lived through tough times—not just in combat but also back home—and yet they cope, usually with help from their friends or former battlefield comrades. I hope I can do the same.

"A lot of stuff I've seen is buried and I hope it stays buried. I'm afraid of some of those memories resurfacing. As long as they stay buried, it's fine," says Cribelar. "It's a hard thing to explain. I've got feelings and everything. I'm not cold. You get the feeling of the war at times, but I won't dwell on it because I think that will get you in trouble. No, I sure don't."

Some of the vets reveal to me the details of events they don't want repeated—stories about prisoners being mistreated, even executed in moments of rage, or shot to end their suffering. Others tell me of mass slaughter. The line of morality in war is not clearly defined. Some cry when they share these memories with me. Others' minds drift to places like Normandy or Tarawa. Iwo Jima or Bastogne. Many sit in silence. Some begin sharing and abruptly stop. When they returned from war decades ago they were left to sort their actions out for themselves. For me this is all too familiar.

Sharing stories seems to make the veterans feel better. In order to move on with my life, I realize I have to confront my own dark history—the rage, the violence, the killing—and come to terms with the things I've done. I've learned the best way to do so is to share it with a friend. I'm less afraid of being judged.

During combat I had my squad around me to confide in. Years later we are spread across the United States. Phone calls and text messages are great—Facebook and other social media provide a way for us to connect despite being apart—but they cannot replace the antics and kinship between bored, disgruntled men on the battlefield. I'm still looking for my grunt bromance. That's when I run into Geoff at a meeting for the local chapter of the Military Order of the Purple Heart—an organization made up entirely of combat-wounded veterans. We're the only two that day under the age of sixty. We get to talking and it turns out Geoff served with First Battalion, Sixth Marines in Marjah, Afghanistan, and earlier in Ramadi, Iraq, with Third Battalion, Seventh Marines. He's a foul-mouthed smart-ass just like me. We hit it off. And we love to bust each other's balls—or, in his case, ball. He lost a nard to an IED blast in Afghanistan. Thank you for your service, pal.

Meeting Geoff is a relief. Just linking up with vets in general is not much help, because those who see combat make up a fraction of the millions of veterans of Iraq and Afghanistan. Some of us know the thrill of a bullet ricocheting off a wall inches from our face. Others do not. And that's fine. But deploying to a combat zone is not the same as being in combat. The vast majority of veterans never left their bases in Afghanistan or Iraq. This is not to say that they had it easy. The ever-present threat of a stray mortar or rocket attack can certainly be stressful, even while checking your e-mail on a big base protected by dozens of lookout towers, concertina wire, and checkpoints. But the stress of potentially getting your entire squad of fifteen Marines and your Corpsman killed while out on foot patrol is a different order of magnitude. This stress multiplies exponentially when you don't have helicopters, jets, vehicles, or artillery in direct support of your mission. The closest Marines to help us if we suffered a mass casualty in Afghanistan were at best fifteen minutes away by vehicle. Longer on foot. In Iraq it could be hours.

Knowing that I killed people—men, children, teenagers—is sickening. Killing them violated every ingrained moral and social code. I had to rationalize that another person should die. Because I wanted them to. That power over life becomes addicting. Very addicting. You miss it. You daydream about it. When I pulled the trigger, I was God. And Geoff understands how that feels. He helps me feel less alone, less like a murderous freak.

We've experienced the most terrifying and inhumane side of humanity. After everything we've seen—ruptured and rotting corpses eaten by dogs, the broken bodies and minds of boys and women gang-raped for amusement or punishment—after watching friends die and then fighting off birds for their body parts, I'm afraid that if there is a hell, and I go there, the eternity of emotional torture will be even worse than the memories haunting my mind. No day passes that I don't visualize the children I accidentally killed. On bad days I see the trail of tears that marked the dust on their lifeless faces. Those children were curled into a fetal position and died clinging to each other for safety. The older shielded the younger. That's how I found them. I need someone like Geoff around to understand what that feels like. He knows what I'm going through and understands my frustration with medications the VA continues to send me by mail—antidepressants, sedatives, amphetamines, and mood stabilizers. Stuff to wake me up. Stuff to put me down. Stuff to keep me calm. Stuff to rile me up. Like a human drone. Numb from the effects of war. Numb from the world around it. I'm sick of the regimen. More pills isn't the answer for me anymore. Between my hospitalization and attending appointments at the VA, the answer always seems to be more pills. And higher doses. And more pills to counteract the side effects of those higher doses. And then swapping pills for other pills. Lots and lots of pills. My doctors try to dissuade me from objecting to pills. They don't want to try reducing my medications. At one point my doctor—a general practitioner, not a psychiatrist—prescribes me Risperdal, an antipsychotic usually prescribed to minimize symptoms of bipolar disorder or schizophrenia. The pills come in the mail. The "voices in my head" tell me to throw them in the trash.

I express my concerns to friends I've served with, and they suggest I try cannabis. The first time I smoke it, I sleep ten hours instead of my usual five or six. I wake up feeling energized and well rested. I don't have nightmares or remember tossing or turning throughout the night. Cannabis becomes my gateway away from the hard drugs the VA wants to feed me. I start to trade my pill bottles for pipes and papers. I begin to feel less numb and I start to smile more often.

The more I interact with the VA, the more I want to distance myself from them. I'm repeatedly told cannabis is evil but asked whether I need opiates for chronic pain. My local VA is not worth my effort. I'm never seen for appointments on time. Cancellations are never communicated to me. When the VA reevaluates my traumatic brain injury twelve months after my retirement, a family medicine doctor and a psychologist rather than a neurologist do my neurological assessments. My appointments normally last about fifteen minutes. I fought in Iraq and Afghanistan and now, as Geoff likes to say, "I fight the VA." I'd rather allocate a portion of my monthly disability payment toward not using, interacting, or depending on the VA. To ease my stress levels, I avoid a broken system by using the very money they pay me to seek help elsewhere. I can focus on assimilating into civilian life and continuing to heal without the added stress of not being able to pay our bills. I'm grateful because some veterans aren't so lucky. They didn't retire with health insurance like me. They rely solely on a system that struggles to answer calls from suicidal veterans in crisis. A return phone call is a rarity. Keeping an appointment or seeing a patient on time seems impossible. But don't worry about your pills—the opiates and antipsychotics will be in your mailbox on time.

I begin seeing a civilian psychiatrist outside the VA network. I choose him because his office has the highest online rating. After a few months of working together I ask him if he is willing to help me reduce the dose of my psychiatric meds as I begin to smoke cannabis. My doctor worries about helping me because of my profession, but I promise him he shouldn't worry about whether I'll report on him. He is in favor of cannabis legalization and is supportive, but under North Carolina law cannabis is illegal. He could lose his medical license. I could be imprisoned or labeled noncompliant and lose my VA benefits. Lose my freedom. Lose our daughter. But it's worth it.

I'm taking fewer pills as I'm burning through rolling papers. I'm happier. I feel amazing. Less clouded. I'm feeling less physical and emotional pain. I'm more hopeful, less woeful. My relationship with Mel is getting stronger. Maddie and I are growing closer. Writing is much more fun. My past is easier to remember and talk about. It feels good to feel again. The numbness and fog are lifting. Using the "devil's lettuce" is yet another thing I have in common with many veterans I speak with, both old and young. Buying cannabis illegally from a drug dealer is far less stressful than interacting with the VA.

Meanwhile, some of my friends are thriving in school or moving up the corporate ladder; others are sinking to the bottom of a bottle or developing other addictions. Marriages are failing. Children are born in and out of wedlock. Affairs tear relationships apart. Friends are finding solace at the finish line of a marathon. Others volunteer with youth or disenfranchised teens. Many delve into the arts—painting, pottery, writing, and photography. A few pursue medicine. Some embrace community. Others want to be left alone. Friends continue to die at war. Friends continue to kill themselves at home. Some swallow pills. Others swallow bullets. It's a lot of what I'm used to, but confusing nonetheless. The Marine Corps forced me to come back from war. It's up to me to allow myself to come home.

Chapter 18

Moving Forward, Sliding Back

We do not see things as they are, we see them as we are.

—Anaïs Nin

Finbarr, Dakar and Dublin, September–December 2013

Senegal in early September means the sweltering heat of the rainy season. Torrential downpours flood roads and bring Dakar's creeping traffic to a standstill. An open sewer overflows onto the muddy track leading to my house. The radio and air-conditioning in my twenty-year-old company 4x4 stop working, as do the brakes, my cell phone, my Internet (my wireless modem has rusted and died in the humidity), and the air-conditioning in my bedroom, the only place in the house that offers respite from the crushing heat. A section of my roof is leaking, and with each downpour wet patches spread across my ceiling, paint and plaster crumble to the floor, and water drips onto the tiles and runs down the walls. My kitchen stove runs out of gas and my fridge coughs and shudders against the heat. Adding insult to injury, Senegal has also just implemented a new immigration law obliging foreigners to apply for a resident visa, a process involving tedious bureaucratic obstacles.

Such irritations are part of living in Africa, but it's still a reality check after a year of American comforts and convenience. Then the usually reliable water supply serving Dakar suffers a burst main pipeline, leaving the capital's population of nearly three million people without running water for almost a month. The country plunges into the grip of a major infrastructure crisis, the worst of its postcolonial history.

For weeks a proud and modern African city with sophisticated bars, restaurants, and nightclubs reverts to the traditional village rhythm of collecting water from hand-pumped wells or from central distribution points and delivery trucks. Shops ration and then sell out of bottled mineral water. People walk miles to line up for hours to fill jerricans or buckets, then trek home again carrying sloshing loads on heads and shoulders. Thousands more dig holes along the beach and tap into a brackish liquid that at least allows them to wash. With my injured leg I'm still not mobile enough to run around collecting water, so I use my one-hundred-liter blue plastic garbage bin to collect rain runoff spilling from my roof during the downpours. I also collect the water dripping inside the house and use it to flush toilets. But it's just too much, and tempers flare. Angry youths burn tires on the streets and riot in protest over the lack of basic services. I'm tempted to join them. The mobs take perverse pleasure in knowing the security forces can't use water cannons to disperse the crowds or put out the burning tires spinning black smoke into the sky across the city. Still, there's little the government can do about the broken pipeline until engineers and spare parts are shipped from France and China to repair the damage.

On my first Friday back, and after an especially frustrating day, I'm desperate to get home to relax. My Achilles is only halfway through the expected recovery period, and it's swollen and throbbing from the heat and from the strain of hauling buckets of water upstairs to my bathroom. I drive my 4x4 home through heavy traffic, using the gears and hand brake to control my speed (the brakes still don't work and my mechanic is unavailable). Torrential rain and flooding mean the fifteen-minute drive from the office takes more than an hour. It's just after twilight as I pull into my driveway. I switch on a porch light and hear a small *pop* as the interrupter on my circuit breaker explodes and kicks up a puff of smoke, plunging the house into darkness. I'll be without electricity for the night, and, unless I can find an electrician working over the weekend, I'll have no power until Monday.

Returning to Dakar after my Nieman year feels like a big step backward. By now I've lived and worked in Africa for Reuters since 2001—nearly twelve years, eight of them based in Senegal. Harvard put into sharp relief just how isolating my life in Africa has been and how vulnerable it has made me to prolonged bouts of depression. The obvious solution is to be closer to home, but Reuters can't seem to find a way there. I feel as if management now wants to remind me I'm just a cog in the machine. My morale plummets, and not just because of the onslaught of daily frustrations in Dakar. I feel trapped and anxious. I used to focus on my friends, the beaches, the surfing, the vibrant music and nightclub scene, the delicious food and relaxed atmosphere. Now things beyond my control overwhelm me: traffic jams, bad drivers, bureaucratic inefficiency, corrupt police shaking me down on the roadside, overpersistent street vendors, child beggars, broken sidewalks, people arriving hours late for meetings. The frequent machine-gun beat of Senegal's famous djembe drums becomes like a hammer inside my skull and makes me want to punch someone in the face.

The Voice has returned, and it's louder than ever. The thought of confronting the logistical nightmare of traveling to other West African countries, or working in the kinds of places where I've spent the previous decade, makes me crazed. I start to imagine the worst possible outcome from any scenario. I can recall only the hassles, the violence, the detentions, and the failures, rather than the successful assignments. I withdraw to my leaky, waterless home. I can't shake the feeling of being stuck.

I'm at home doing my daily Achilles rehab exercises—a series of controlled heel lifts—when a *pop-pop* sound and a sharp jab of pain suck the breath from my lungs. My heart hammers in my chest and my fingers tremble as I look down to see a section of my left leg just above my ankle swell up to the size of a Ping-Pong ball. The heat, the strain of hauling water, and perhaps the burden of everything else weighing me down have caused something to give. An MRI eventually reveals that the soleus muscle has torn away from my injured Achilles. My recovery is set back another four months or more. I'm crushed. I can't even take a shower, let alone get the medical care I need. I've been back in Dakar for little more than a week.

Eventually I'm medically evacuated in a wheelchair back to London, where another doctor confirms my condition and I'm granted an additional three months' medical leave, this time at half pay. I head for Dublin, where there's more space to stay at my mother's house and where getting to and from rehab sessions at a nearby gym will be easier and less expensive than in London.

Just as I'm leaving for Dublin, my boss calls. My position as West Africa photographer is being eliminated as part of companywide cutbacks. I'm being offered a severance package that will take effect on January 1, 2014, the day my medical leave is due to end.

It's as if the Voice has come alive and assumed a physical presence, a brittle texture. It's taunting me, mocking the idea that I might actually be worth something: *You're a hobbled forty-two-year-old bachelor living at home with your mother—in the attic, no less—and facing unemployment. Put that in your online dating profile, and see how you do.*

It's a humbling fall from grace. Until my sabbatical year at Harvard, I'd been doing well. I'd won some big awards, company bosses favored me, and my byline was known and sought by editors at top publications. Reuters organized a traveling solo exhibition of my Congo work, and I had the luxury of being mostly self-assigning, with a generous budget for travel, equipment, and perks. I loved my job, my future looked promising, and my place within Reuters seemed assured.

"You're probably one of the two people Reuters can never get rid of," one colleague told me. The other was Peter Apps, a journalist who had been paralyzed from the neck down in a car accident while covering the war in Sri Lanka. It was Peter himself who made the comment.

Now, suddenly, I'm a number on a corporate spreadsheet that needs to be balanced. There were management changes at Reuters while I was on sabbatical, and new managers with different priorities have replaced the top editors who championed me. Media outlets worldwide are facing financial difficulties in a shrinking global market and there are industry-wide cutbacks and layoffs. I long assumed I was safe, but institutional memory seems short. All I've done lately is cost the company money. Resentment is a normal reaction to being laid off but, like TJ, I feel betrayed by the very institution to which I've devoted a huge chunk of my life, and for which I've often risked my personal safety. For most of my career I've been a Reuters journalist. The threat to my sense of identity is as palpable as my feelings of betrayal.

Then, a week later, my boss, Steve Crisp, calls me back to say there's a new chance: He's been given approval to create a position for me as senior photographer for Israel and the Palestinian territories. It's a good offer for a high-profile job—a promotion, in fact—but it's not exactly in a peaceful region close to home. I worked in Israel during the 2006 war with Lebanon and didn't enjoy the experience. I left thinking I would never want to live in a place with so much pressure, scrutiny, conflict, and hatred.

Steve gives me a few weeks to decide. It's a difficult choice. I can accept the buyout and return to the kind of freedom I enjoyed while on sabbatical, only without the support of fellowship colleagues. Or I can carry on with a global media corporation in yet another hostile environment while unsure of both my standing within the company and my own motivation.

Perhaps the biggest question, though, is that of identity. If I walk away, then who am I, and what will I become? My fellowship was meant to prepare me for my next career move, to provide me with the skills to take on new challenges and instill the confidence required to reinvent myself, but I actually just came back injured and depressed and reentered an industry itself in a state of near collapse. The market for freelance photographers is brutal and ever shrinking, I haven't published new work in almost eighteen months, and I've got a debilitating leg injury. Returning to Reuters feels like a cop-out, but in my current state of mind, I don't have what it takes to map out an alternate future.

Before making a final decision, I take a five-day trip to Israel to see how it feels. I stay in Jaffa, the four-thousand-year-old seaport adjacent to the country's business capital, Tel Aviv. The city's leafy boulevards, the European-style cafés, and the beach promenade stretching the length of the Mediterranean waterfront immediately seduce me. It seems like a weird combination of Paris and Miami, grafted onto the Middle East, with a blend of languages and religions. At one end of town is Jaffa, with crumbling old stone buildings and the sound of Muslim calls to prayer intermingling with the ringing of church bells. In the other direction Tel Aviv's gleaming skyscrapers rise above the din of heavy traffic and animated conversations in Hebrew, Arabic, Russian, French, and English. The city has none of the stifling religious conservatism of Jerusalem, and the tension of the conflict doesn't seem like such a daily personal assault in the material comfort of the "Tel Aviv bubble." A modern infrastructure and lifestyle are appealing after so long in Africa. After a few more days of soul-searching, I decide: Israel it is.

Chapter 19

No Easy Fix

I mean, it's affected my life. It surely has. But I'm not out there cry-ing about it. I know that I went to war, and I came out of the battle with what I got.

—Jim Otto, Oakland Raiders player 1960–74, in the
PBS documentary film *League of Denial*

TJ, Camp Lejeune, North Carolina, early 2014

I've found my beat. I want to report on how others are coping with the transition to postwar life. With my editor's encouragement, I contact Camp Lejeune's Wounded Warrior Battalion East. I talk to the new commander, Lieutenant Colonel Leland Suttee, Marine to Marine, about my own experiences, including the administrative issues I faced during my exit from the military. Suttee recognizes that I, the journalist and the Marine, could be a valuable ally in battles against bureaucracy and insti-tutional delays. He grants me access.

I still have to earn the confidence of Marines and sailors who are still on active duty and stuck in that same place I was not so long ago—physically or mentally damaged, or both, and unsure what their new lives will hold. It doesn't take me long. Once again I use my own strug-gles to build trust. Once the men know I've been through similar trials, they don't hide much. Over the following twelve months, I write dozens of articles on mental health, TBI, PTSD, moral injury, suicide, therapy, the overuse of medication, and life as an amputee. I become a public out-let for wounded warriors and veterans, but my work also allows me to reconnect with my old "brotherhood." Although building my new life as a civilian, I'm still a Marine at heart. Being accepted by the men I inter-view allows me the sense of kinship and belonging I've missed. And it eases the sting of my final months in the military, when I felt ostracized as a malingerer and rejected as a Marine. Through my reporting I get to be close with the Corps again, talking with other Marines about issues affecting us all.

Together Lieutenant Colonel Suttee and I develop the idea for Alive Day Dinners at the battalion. Each month we invite Purple Heart recipients and their families to come together for dinner and share as much of their story as they wish. No pressure, no judgment. It's a time to be among fellow wounded, to realize that none of us are as alone as we often feel. Suttee asks me to be the first guest speaker at one of our gatherings. It's a spaghetti dinner sponsored by the Semper Fi Fund and Hope for the Warriors, two nonprofits that provide emergency funding, assistance, and resources for wounded veterans and their families. Dinner is at a rustic dining hall adjacent to the base stables, with horses grazing in a nearby field. As the Marines and Corpsmen eat, I share some of my war stories and discuss what has helped me during my recovery. When I'm done, a Marine raises his hand.

"What do you think helped you the most when you got out?"

I pause. Look him in the eye. Then answer, "My suicide attempt."

It's not the answer Suttee wants to hear in such a setting, but it's the truth. I'm not proud of having tried to kill myself, and suicide is never the answer, but hitting that ultimate low was like a boomerang reaching the end of its trajectory, a turning point that had to be met before I could loop back along another path to where I'd come from. I'm not ashamed—there's no way I can change what I did—but coming close to dying, just as I had so many times in combat, allowed me to finally feel alive again, and to see why life was still worth living. It was my jump start, the shock that revived me.

My message is blunt: I hit rock bottom, but you don't have to. Everyone has bad days. You have to know when enough is enough. Get help. Don't be a stubborn asshole like me.

Over two months the Alive Day Dinners triple in attendance from ten to thirty as more wounded Marines and sailors become involved. Dinners revolve around turning the negatives of combat into lessons learned, the positive things we hold close to us after losing a friend or being shot or burned or losing limbs. We talk about funny memories—dressing up while in combat or someone's epic face-plant during a firefight. We share the happy parts of our terrible memories. One burn survivor jokes that his wife enjoys him "well done." Amputees laugh about how they're often asked whether it hurt when their limbs were blown off. The dinners and conversation are mostly among lower enlisted Marines and sailors, who make up the majority of the patients at the battalion, but one evening a decorated Marine officer and combat-wounded infantryman speaks to our group. He addresses the stigma of seeking mental health care and says he admires those of us sitting in front of him. Because of his rank and position within the Marine Corps, he asks that his remarks not leave the room. He tells us that he knows he himself needs help but that the consequences of asking for it as a senior field grade Marine officer are too great. He tells us we're part of a generation making it okay to ask for help. Someday, he says, seeking help will become an accepted part of the job, but for now, he'll have to wait until he retires. None of us fault him for his decision.

There's always some new problem. Government sequestration—the Defense Department's mandatory budget cuts that reduce spending on everything from active-duty troops to supplies, from fighter jets right down to wag bags—and the resulting furlough of mental health workers have a severe impact on the availability of treatment, not only for the Wounded Warrior Battalion but for the entire military. The financial cutbacks are a blow to a military already struggling with a massive backlog of mental health claims. I take the issue personally, launching an investigation into the impact it will have on Marines seeking treatment at Camp Lejeune as well as service members farther afield. I publish reports revealing how the large number of government mental-health care workers furloughed is having a dramatic and harmful impact on service members unable to receive adequate treatment for mental health. Wait times for nonemergency care have increased 14 percent and more than sixty appointments are being rescheduled each week at Camp Lejeune alone. North Carolina congressman Walter Jones picks up on my stories.

In a letter written the day of publication, Jones challenges Secretary of Defense Chuck Hagel to give servicemen and servicewomen "the high quality mental health care they desperately need." In response, two days later Hagel exempts mental health workers from furlough, returning them to work and restoring treatment of personnel back to full capacity across the Department of Defense.

Seeing my reporting reach high-level decision makers and influence public policy is another personal victory for me—one more step toward the kind of purposeful life I'm seeking. I've also decided to resume therapy sessions twice monthly with a civilian psychologist in addition to seeing my psychiatrist. During my initial intake appointment I tell them I'm looking for someone who isn't timid. While I was still on active duty, I grew to respect Dr. Webster and Frank for their honest conversations and advice. They weren't afraid to call me out on my bullshit when I tried to feel sorry for myself, but I no longer have access to them since retiring from the Marine Corps. My new psychologist, Gail, is a military spouse and doesn't sugarcoat anything. My trust in her and the civilian medical staff in charge of my treatment grows. The access to care, ambience, staffing, and patient satisfaction exceed that offered by the VA. By the end of 2013, I'm only a few months away from completing my online bachelor's degree in journalism and have set my sights on pursuing a master's degree at Columbia University's Graduate School of Journalism.

Things are going well. Then, over the span of three days in January 2014—fourteen months after my retirement—I'm required by the DOD to undergo ten hours of neuropsychological testing. The evaluation is required annually for five years to monitor my level of disability. The tests measure behavioral and cognitive changes resulting from central nervous system disease or injury. If the evaluation reveals a drastic improvement, I could lose my retirement benefits and even be recalled to active duty. There's temptation to deliberately perform poorly, but I'm confident that my progress hasn't been significant enough for it to affect my status. Still, appealing the decision isn't something I want to go through. It's too much paperwork and added stress. I'm ready to move on.

After the same battery of exams in 2012, I was depressed for a month.

Any progress I'd made felt like it had been reversed. The examinations felt like some kind of punishment. The results of the neuropsychological tests pointed out my every deficiency, labeling me "below average" or "poor" in certain brain functions. My therapy and new outlook on life were focused on recovery and moving forward, but with each test I was reminded of all the ways my injury had depleted me.

For all my progress, I still rely on a cocktail of drugs—Zoloft, Abilify, Adderall XR, and clonazepam—to get through each day. The slightest triggers—large crowds, potential threats, an emotional conversation with Mel—still plunge me into bouts of depression that can last weeks. I still draw support from my terrific dog too. Mr. Luke isn't a cure for my anxiety, but when I need a break from stressful situations, he's the perfect excuse to escape. I just tell people he needs to poop. Taking him outside gives me room to breathe and relax. I want to let go of these fears, but I can't shake them. My anxiety also makes sleeping difficult, and I still have frequent intrusive thoughts and headaches. Balance is a major problem. I often get dizzy walking up stairs. When I wake up each morning, I sit on the edge of my bed for several minutes before I can walk. This also limits my physical activity. I can't play with Maddie in the yard without fear of falling. I can't run or exercise. My iPhone is filled with daily task reminders and my work space and home office are plastered with Post-it notes and to-do lists to keep me from forgetting things. Life has become a collection of compensatory strategies to keep me from failing. My brain injury affects my judgment, and the frustration of these daily challenges sometimes overwhelms me and leads to angry outbursts. During my first year at the *Daily News*, I've twice been reprimanded for raising my voice in disputes with editors. On another occasion I suffered a manic episode after covering a story about a Marine who fell out of a helicopter and died during a training exercise. The accident triggered memories from Iraq and I was unable to sleep for four days. During the episode I impulsively got three expensive tattoos our family couldn't afford.

Amazingly, despite all this, my mood and state of mind are generally improving. The occasional cannabis use is helping. I still have bad days, but the coping strategies and mindfulness I've learned during my sessions with Frank and Dr. Webster have been working. So this year's round of tests has me wound up again. It doesn't help that they fall on Mel's birthday, so instead of enjoying the day with her, I will be tired, mentally drained, and agitated. I expect that the emotional toll of the tests will be heavy and leave me hating myself again. My TBI wiped away many of my best memories, and this is something that a neuropsychological evaluation cannot quantify or evaluate. I cannot fathom why I must do these tests four more times just to prove I'm still as damaged as ever. Just because I've developed coping mechanisms and compensatory strategies doesn't mean my deficiencies and stressors have disappeared. I've just learned how to manage them better.

My first appointment is at Camp Lejeune's Intrepid Spirit Concussion Recovery Center on January 13. As usual, Mr. Luke is by my side, a calming, furry presence I can trust. Still, as I fill out the paperwork at the clinic, my palms are damp and my knees feel weak. When my name is called, I barely have the strength to stand. I want to leave, but I can't. If I don't stay for the tests, I could lose my benefits, including pay and medical coverage for my family. I have no choice but to submit to a process that dredges up the trauma I've been trying for years to process and overcome.

During the ninety-minute session with a neuropsychologist, Mr. Luke keeps his head on my lap. I massage behind his ears to calm my nerves. The doctor asks about the two mild concussions I sustained while fighting in Fallujah, about my suicidal thinking and suicide attempt, about my injury in Afghanistan, about friends who have been killed, about how I feel about having killed, and about how my various symptoms affect my relationships with Mel and Maddie. It's all about my cognitive difficulties and failures. I'd rather he focus on my coping mechanisms and how far I've come with implementing them. But it's all negatives. No positives.

The crudeness of the tests is an indication that, despite millions of dollars in research, little is known about how to diagnose and treat mild to moderate traumatic brain injuries.

I leave the interview too depressed to feel angry. And I know it's only the beginning. I still face hours of cognitive testing during the days ahead; then I'll have to wait another week to find out just how deficient the tests deem me to be. The indignity is infuriating.

I vent my frustrations by writing another piece for *At War* detailing my experience. Most of the twenty-eight responses posted online are from sympathetic civilians, but two entries from former servicemen typify attitudes that linger within the military despite attempts to advance thinking about trauma.

"Stop crying. You have a job. . . . Get to work," writes Mel Garten of Portland, Oregon, who identifies himself as a parachute infantry colonel who commanded troops in World War II, Korea, and Vietnam. "I have known more men wounded in combat by weapons, not trucks blown up, in one year than in 12 in what you call wars. I was 100% disabled in Vietnam and taught for 20 years after. What do you want the citizens to do now?"

Another unidentified reader from Maryland is equally unsympathetic, writing, "After serving in and with the Army for 39 years, I've met my share of traumatized returnees, many of whom were medically retired, but damned few whine about their medical follow-up as much as the author."

Making matters worse, the tests coincide with news from Iraq that Fallujah has fallen to Islamic State militants. The same streets I fought on in 2004. I watch television images of the militants raising their flag in victory and I'm transported back to Fallujah's cinder-block buildings and rebar. The dust. The heat. The smell. The loss of friends like Demarcus Brown, Bradley Faircloth, Travis Desiato, and so many other fellow Marines. Should their loved ones feel as though those lives were lost in vain?

Before I deployed, I thought I understood war. Bullets and blood. Bodies and bandages. Some live. Some die. Oohrah. In combat, your circle shrinks to those who are there with you. Nobody else matters. Fuck the flag. Fuck politics. Mel didn't matter. Neither did Maddie. Our families couldn't save us—we'd only burden them if we were injured or killed, a flag draped over our coffin. Politicians would offer hollow condolences

and talk shit. Family would mourn my death. My men were all that mattered when push came to shove. I was all that mattered to them. Coming
home is the luck of the draw. And as I told my men before every patrol, if
today's the day, today's the day. We'll worry about the flag, the bills, our
families, and the Washington boondoggle if we ever get home. If we're
lucky.

Being home still doesn't make me feel very lucky, though. I'm trying
to refocus on a career and redefine myself, but focusing solely on work
bores me. I still miss the campfire at Kunjak and choking down greasy
chicken with my boys. I sit out by my fire pit in my backyard or by a tiki
torch on my front porch as I write. The flicker of the flame reminds me of
my happiest times in Afghanistan—by the fire with my guys. Laughing
about fetishes and pet peeves, joking about sex. It reminds me of when I
always had someone to talk to.

While working in the newsroom, I turn my focus toward finishing
my undergraduate degree and getting into Columbia. Keeping myself
busy occupies my mind, and at least the thought of going to grad school
is something I can feel hopeful about, something to dispel my feelings of
failure. I view Columbia as the Parris Island for reporting—it has the
reputation for being the best and most challenging.

At work I put my anguish into print. I write about how my brain injury has robbed me of countless memories, including my wedding day. I
married Mel in a quaint waterfront ceremony at North Carolina's Lake
Lure on April 15, 2007. A handful of fellow Marines and close family
were in attendance. I watched her walk down the aisle following a trail
of white rose petals. She looked stunning in her flowing white dress, cradling a bouquet of flowers, a gorgeous smile lighting up her face. The
only way I remember any of these details is from looking at photographs.
I have no emotional memories from the day Mel and I got hitched. They
have been erased. It's the same for the day I was injured in Afghanistan.
Only Fin's photographs give shape to memories clouded by a thick gray
fog. And there are parts of Maddie's birth I cannot recall—holding Mel's
hand as she pushed and staring in awe as Maddie's head crowned. I know
only because Mel reminds me. I often lie. I say I remember shared memo-

ries with Mel and Maddie—events from when we dated, birthdays, vacations. I can recall plenty of other memories, often the unimportant details of less significant events. Meanwhile, countless moments that have shaped my life are like Polaroid pictures developing in reverse, fading to blankness instead of sharpening to capture a moment in time.

It's a slow afternoon at the office on Friday, March 14. I'm working on a story about Sergeant Major Lanette N. Wright, the first female commanding officer of the Twenty-fourth Marine Expeditionary Unit. It's a significant milestone for the Marines, but I'm unable to make sense of the story on my page. I'm sitting in my cubicle staring at my computer screen when an e-mail drops into my in-box. As I scan the message, another lands, and then a minute later, another.

"Wow," I say to nobody in particular, "I got into Columbia."

Two reporters sitting near me ask me to repeat what I've just said. I'm a bit stunned. I quickly call Mel and then I send a message to Fin. They're both thrilled. It's phenomenal news, and it couldn't have come at a better time. I need to get away from the military mind-set of Jacksonville and of the Marine Corps at Camp Lejeune. But I also need a new challenge, a new community, which I hope I can find in Columbia's elite investigative reporting program. After calling more friends and family, I update my Facebook profile with the latest news.

The duty editor at the *Daily News* that day is happy for me but has more pressing concerns.

"Yay! Congrats!" she comments on my post. "I need your story—we're on deadline."

Chapter 20

Another War

When you're willing to die for something and then you realize it doesn't make any difference, it's a shock. And when you lose that faith, it's time to quit and move on.

—Emma Sky, author of *The Unraveling*

Finbarr, Israel and Gaza, February–August 2014

I arrive in Tel Aviv in February 2014. Our office in Jerusalem is about an hour's drive from my rented apartment in Jaffa. Aside from short stints on desks in London, Berlin, and New York, this is my first time posted to a large bureau with a steady flow of daily news assignments.

During my time in sub-Saharan Africa, Reuters had four staff photographers, myself included, covering more than fifty countries spread across an area greater than the United States, China, India, and Eastern Europe combined. By contrast, we have four staff photographers working from our Jerusalem office alone, and half a dozen more staff and full-time contract photographers across Israel, the West Bank, and Gaza, a combined area only slightly larger than New Jersey, America's fifth-smallest state. In media terms, Africa is a forgotten continent that grabs occasional international headlines while tiny Israel and the Palestinian territories are likely the world's most scrutinized place. It's quite an adjustment. Back in Dakar I would stop by the small villa housing our West Africa bureau every few weeks to file expenses and greet my half dozen local and international colleagues from text and TV. I determined my own working hours and days off.

In Israel I'm part of a regular shift rotation and often make my way into the office on the twelfth floor of a commercial tower above one of the country's largest shopping malls. The news desk determines coverage and photographers send pictures back to local editors in Jerusalem. There's a steady flow of daily assignments, often covering press conferences or events I would not normally consider newsworthy. But unlike Africa, news from Israel is always in high demand.

I was spoiled in Africa, despite my whining. I took my autonomy for granted, and I'd moved there because of a deep-rooted interest in the continent. I'd spent a year after college backpacking from Kenya to South Africa, passing along the way through the mountains of eastern Congo and Rwanda, leaving the region just as the 1994 genocide erupted and arriving in South Africa in time to experience Nelson Mandela's election as the country's first black president. On that trip I encountered some of the best and worst sides of human nature. In each country I visited over the years, I learned as best I could the local languages and immersed myself in the lives of those I met, looking for glimpses of joy. These small moments offered glimmers of hope and redemption in difficult times.

By contrast, in Israel I soon find myself confronted by the challenges of living in a foreign land saturated by media and plagued by an endless conflict between people with whom I share no sense of connection.

Unlike in Africa, I can't speak or read the local languages, which leaves me unable to communicate or even navigate much of daily life. Even though many Israelis and Palestinians speak English, many do not. Fuel stations in Israel, for example, function only in Hebrew and require a complicated sequence of steps to pay by credit card at the unmanned pumps. They also have a limit of fifty dollars for foreign cards. With all the driving I'm doing for work, I frequently spend absurd amounts of time seeking help to fuel my tank. Banking is equally complicated. At supermarkets—which are surprisingly difficult to find in Tel Aviv—I'm unable to read any of the labels. Many staff members at the supermarkets I do find are Russian speakers who know little English. It's a struggle just to find basic household necessities. On one occasion I buy from an illogically organized shop what I think is salad dressing, only to discover when I get home that it's some kind of floor cleaner. The solution, of course, would be to learn at least some Hebrew, but for whatever reason—possibly stubbornness—I resist. While traveling across Africa, I was constantly exposed to a tradition of inclusion typified by the ancient word *ubuntu*, meaning "humanity to others" or, more broadly, "I am what I am because of who we all are." Nelson Mandela embodied this spirit of connection, community, and mutual caring. Life in Israel, however, seems insular and frozen by a culture of exclusion, symbolized most powerfully by the towering concrete separation barrier between Israel and the West Bank.

I find Israel bewildering and unsettling, and the feeling of isolation and the sense of alienation land me back inside the cage of depression. The view from inside is grim.

An undercurrent of tension compounds the feeling. Security is omnipresent. Driving to Jerusalem or the West Bank involves passing through military checkpoints guarded by Israeli soldiers carrying machine guns. Entrances to shopping malls and supermarkets feature metal detectors and armed guards who search bags and ask, "Any weapons?" This is normal to people living in Israel, but it seems strange to a newcomer and an outsider like me.

The initial charm of Tel Aviv's cafés quickly fades, and once again I become transfixed by the litany of irritations that compound to make life unpleasant, starting with a flea-infested apartment and a neighbor's rogue and instrusive cat.

These are trivial complaints, of course. Far more disturbing is the constant, overt racism and unabashed prejudice. People slip off-color comments into casual conversations without shame.

"You don't want to live in Jaffa," an Israeli real estate agent tells me while showing me apartments upon my arrival. "Too many Arabs. Very dirty and noisy."

The Arab presence in Jaffa is exactly why I chose it as a place to live. By comparison, the rest of Tel Aviv and much of Israel is segregated and socially sterile. Such divisions make me uncomfortable. There is, of course, a degree of hypocrisy in this. Here I am, unsettled by the distance imposed between various social groups, and yet what I crave most is the familiarity of my own kind, to be around people with whom I feel some cultural connection. It's pretty confusing. Still, I need a cosmopolitan environment where people of different religions, colors, and cultures brush shoulders and share space without rancor. In Israel, Jaffa is about as close as I can get.

Comments like the real estate agent's are common and not directed only toward Palestinians (who are often referred to broadly as "terrorists"). Tens of thousands of Africans, most of whom have fled wars or oppression in Sudan and Eritrea, are viewed with general disdain. Israel's prime minister, Benjamin Netanyahu, calls them "infiltrators" and has said that the mostly Christian and Muslim asylum seekers "threaten the Jewish character of the state." Some three thousand African men are held in a grim detention center in the desert near the Egyptian border. I find all this shocking. I assumed that a country forged in the aftermath of the Holocaust would be sensitive to the plight of those facing persecution and genocide, no matter their religion or ethnicity. Instead the African migrants, many of whom have survived horrific overland journeys on their way to Israel, are belittled, held in a legal limbo, and treated as criminals. Yet their situation exists in the shadow of the dominant political narrative of the Israeli-Palestinian conflict and receives little attention or sympathy. There's an active and vociferous liberal Left in Israel, but it's roundly ignored or dismissed by the more strident and pervasive attitudes of a conservative society. To raise any of these issues in conversation—or to criticize Israel's right-wing policies in any way—means being branded an anti-Semite or, if you are Jewish, a self-hating Jew. The paranoia of the national psyche is historically justified, but it carries with it a deep sense of menace and injustice.

The one bright spot in this tangled mess is Helen, an American woman I met during my brief scouting trip to Israel back in November. We quickly fell for each other and, now reunited, bond over the difficulty of living as outsiders in Israel. Helen is twenty-five and exudes a kind and gentle sweetness. She was born in California and grew up there, but her parents are Eritrean and she works with African asylum seekers in Israel. Being together keeps us both sane in an insane place. Helen is studying psychology, and the stories she hears while helping with Tigrinya translations in the therapist's office often leave her in tears. She's new to the kind of cruelty and injustice that define daily life for refugees in this part of the world. She identifies with the struggle of the Eritreans, and her stories, along with her own experiences with racism in Israel, only further cloud my view of the country.

It's somehow easier to accept that in Africa, where vast swaths of the population are uneducated, disenfranchised, and impoverished, cynical leaders can manipulate people into moral gray areas that allow for extreme behavior. Israel, by contrast, is a highly educated, developed, and in many ways Westernized democratic society. With the experience of centuries of anti-Semitism to draw from, it seems that its people should know better than to treat minorities and those fleeing persecution with such hostility and contempt.

The simplest take on the broader conflict goes something like this: Either you believe that Palestinians are oppressed and driven to stand up to Israel's power or you believe that beleaguered Israelis are under constant threat of annihilation from hostile Arab neighbors. Of course, it's far more complicated than that. My job is not to get entangled in the politics and propaganda put forth by each side. I'm just here to take pictures. Which is part of my problem. Many of my concerns would evaporate if I felt more professionally satisfied. But working in Israel means I'm shooting alongside crowds of other photographers covering the same events day in and day out. After eighteen months away from photography, I'm rusty, and it shows. There is little coherence or vision to what I produce, largely because I have no idea what I want to say, or whether I even have anything worth adding to the conversation. Photographers in Israel and the Palestinian territories are savvy operators accustomed to working in a competitive environment. They always seem to get the shot. I don't. I feel like I've lost my touch.

I've also made a conscious decision, which I've relayed to my bosses, that I won't cover the regular clashes between stone-throwing Palestinian youths and Israeli security forces, who habitually fire back with tear-gas canisters and rubber bullets aimed not only at the protesters but also at members of the media. Hardly a month goes by without a journalist getting shot with pellets, beaten, or physically harassed by Israeli security forces. I understand why newswires maintain their coverage, but I don't want to be the one to do it. My main excuse for abstaining is my injured leg. But there's more to it than that. The truth is that I'm scared. It feels cowardly to admit it, but I want to be as far away from violence as possible. My self-confidence has melted and I feel too emotionally vulnerable. I feel brittle, as if I could crack. I try to hide it, perhaps the same way TJ tried to mask his symptoms from his men after he was injured in Afghanistan.

The threat of violence has been on my mind. Two more photographers have been killed covering wars during my initial months in Israel. Anja Niedringhaus, a German photographer for the AP, is shot by an Afghan policeman while sitting in the back of a car during an assignment to cover local elections. She was a twenty-five-year veteran of many wars and had been shot once before in Bosnia. She had also been hit by shrapnel in Afghanistan. She was tough yet gentle and was known for her big laugh. We crossed paths in Kandahar and Libya. Her death sends another painful ripple through the journalism world. Camille Lepage, a young French photographer, is caught in an ambush between rival militias in the jungles of the Central African Republic. She isn't as well known as Anja, but her work is powerful and her violent death again rattles a profession that seems to be losing members at an ever-increasing pace.

When I get the news from TJ that he's been accepted to Columbia, it's one of the few occasions during my first months in Tel Aviv when I allow myself to feel optimistic. Through his openness and determination, he's shown that there's always reason to hope, that no matter how bad things are, something good might be just around the corner.

And then the Gaza war starts. I'm getting out of bed on the morning of July 9, 2014, when the metallic wail of an air-raid siren sounds over Tel Aviv. Rocket attack. I grab my cameras and run outside in my flip-flops. Nobody in sight. The mournful drone of the siren has emptied the streets. Stillness hangs in the air, as if a pause button has been pressed. A cat skulks across the road and hides under a parked car. Then the *crump* and *boom* of an explosion sound somewhere overhead. The next seven weeks will become the bloodiest period of the Israeli-Palestinian conflict in years.

I spend the first week of the violence roaming the Israeli side of the Gaza border as the country moves tens of thousands of troops and war machines into the dusty scrubland along the dividing line between two peoples bracing for another round of killing. Hamas rockets and mortars trigger sirens across southern Israel, sending the residents of nearby towns and kibbutzim running for concrete bomb shelters. In the towns nearest to Gaza—many of them with views into the Strip—Israelis have as little as fifteen seconds from the moment an alarm sounds to take cover before the Hamas projectiles hit. The incoming rockets and corresponding sirens soon reach farther north, to Tel Aviv, Jerusalem, and even Haifa, at the opposite end of the country from Gaza. Tech-savvy Israel has an app called Red Alert that delivers area-specific real-time warnings directly to mobile phones every time Hamas fires a rocket or mortar across the border. The app's "code red" alarm sounds the same as the sirens, and Hamas attacks become so intense and so frequent that the app sometimes crashes.

When the sirens sound, people momentarily freeze, look skyward, then run for cover. When not roaming the border, I sit in cafés or stalk Tel Aviv's streets and beaches, waiting for the sirens and for Israel's Iron Dome defense system to intercept incoming rockets in a dramatic aerial display. The Iron Dome is so effective that many Tel Aviv residents become nonchalant about the sirens and, instead of running for cover, gather to stare skyward, waiting for the explosions to leave bell-shaped puffs of white smoke with tentacles that look like deadly jellyfish floating in a sky blue ocean. The only damage caused to the city by Hamas during the first week of the war is when shrapnel from an intercepted rocket lands near a fuel station and shatters a car windshield. In Gaza more than two hundred Palestinians have been killed by the end of the first week. There's still hope things might end quickly, as they did after eight days of intense Israeli bombing in 2012, but this time Israel's campaign, known as Operation Protective Edge, lasts fifty days.

By the time it ends in a shaky cease-fire in September, it will have been Israel's longest military campaign in decades. For Gaza residents it will be the deadliest. More than 2,100 Palestinians, many of them civilians, will be killed. Sixty-seven soldiers and six civilians will also be killed on the Israeli side. The numbers reflect the asymmetrical nature of the war, with Hamas using guerrilla tactics and tunnel networks beneath Gaza's cramped urban landscape and Israel pounding the tiny enclave with F-16 jets, artillery, mortars, and drone strikes and sending in ground troops and tanks.

Even though our offices in Jerusalem and the Palestinian territories employ more than a dozen photographers, they are all either Israeli or Palestinian and can work only in the specific areas they are permitted to travel; Israelis can't enter Gaza and aren't supposed to enter the West Bank, whereas our Palestinian colleagues in Gaza can't cross into Israel. I'm the only member of our pictures team who can move back and forth to cover the war from both sides.

The images coming out of Gaza show destroyed buildings, dead bodies, grieving relatives, and funerals. On the Israeli side, despite the frequency of sirens and the occasional *boom* of intercepted rockets, the war feels distant, invisible. The only way for me to see it up close is to cross into Gaza.

I'm outside my apartment loading bags into the trunk of my car when another 8:00 A.M. rocket siren sounds. It's a week into the war and the wailing noise had become part of the morning routine—wake up, shower, coffee, breakfast, siren, explosions, though not always in that order. The Hamas rockets are usually intercepted before they get too close, but this time I look up as the rockets explode a few hundred feet overhead. I snap pictures of onlookers before setting off for the forty-five-minute drive to the Erez border crossing into Gaza. I was there yesterday with several other foreign journalists and crossed briefly into Gaza, but we had to turn back. Israel had bombed the Hamas checkpoint. Shelling and the steady chatter of small-arms fire meant no vehicles could reach the crossing to pick us up. We returned to the Israeli side and, just after we left, a Hamas mortar round exploded at the crossing, killing an Israeli civilian handing out food to soldiers. It was Israel's first fatality of the war. The explosion shattered a window at the crossing, which resembles a vacant airport terminal guarded by tense Israeli security forces.

As I try to cross for the second time in two days, the female passport-control agent behind bulletproof glass waves at me to move.

"Go! Go! Go!" her muffled voice shouts. "Rocket! Rocket!"

I'm trapped in a Plexiglas passport booth between two magnetically locked doors, but one of the locks releases as I push through and run toward a wall, dragging my rolling luggage behind me. A security guard runs toward me and steers me into a safe room. I kneel by the door and wait. For all its size and space, the mostly cavernous terminal looks like it has a roof made from aluminum foil. A bird swoops down from the rafters, then—*boom! boom!*—another mortar attack shakes the building. It's been a long time since I've been under fire—the vague threat of rockets notwithstanding—and this is a sharp reminder of how much I dislike it. I've been hoping the war might still end quickly and that more violence will be averted, but a proposed cease-fire is rejected by Hamas. Things are only going to get worse. I told my family and friends—including Helen and TJ—that I would no longer put myself in harm's way on the front lines of war. I've even tried to convince myself that was true, but here I am again, heading straight into the fray. I could turn back. There's no overt pressure from my employers to go into Gaza. But I'm now part of a team. Others count on me to deliver. Times like these are why international media keeps the region so heavily staffed—and why I've been posted to Israel. I know what's expected of me. My reputation, my standing within Reuters, and my own sense of self-worth are at stake. I have little choice. I have to keep going.

Once the all-clear is given, I continue through the crossing's labyrinth of unmanned turnstiles and mechanized metal doors until I emerge at the lengthy covered walkway into Gaza. Moving in a matter of minutes from Tel Aviv's modern world of skyscrapers, superhighways, and tight security into Gaza's deserted sand dunes is like being teleported to another dimension. Smoke from air strikes rises on the horizon and the bombed-out landscape is crisscrossed by dusty footpaths or cracked pavement and littered with debris, including an abandoned wheelchair. Unlike the day before, a lone battered yellow taxi with a nervous driver waits to shuttle journalists to and from the Hamas checkpoint just over the next hill, where officials have erected a makeshift table next to their destroyed immigration and customs building.

A driver with the Reuters armored Land Rover meets me and we drive past shattered buildings to our office on the ninth floor of a tower block in downtown Gaza City, where my Palestinian colleagues greet me. Our Gaza office is staffed by several TV cameramen, three photographers, and a bureau chief. I would normally be welcomed with tea or coffee and lunch, but it's Ramadan and everyone is fasting and busy filing stories and images.

Within minutes two huge explosions shake the building. I run downstairs, jump into a car with my new driver, Zuhair, and race toward the sound of the explosions by the port. We pull up by the beach to find medics carrying the limp body of a boy across the sand. The boy's shin and forearm are gouged to the bone, his flesh peeled back by shrapnel. The skin of his bare chest is charred, his dark hair covered in dust. Dozens of cameramen and photographers follow the stretcher bearers toward a waiting ambulance. Video cameras roll, shutters whir. The body on the stretcher is one of four boys—cousins Ismail, Zakaria, Ahmed, and Mohamed, all from the Bakr family—killed by an Israeli air strike below a row of beachfront hotels filled with Western journalists. Moments earlier the Bakr boys had been playing soccer on the sand.

Outside the hospital morgue, crowds gather and relatives wail. Inside, the children's bodies are shut into metal drawers as more and more people press into the building, elbowing and pushing through the crush and the heat and the smell, trying to get a look at the corpses. Photographers and TV cameramen are part of the chaotic swarm pressed into the tiny, sweltering room. A brother of one of the boys pulls a body from a drawer and hugs the corpse tight to his chest, his head tilted back in a scream that pierces the clamor and din of shouting, crying, weeping Palestinians. The four bodies are wrapped in white shrouds and paraded across the hospital yard on blue stretchers. The dead children's faces are open to the sky as the crowd of mourners runs with them carried high on their shoulders through streets toward the cemetery.

Israel's killing of four children playing on a beach sparks international outrage. The bombings continue. The death toll mounts.

The next morning I begin a routine that runs for the next three weeks: I wake up at 5:00 A.M., find out what areas have been shelled overnight, grab a quick coffee, then drive through the empty streets to photograph destroyed buildings. Survivors pick through the rubble, collecting valuables, appliances, and personal effects. Along the way I run into other photographers and cameramen doing the same in one of the world's most choreographed war zones. The massive media presence in previous wars between Israel and Gaza means that the imagery repeats itself. Photographs and video footage show huge explosions and smoke clouds billowing skyward, and the pictures of destruction, death, and mourning that follow are almost interchangeable.

By midmorning the routine takes me back to the office or hotel to file the day's first set of pictures. Then I wait for the next round of air strikes or artillery. It rarely takes long. Each day the heavy shelling creeps closer to our office, providing a constant soundtrack of explosions, sometimes every five or ten seconds when Israel's assaults are at their peak. Occasionally a projectile screams past our building and slams into one of the nearby towers, and the shock waves rattle our windows and lift the curtains. After a while we remove all the windows from one side of the building to avoid the risk of glass shards being blown through the office.

The summer heat is too oppressive to wear flak vests and helmets except when things get really bad. Reuters only has one armored vehicle in Gaza, so I travel in a normal "soft" car and keep my body armor on the backseat. The roof, windows, and hood are emblazoned with "TV" and "Reuters" in red tape to be visible to the Israeli surveillance cameras and drones hovering overhead. The constant high-pitched whine of their engines weaves its way into the acoustic fabric of the war. Moving anywhere is dangerous, but then again, so is sitting still. Driving through Gaza's rubble-strewn streets knowing that at any moment a shell could explode nearby is exhausting. With the intensity of the bombing and Gaza's confined urban geography, the threat feels even more intense and immediate than that of IEDs in Afghanistan. Fear, combined with the heat, kills my appetite and drains my energy. It doesn't help that my driver, Zuhair, is hopeless at his job. Zuhair is an intellectual who studied physics and philosophy in Germany long ago, but his only qualifications as a driver seem to be his possession of a car, his ability to speak English, and the fact that he'll actually drive me (many drivers have stopped because of the war). His driving is almost as frightening as the threat of incoming Israeli bombs. His talent for making the worst possible decisions at the most critical times magnifies my stress level. For safety and to be more visible to Israel's "eyes in the sky," journalists often travel in convoys from place to place, but Zuhair can rarely keep pace and we often end up separated from other vehicles and lost on deserted streets that give me the creeps or, worse, trying to find our way as tank shells and mortar rounds slam into crumbling buildings less than a block away. The tension becomes almost unbearable. All I want is to be somewhere safe. I've always justified taking risks and coped with my fear by covering stories I felt were underreported, or ones I felt connected to and to which I believed I could contribute something worthwhile. And, if I'm honest, the thrill was as compelling as any other motive. Not anymore. Now I want to be anywhere else but here.

The most difficult thing is photographing injured children. And there are many. Every day, one after another, and often in groups. Bewildered, in pain, and sometimes just orphaned, they seem out of place in a world of such violence. One afternoon I roam the hospital halls away from the chaotic scenes closer to the entrance. I peer through the door of an operating room where three medics are treating an infant. I slip in and photograph over their shoulders. The latex-gloved hands of one of the medics massage the child's tiny rib cage. Her skin is pale and waxy, and her eyes blink slowly. Her fists and feet are clenched. And then they aren't. Her eyes go blank.

"Finished," says a medic. "Parents also."

Compared with the emergency ward, the morgue behind the hospital almost offers respite. At least the suffering of those resting here has ended, even as their relatives absorb the shock of loss.

I'm still struggling to find my photographic way. I feel unable to capture the enormity of what's unfolding. Standing in the midst of street after street of ruins or in a morgue filled with bodies and relatives over-come with grief, or facing children shaking and convulsing from shock and fear, I fail to see how I can cram the scale of the suffering, heart-break, and destruction into the confines of a single frame of my camera. The trauma runs so deep.

Each evening I call Helen in Tel Aviv and she tells me about her day on the other side of the war—her frustrations at work, the bursts of fear triggered by frequent air-raid sirens and the sounds of explosions as missiles are intercepted midair, and the shock and anger she feels at witnessing a war where so many Palestinian civilians are being killed—and at finding so little sympathy for them among Israelis. She's barely able to articulate her distress, but her hair has begun to fall out, leaving a bald spot atop her scalp. She tries to calm herself by cycling daily along the city's waterfront promenade and sometimes goes at night to sit on the beach near my apartment in Jaffa, listening to the waves under the moonlight, the sand cool beneath her feet on a warm August night.

"I cry and release all that pent-up sadness and frustration from the day," she says. Helen also tells me she has begun to question her faith for the first time in her life, but she still goes to St. Peter's Church in Old Jaffa to pray. She says she prays for me. Every night she asks when I'll be com-ing home. And every night I tell her I don't know.

During my second week in Gaza, I get a boost when my old friend Marco Longari arrives. Marco was the one who called me, warning me to get out of the stadium, that day in Kinshasa. An Italian photographer for Agence France-Presse, he spent five years working in Israel and Gaza before recently moving to South Africa. He's one of the world's most re-spected newswire photographers and is generous with his virtuoso tal-ents, but also a good listener. For all the conflict I've covered, I've never seen industrial killing on such a scale nor witnessed the kind of collective glorification and documentation of death. It introduces a strange new level of torment. Every day in Gaza's morgues I elbow my way through crowds of mourners and photographers, step through pools of blood, and take pictures of mutilated bodies and piles of corpses. Anywhere else such behavior would be absurd, unconscionable even, but here it's part of the war routine. I struggle to reconcile my own behavior with the lack of dignity accorded the dead.

"I struggled with this too at first," Marco says. "Then, after a while, I realized that it's actually kind of a ritual. It has become so much a part of what happens here that people expect it to happen and need it to happen. It's part of the mourning process."

Such rituals help people cope with the immensity of the tragedy consuming them, Marco argues, and we would all evoke rituals of our own if confronted with such grief.

One afternoon I'm inside a morgue during a relative lull. There are only a few other people inside the room when a worker opens a drawer containing the bodies of three children. Their bright clothes are covered in that gray dust, their hair tousled and their limbs intertwined, as if they passed out together on a sleepover. It's nothing I haven't seen and photographed a dozen times already, but for some reason, perhaps the relative quiet at that moment, the scene freezes me. I can't photograph. I'm overcome by a physical wave of sadness. I can hardly breathe. There's a weight on my chest and I feel the prickle of hot tears. I leave the gloom of the morgue and step out into the bright afternoon sun.

I no longer want any part in this ritual. The media is one of the most powerful weapons in a war where the Palestinians are outgunned on the battlefield. The staggering number of civilian deaths—especially of women and children—is used by the Palestinians to convey the message that Israel is slaughtering innocents on a massive scale. That much is true. But the propaganda machines and lobby groups on both sides of the conflict are working around the clock to get their version of the story heard. It's a cynical game with civilians trapped in the middle. Photography for me has always been about illustrating the common threads connecting disparate lives, with a view to building empathy and understanding. But the only common thread here seems to be a mutual hatred and the lust for destruction of the other. By contributing to the steady flow of images from the war, I feel somehow complicit in perpetuating the endless spectacle of violence, with mass media amplifying and even romanticizing the very thing we seek to condemn. It's as if, as Don DeLillo writes in *White Noise*, "we're not here to capture an image, we're here to maintain one."

Even in the relative safety of my hotel room, the nighttime bombing is unnerving. The Israeli navy is positioned offshore and fires artillery barrages over the hotel. From my window overlooking Gaza's port, I watch red tracer fire zipping across the horizon from the invisible warships and hear it slamming into beachside targets a few blocks away.

The night of July 28 is especially bad. Most nights the heaviest bombing is a distant rumble punctuated by the occasional nearby explosion, but on the twenty-second night of the war, a constant artillery barrage brings hour after hour of room-rattling concussions. The bombing is heavy and close. I put on my flak jacket and lean my mattress against the large window to shield myself from any flying glass. At about 4:30 A.M. the screech of an incoming shell makes me curl away from the window as the flash from a massive explosion lights up my room. The foundations of the hotel shake and my bed sways as if in an earthquake. The downstairs windows of the hotel shatter. An air strike from an F-16 jet has struck the adjacent port. I crawl away from my window and take cover on the floor as the whistle of another incoming bomb pierces the darkness. The screech of incoming ordnance is harrowing. It means the air strike is close, but there's no way of knowing how close. I've been to the scenes of too many bombings and seen the shredded remains of those who have gone to sleep in their homes only never to wake up. Entire neighborhoods are reduced to rubble and covered in a blanket of fine gray dust, turning vast cityscapes into a jagged monochrome. Just like the beige moondust at Outpost Kunjak, this dark powder hangs in the air, sticks to skin, floats into lungs, coats the insides of my nostrils and mouth, and crunches between my teeth. When I shower in Gaza's salty water each night, gray ash swirls down the drain and stains my towel even after I've washed. Like a bad memory, it's hard to be rid of it.

In the evenings I exchange brief online messages with TJ, who is upbeat and busy preparing for Columbia. His move to New York will carry him one step further from the kind of violence and madness enveloping Gaza.

I too wish to be away from the drumbeat of war. I can no longer stand the noise—least of all inside my own head. War has become too sad for me to endure.

I know TJ is worried about my safety, although he doesn't reveal just how concerned he is at the time. Only later does he tell me how he sits with Mel on the couch, watching the news and scanning the Internet for my pictures. He says he'd have been less worried if I'd gone back to Afghanistan with the Marines. At least he knows what that looks like. He can't grasp what it's like on the ground in Gaza.

"I know the reality is probably even worse than we can see," he tells me when we talk about it later. "And watching those pictures coming out of Gaza, it was as close as I could get to my mom or Mel seeing pictures from Afghanistan when I was there. It's the first time I felt helpless for someone else who was at war.

"I was like the wife back home, all worried and concerned," he adds, joking that Mel is well aware of his fears and his affection. "At least it was an open relationship. We were both worried about you."

My inability to make sense of my situation is weighing on Helen, who can't understand why I agreed to go into Gaza.

"I opposed the idea of Gaza from day one because it was evident that you weren't well and all of the outcomes were negative," she tells me later, adding that images of dead Palestinian children are made even more upsetting by knowing I'm making pictures in the midst of all the violence. "My perspective was you'd either not return or you'd return with inevitable trauma. I couldn't even try to rationalize the possibility of you dying. I thought it was fucking crazy. I still think it's fucking crazy. I tried every day to understand your position. I couldn't make sense of it. Our text conversations consisted of you telling me how unhappy you were with your photos and the conflict. You felt like you didn't have that spark anymore and you were beating yourself up about it. And then you'd completely shut down on me. Part of me was like, *Okay, he might just not be into this anymore.*"

Day after day the war grinds on. Israeli mortar rounds and artillery shells strike United Nations schools, killing civilians and children who have fled their homes in search of shelter in supposedly protected compounds, cease-fires are broken, and the killing continues. Then, after I've been in Gaza for three weeks, another cease-fire is declared and Israel's ground troops withdraw from the Strip. It's my own chance to retreat. I agree with my bosses and colleagues that it's time for me to return to my base in Tel Aviv. The shaky truce is holding and heavy fighting is finally winding down, though several more spasms of violence extend the bombing another two weeks until a comprehensive cease-fire finally ends the war, not before Simone Camilli, a thirty-five-year-old Italian cameraman working for the AP, is killed while filming Gaza police engineers trying to defuse an unexploded Israeli bomb. The blast kills the four engineers and a freelance Palestinian translator and seriously injures four others, including Palestinian AP photographer Hatem Moussa. Camilli leaves behind his longtime partner and a three-year-old daughter. Another day, another death, another ghost.

Leaving Gaza, I walk alone under the kilometer-long covered walkway leading to Erez, that steel-and-glass portal back into Israel. The core issues that sparked the conflagration remain unsolved, but both sides are deflated and tired of fighting, at least for now. The war machines have fallen silent and the summer hum of insects fills the air. Bright sunlight bounces off the yellow sand dunes lining the caged passageway. I walk slowly, taking it all in, senses alert. Off to one side are craters and tank tracks in the sand. Halfway along the walkway I pass an unexploded mortar shell lying beside the footpath. I try to imagine how many more bombs and missiles are scattered across the Gaza Strip. I've seen them all over the place, lodged in apartment walls, lying on the cracked pavement of school playgrounds, and wedged into splintered tree trunks. I saw one Israeli bomb the size of a sofa sitting in the middle of a main road, a bulging symbol of unfinished business.

When I reach the parking lot on the Israeli side, where I left my car more than three weeks ago, my vehicle is coated in a thick layer of dust kicked up by tanks and armored vehicles churning the earth as they passed. One of my Israeli Reuters colleagues stopped by yesterday and has written "Welcome Back Finbarr" in the dust on the windshield.

After the forty-five minute drive to Tel Aviv, I carry my bags up the flight of stairs to my front door. I remove my socks and filthy boots and leave them outside. I dump my bags on the floor and wash my face in the bathroom sink. My reflection in the mirror is gaunt. Weight has melted from my face and my body is all sharp angles. I want to collapse. But when I walk barefoot across the wooden floorboards, I feel a thick layer of dust underfoot. I've left a window open and weeks of grunge has blown in on the sea breeze. It's everywhere, coating the floor, counters, table-tops, and furniture. I can't bear it. I dig cleaning products out from under my kitchen sink and spend two hours scrubbing and vacuuming. When I finish, I put away the mop and bucket and throw away the dirty rags. Then I climb into the shower and stand there, too tired and weak to move, hot water washing over me, scalding my skin. I towel off, retreat to my bedroom, and close the curtain against the afternoon sun. The room goes dark. I slip between the cool cotton sheets and close my eyes. I take a deep breath, then fall asleep. There will always be another war. Just not for me.

Chapter 21

Yellow Footprints

You are now aboard Marine Corps Recruit Depot Parris Island, South Carolina, and you have just taken the first step toward becoming a member of the world's finest fighting force, the United States Marine Corps.

—The first words all recruits hear from a drill instructor
once they step onto the yellow footprints

TJ, Camp Lejeune, North Carolina, June 2014

Mel looks ethereal in a strapless, blood orange dress. The sheer fabric sways with her hips as she glides across the ballroom floor. Her straight hair falls across her shoulders to a fresh tattoo by her collarbone that reads "Learn to fly with broken wings." A diamond necklace rests against her chest. I inhale her perfume and am captivated anew by her eyes. She smiles and presses her lips against mine, and I ache for her in a way I haven't in a long time. I'm in love again.

We're at a fund-raising event for the Semper Fi Fund, one of the veteran-focused charities that assists wounded Marines and sailors. The event is the Fourth Annual Burn Your Own Steak dinner. It includes a silent auction for firearms, a motorcycle, stained glass, and other artwork created by wounded veterans of the Iraq and Afghanistan wars. The Semper Fi Fund and my case managers, Lisa Killeen and Jean Hislop, have helped me whenever I've asked. They paid for Mr. Luke to be trained as my service dog. They also provided me with an iPad so I can take notes on the go. They gave me gas cards while I was working in Lumberton. They call and e-mail to check on my progress and to remind me I'm not alone. Plus, the "ladies in red," as we call them, give awesome hugs. They've asked me to be the guest speaker and I've got a case of nerves. It's the first time I'll speak in public with Mel present, and I have some things I want to say to her.

I'm introduced, and I take the podium with Mr. Luke at my side. He's almost better dressed than I am, wearing a black vest with vibrant yellow and red decorative patches. His collar is dotted with stainless-steel hooks and rivets, and I even brushed his fur for the occasion.

Mel makes goofy faces at me from her chair. Just before I start to speak, she gives me a thumbs-up. I tell the audience about Mr. Luke. About what a gift he has been, and how he was a rescue dog. Two lives saved. How my little buddy helps me regain my ability to explore the world. Then, in front of the crowd of a hundred people, I address Mel, my wife, the woman who enlisted in the Corps alongside me with the words "I do." I stare out at the audience and tell them about Mel's and my journey, about my best friend, the one who never stops trying to reclaim our marriage from the shadow of war. I admit I've been a terrible person at times, that no person deserves to be treated the way I tormented Mel. I tried to emotionally destroy her. Misery loves company, see? She was the closest target. I burdened her with my own guilt, my shame. I called her names I now regret. I pushed her away. I don't want to be without her because she makes me a better person. She's strong, inspiring, and the mother of our daughter. She's the most resilient, compassionate person I know.

"I love you," I say. "Thank you for saving me."

I've never been able to pinpoint what it is about Mel that draws me in. The way she moves, the way she talks, the way she presents herself to the world. Sometimes it's her playfulness. Other times it's her shyness, or her passion, her drive, her approach to life, her fire, her calling to heal others as a nurse, or her love for Maddie. It's the intangibles that keep me wanting more. It's everything about her, knowing that she's mine and I'm hers. Plus, she has a great ass.

I step down from the podium. Mel stands at her chair.

"You didn't have to say that. Thank you. I love you," she says, wiping away her tears. We embrace. I longed for Mel in Afghanistan. The few moments I hold her in my arms are the embrace I wish I had given her when I first stepped off the bus. For the rest of the night she glows. So do I.

On July 9, my second-to-last day at the *Daily News*, I put on a new shirt and sunglasses and drive with Mel and Maddie to the Wounded Warrior Battalion at Camp Lejeune. In front of the Warrior Hope and Care Center stands the No Man Left Behind Memorial, a ten-foot-tall bronze sculpture of two Marines carrying an injured comrade. The statue was created by John Phelps, the father of Private First Class Chance Phelps, a Marine killed during the battle of Fallujah, and is based on a photograph taken by Lucian Read during a firefight in 2004. The statue was created to honor all wounded and fallen service members and to symbolize the hope required for survivors to move on to the next phase of their lives. I covered the statue's unveiling a few months ago. I'm about to have my official Marine Corps retirement ceremony.

When I was medically retired in December 2012, a senior enlisted Marine told me I "didn't rate" a retirement ceremony, that I didn't do my time. I didn't dispute his assertion even though in fact he was wrong: I was officially entitled to a formal retirement ceremony. I was too tired of fighting and feeling ashamed to push back. I was ready to take off my uniform despite how conflicted my emotions were at the time. That painful rejection has weighed on me since. As a show of respect, Lieutenant Colonel Leland Suttee, the commander of the Wounded Warrior Battalion, wanted to correct that. Even though I'm retired now, he offered to arrange a formal retirement ceremony, complete with an official retirement certificate ordered from Headquarters Marine Corps and a folded American flag. This surprised me, but then I realized how fitting it would be for my retirement to be hosted by those I had met as a reporter. When I started at the *Daily News*, I worried that surrounding myself with members of the military and reporting on them so soon after my discharge would only make me miss it even more. It didn't to that, but it did remind me why I had served for nine years and why I had reenlisted after my first tour in Iraq. I loved being a Marine. I love Marines. And I was great at blowing shit up.

I arrive to the ceremony with Mel and Maddie. Chairs are arranged in a semicircle facing the monument. More than twenty Marines, sailors, and friends are waiting. The active-duty Marines are ones I met as a journalist rather than while I was in the service. Matthew Brown, a machine gunner with my platoon in Iraq, is here, as well as Geoff, Semper Fi Fund case managers, generals, an admiral, and two public affairs officers. It's as if two separate worlds—military and civilian—are merging. The attendance of this small handful of people means more to me than the hundred indifferent Marines who would be obliged to attend such a ceremony normally, which is usually how these things unfold. Sadly, Fin can't make it. He's still in Israel and will have to settle for photographs instead.

Lieutenant Colonel Suttee gives a short speech, saying that while I was not a member of the Wounded Warrior Battalion, every Marine deserves a retirement ceremony. This is his attempt to right a wrong, he says. I'm handed my folded American flag. Suttee also presents Mel and Maddie with formal USMC Certificates of Appreciation. I make a short speech thanking everyone for attending. I hug them all. Then it's time for cake, and the sense of resolution I've been seeking for the past eighteen months.

Reporting on the military has allowed me to continue serving beside those I love. I may no longer be in uniform, but writing about those who are has been an honor. Through it all I have forged new friendships in ways I never imagined possible. I've gotten to know Marines and sailors I never would have met. I've cried and shared painful memories with families who have suffered, and I've laughed with others. I'm thankful for what each has taught me. The day is a perfect ending to what will always be the most memorable chapter of my life.

Later Lieutenant Colonel Suttee tells me he's been selected for promotion to colonel. Few enlisted Marines become officers—and most Marines don't do thirty years like Suttee. His promotion doesn't surprise me. For months I watched as Suttee and his team at Wounded Warrior Battalion pushed the Marines and sailors to engage with life and find a renewed sense of purpose, to keep faith that life goes on. He encourages them to seek help, and means it. His promotion is a reflection of a rare kind of leadership. More than any other Marine, Leland Suttee restores my faith that good leaders don't just acknowledge the pain of their subordinates; they stand beside them. They help them get back in the fight, whatever that fight may be.

SHOOTING GHOSTS

The ceremony is a just few weeks before I leave for New York to start my studies at Columbia, and I want a family vacation before I go. I take Mel and Maddie on a ten-day Caribbean cruise to Grand Turk, Puerto Rico, Saint Martin, and the Bahamas. Driving home afterward, we travel up the southeast coast. Along the way we make a diversion to the Marine Corps Recruit Depot at Parris Island in South Carolina. As a teenager I did thirteen grueling weeks of recruit training here. Now that my military career is officially over, I want to show my girls where it began.

I walk Mel and Maddie to building 6000 on Panama Street, where eighteen rows of yellow footprints are painted on the tarmac outside. When recruits step off the bus for boot camp, they stand in the footprints four abreast. Recruits are told about the millions of men and women who have stood on the same spots before them, and what it means to be a United States Marine. It isn't something any recruit understands at that moment. They can't yet comprehend what it means or what it's like to go to war. The recruits are marched through two large silver doors, never to pass through them again. This tradition marks the beginning of the transformation from civilian to Marine.

Perhaps it's the afterglow of my holiday or the prospect of embarking upon another adventure into the unknown—or perhaps even the memory of my naive and youthful self—but being back where it all began reminds me of the good things brought about by my decision to become a Marine. Despite everything that has happened, I have no regrets.

Wearing sunglasses, flip-flops, Bermuda shorts, and a short-sleeved checkered shirt, I stand on a pair of yellow footprints at the front of an imaginary column. Ghosts in front of me, ghosts behind. I'm a few pounds heavier now, with more tattoos and thinner hair, but the pair of footprints I stand on are the same ones I stepped onto nearly eleven years ago. With my heels turned in and toes turned out, my fingertips curled into my palms, and my knuckles pressed against the seams of my shorts, I raise my chin and stand to attention.

Able 3-4, entering friendly lines. I'm home.

Chapter 22

No Wars and No Jobs, but Another Tasty Chicken

For the more haunted among us, only looking back at the past can permit it finally to become past.

—Mary Karr, *The Art of Memoir*

Finbarr, Tel Aviv, November 2014

On November 18 I'm sent to a Jerusalem synagogue to cover the aftermath of an attack: Two Palestinians, armed with a meat cleaver and a gun, have shot and hacked to death four ultra-Orthodox Jews before being shot dead by police. It's the deadliest such incident in six years in the holy city, part of yet another surge of violence. I photograph blood being washed from the pavement and walls, the removal of the corpses, and then the funeral, where hundreds of people gather to bury the latest victims of an endless conflict.

The next day I'm invited into a room in the Reuters office in Jerusalem and told over speakerphone by a voice from Human Resources in London that I no longer have a job. That's it. After fourteen years, four international postings, countless miles traveled through dozens of countries, numerous conflicts covered, some 8,700 photographs moved to the wire, and a handful of awards, my time with Reuters is over. A few weeks before Christmas, the company is eliminating my position as part of another round of corporate cost cutting. I look up at the wall-mounted clock. It's five minutes past one. I watch the red second hand ticking. For a fleeting moment I'm relieved. This is what I wanted—an escape route, and this one comes with a buyout. But it's a hollow victory. Orchestrating my own departure is one thing; being cast aside is another. Like anyone else, I want to be valued and respected, and the realization that

I've just been deemed expendable hits me with concussive force. In the days that follow, I'm in a daze. I have no appetite. It's as though all the blood has drained from my body. I can't sleep, and when I do, my dreams are fraught and I awake to an unbearable weight bearing down on my chest. I can barely breathe. Helen has tried to comfort me since I returned from Gaza, but there's little she can do, especially now.

"I was determined to keep you in happy spirits and get you out and about to help you bounce back," she says when we talk about it later. "It was a struggle, though, because you didn't want it. I felt like you were detached from me. I remember I used to get fed up with you sometimes because there was very minimal cooperation from you. November came quick. That month was sort of like the beginning and the end of us. It started out with us meeting each other on that Jaffa rooftop and then ended that afternoon you called and told me you were leaving Israel."

My last weeks in the country are anxious. Where will I live? Where is home? There's no obvious place for me to go. I'm officially a London-based photographer on assignment in Israel, and Reuters is contractually bound to ship my worldly belongings to the UK, but aside from those few months during my therapy sessions, I've never lived in Britain. It's been fifteen years since I left Canada, and I have no real links left there either. The idea of finding another job in journalism, an industry beset by layoffs, seems impossible, as does the prospect of freelancing. And I'm in no shape to keep working as a photographer, at least not now. I have no energy, no drive. My spirit, my sense of curiosity, and my faith in photojournalism have all been crushed.

"War journalists, like all who have prolonged exposure to violence, come home emotionally maimed and often broken," writes Chris Hedges, a former *New York Times* war correspondent and the author of *War Is a Force That Gives Us Meaning.* "And yet, a news culture in denial has pretended that war journalists are immune from trauma. This fits into the macho culture of war journalism. It also assuaged the consciences of those running news organizations, who often crumple up and discard, years later, those they send to war."

Hedges is among those featured with me in *Under Fire*, the documentary film adaptation of my Toronto psychologist Anthony Feinstein's book about the psychological hazards of covering conflict. He writes that Dr. Feinstein's research is "a searing indictment of major news conglomerates who have refused to acknowledge or address the suffering of their own."

I have to pack up my life and leave Israel. The end of my time in the country will eventually bring my relationship with Helen to an end as well. She's headed back to the United States, and, as much as we care for each other, things will soon fall apart once I get to London, where I feel the need to leave behind everything I've known in Israel, even the one good thing.

On the day of my departure from Tel Aviv, Helen and I walk down to the beach near my apartment in Jaffa in search of a quiet moment. We sit on the boulders overlooking the breaking waves. Within seconds, an irate middle-aged Palestinian woman is shouting and gesturing at us. She and her husband are fishing about fifty yards away and—perhaps assuming we are Jewish—they take issue with our presence. When we respond in English, she does the same.

"Go away! This is not your place! Leave here now!"

We ignore her. She continues.

"I hope you fucking die and all your family too! All of you, I hope you burn in fucking hell forever!"

Then she spits on the ground.

Finbarr, London, January 2015, and Dublin, February 2015 onward

From the small desk in my temporary one-bedroom rental, I have a clear view beyond the curtains to the nearby Shard, London's tallest building, a ninety-five-story, 1,016-foot spire.

I've lived for years in a kind of alternate reality, one in which I've isolated myself from those closest to me to venture into some of the world's most hostile places. I put my work ahead of everything else because that's what gave me the greatest sense of satisfaction, purpose, and reward. But that faded over time and now I've reached an end point in a journey that has marked me for life. I had a good run before things went sideways and

SHOOTING GHOSTS

it's easy to be nostalgic, just as British writer A. A. Gill was about his years as an alcoholic, which he described as "an optimum inebriation, a time when it was all golden, when the drink and pleasure made sense and were brilliant."

Now it's time to plot a new course. Easier said than done. The thing that made me good at my job—my ability to empathize with others—feels exhausted. I find it hard to relate to the people I photograph, or even the people I care about in my own life. I'll have to rebuild my ability to do that, just as TJ had to learn how to reconnect with Mel and Maddie when he came home.

I realize that I'm in a situation similar to the one TJ faced. The termination of his military career deprived him of pride in his duty and the sense of service to his fellow Marines, the very things that had defined his life since he was a teenager.

He knows what it's like to be culled from the herd, to lose faith in the institution that sent him to war. His dismissal, like mine, provoked feelings of loss, abandonment, betrayal, and vulnerability. Being cast aside by the Corps was as damaging to him as anything that happened in Iraq or Afghanistan, and it plunged him into a suicidal tailspin. Dark thoughts skitter through my mind too: Where do I belong now? How can I build a new life that matters? What would that even look like? Is it even worth trying? What's the point anyway? Maybe I should just check out while the going is bad. I can't explain to my friends or family how low I really feel, which makes the experience even more isolating. But TJ has been where I am now. Twinship.

When TJ and I sat on his porch in Jacksonville on that night when he told me about things he'd done in Iraq, I asked him whether he would still join the Marines and do it all again, knowing what he does.

"Fuck, yeah," he answered, and then took a long pull on his cigarette. "I miss it every day. Being around Marines, the grab-assery, blowing shit up. It's hard not to feel nostalgic about it."

Inherent in that tribal sense of belonging lies the communal focus on a collective mission, even if it's just another fuck-fuck game. Nothing seems impossible when you don't have to do it alone, when you've got your buddies by your side watching your back. When that's torn away, though, the bottom drops out, any sense of security evaporates, and the world becomes a very lonely place. It's almost impossible for even the most loving wife, girlfriend, child, or family member to fill that void. It's not just the storm of war that wounds the soul; it's also the silence and emptiness that loom in its wake. Coming home from war means finding ways to fill that haunted space with something else. And without the necessary institutional support, we're forced to figure out our own coping strategies.

It has taken TJ time, but through the hard work of therapy and with Mel's help, he has found a new way to serve his Marine brothers by writing about them. Now he's a few months from earning his master's degree in journalism from Columbia, and upon graduation he plans to launch a digital news platform for investigative reporting on the DoD and the VA. By transforming himself from a Marine into a journalist, he has arrived at a new way of being as a civilian. He's redeeming himself by helping others. And his trajectory allows me to believe I might be able to make a transition of my own.

I start by doing what TJ did after his suicide attempt: I move home, or at least, to my mother's house in Ireland, where I felt safe and grounded last year as I recovered from my Achilles injury. Once again the roiling Irish Sea, the windswept beaches, the craggy headlands, and the smell of turf fires comfort me, as does my mother's cooking and her presence. Spending an extended amount of time with her as an adult after two decades living continents apart—and seeing each other for a few days every couple of years—is a rare midlife opportunity to reconnect. Sometimes, it seems, even a war photographer needs his mummy.

During my fellowship at Harvard, the idea for this book with TJ emerged. In Israel, where the pleasure I once derived from photography was blown away, writing in evenings and on weekends provided a respite, a creative outlet through which I could attempt to make sense of a jumble of violent events and disturbing emotions. Now, from Ireland, I'm in touch with TJ most days. We talk about words, metaphors, and chapters, but what we're really talking about is our lives, and how to right them. After so long venturing into the world to tell other people's stories, our collaboration allows me to engage in a new kind of inquiry, one that traverses an inner terrain, stripping back layers of ego and self-deceit to uncover what really matters.

It will take another year before I feel comfortable wearing the mantle of author, but the transition to life after war is under way, and TJ has shown me what it looks like. By taking control of his own narrative, he has reclaimed something of himself and learned to stand in his new role as a new man, emotionally and psychologically scarred, yes, but stronger for it.

Of course, working closely with TJ is not the only thing that's restorative. As Dr. Feinstein, my Toronto psychiatrist, tells me, there are many tools in the toolbox and it's important to use them all. I spend time with friends I've had time to see only briefly in the past, and I visit often with my uncle Michael. I go back on antidepressants. I wasn't taking them in Israel, which no doubt dimmed my view of things there. The Voice still creeps back from time to time, but writing, much like the meditation I've been practicing, allows me to "start identifying a little bit with that detached, watcher self," as Mary Karr writes in *The Art of Memoir*, and less with my "prattling head."

Exercise also helps. I start working out again at a local gym, this time with a boxing trainer, Simon. Our sparring sessions keep me fit, alert, and motivated, creating clarity of mind. Simon and I will later take up cycling together. At first I can barely manage thirty kilometers on mostly flat roads and I struggle to keep pace with Simon, who is younger by ten years. But I gradually build up my strength and stamina and soon become hooked on the sport; in my first year I ride more than 13,000 kilometers. Cycling forces me to push through discomfort and difficulty—fatigue, a flat tire, a slipped chain, a wrong turn—and I learn to just keep moving forward. I've discovered Noam Chomsky's bicycle theory: "As long as you keep riding, you don't fall off."

In time I also return to Dakar to visit my friend Adama as she hosts another Fashion Week. I take along my cameras and make pictures for the first time in ages, this time just for myself. I'm reminded that photography is a central part of me, something elemental in my spirit and fundamental to how I view the world.

And when I meet a wonderful woman, I'm finally ready to settle down and build a future with her. A serious, long-term relationship presents its own set of challenges, but it also offers stability and hope. Another piece of the puzzle falls into place.

"I don't think I've ever seen you looking so happy and relaxed," my mother tells me one day as we sit chatting in her kitchen. I've just returned from a twelve-hour, 250-kilometer ride over Ireland's Wicklow Mountains. Although physically exhausted, I'm basking in a triumphant afterglow, but she's not just referring to my blissful postride state. The version of me that used to return from assignments irritable and morose has become less present. Bit by bit, life's setbacks, big and small, have ceased to take the shape of insurmountable obstacles. Instead they are reduced to challenges to be met and overcome. And cycling, Dr. Feinstein later tells me, is likely as good for my mental health as any medication.

"Keep pedaling," he says.

Finbarr, New York, May 2015

I walk along the tree-lined northwest edge of Central Park on my way to TJ's apartment near Columbia University. It's a crisp Friday evening. After spending the last few months in London and Dublin, I'm back on the East Coast of the United States, preparing to embark on another fellowship, this time at Yale. Despite our regular contact it's been nearly eighteen months since we last sat together on his porch in Jacksonville. Now TJ is just weeks away from graduating, not that he's waiting for a diploma to get to work. He has pitched a story to the *New York Times* about a Marine who went to Iraq to fight against Islamic State militants, and the piece is published on the paper's front page as the lead story, with a photo spanning four columns. TJ shares the byline with a staff writer and publishes an accompanying article for the *At War* blog titled "The Curious Draw of the Battlefield." It ends with the line "We know the hardships and heartbreaks, the guilt and pain of combat. And yet, we think of going back."

TJ buzzes me into his building. When I get to his doorway, he grins from behind a bushy ginger beard and hugs me. He looks relaxed in jeans and a gray hoodie. He's been off his medication since last year and seems more focused than he was in Jacksonville. His eyes have the same clarity I saw in Afghanistan. He's no longer living in a pharmaceutical fog, as he puts it. His dog, Mr. Luke, is curled around his knees, and TJ reaches down to rub behind the animal's ears.

TJ has planned a surprise gathering and has invited a handful of people, including half a dozen members of his Kunjak squad, some of my Nieman Fellows, one of his professors, and a Columbia faculty member, as well as several other mutual friends. For various reasons, almost everyone cancels at the last minute, except for John Chun, the lance corporal who suffered a concussion, his third, the same day as TJ. The poor showing doesn't matter—I want a mellow evening and am touched that TJ has made such an effort on my behalf. There's no real cause for celebration, other than our reunion. So it's me, TJ, Chun, TJ's two roommates, and a school colleague, plus a mountain of Kunjak chicken that TJ has doused in Texas Pete hot sauce and boiled in a vat on his stove.

Dinner isn't the only reminder of our days together in Afghanistan. TJ's room is an echo of his makeshift bunk at OP Kunjak, with Maddie's drawings and photos of Mel pinned messily to a corkboard and adorning the walls. Camouflage netting hangs above the window near an Afghan flag signed by some of the Afghan policemen who shared OP Kunjak with the Marines. Boxes are stacked under TJ's bed, and clothes, papers, mugs, cameras, and lenses are piled on his desk. In the days ahead Mel and Maddie will fly up to join TJ for Easter, and I will take pictures of them laughing in Central Park as TJ spins Maddie on a tire swing—a typical American family enjoying the spring sunshine. But for now, TJ and Chun and I catch up while gorging on spicy Kunjak chicken with roasted potatoes. (This time we have plenty of beer to wash it down and cake for dessert—no wonder we're getting chunky.)

It turns out that TJ recently met with his former Afghan interpreter and learned that the Afghan policeman who fired the RPG at him has since joined the Taliban. "I guess it wasn't an accident after all," TJ says.

This offhand bit of information seems only to reinforce the misguided futility of the Afghan campaign. TJ was blown up by a member of the Afghan police, the very forces the Americans were trying to help to secure their own country. And of Afghanistan's major provinces, Helmand was perhaps the least strategically important. It's home to about 2 percent of the country's population, but about 20 percent of America's military resources were devoted to the province. (A few months after our dinner in New York, during the summer of 2015, Musa Qala and OP Kunjak fall back under Taliban control, and Helmand becomes a bigger producer of opium than ever before. As one retired Marine tells me, Helmand was the most pointless deployment ever, just an excuse for "Marines to play Marines.")

So was Helmand was just a giant fuck-fuck game, a province-size "happy sock" for the military to jerk off into? That war in its naked essence is masturbatory seems undeniable: the pornographic arousal of training, the deployment boner, and the climax of combat, followed by the detumescence of returning home, complete with feelings of postorgasmic guilt and shame, not to mention the eventual desire to do it again, if only because it's easier than the alternative. No wonder young men like it so much.

"The bigger picture is a lot bigger than I am," TJ told me when I interviewed him in Musa Qala ten days after his injury. "I'm a piece of the puzzle, and if I'm not doing my job, the rest of the puzzle can't fit together. My guys need to trust me, and I need to trust my leaders. If I trust them and accomplish the mission they want done, then the bigger picture will fall into place."

Or fall apart. Rather than bringing about peace and stability, the interventions in Iraq and Afghanistan have only made matters worse, not just for the occupied countries but across the Middle East, and in ways that have disrupted the global balance and upturned the political order in the U.S. and across Europe. On a personal level TJ and I feel bitter and betrayed by our youthful ideals and by the institutions that sent us so willingly to war. They got what they wanted and, I guess, so did we. But now it's up to us to cope on our own. We're dealing with it the only way we can—by surrounding ourselves with the people we know, love, and trust. We've both undertaken the emotional work of therapy and reengaged with life in ways that will continue to steer us toward recovery. But trying to fit back into an individualistic society removed from the unifying experience of combat can leave men nostalgic for the simplicity and urgency of life at war and for the closeness they felt while there. It was easy for me to connect with TJ under the stress and strain of the battlefield. And the bond of hardship and loyalty he shared with his men got them through their deployment. Those bonds can loosen upon coming home, and people can be left dangling. One of TJ's squad members, Serge Huber, the big, baby-faced Russian he calls Drago, summed it up in a Facebook status update: "I just want to do war stuff with my war buddies. Cause this whole being home thing kinda sucks."

As young men we were seduced by the danger and excitement of war as much as by the duty of our jobs. We chose the depth of purpose and meaning war provides over the mundaneness of regular life. Or so we told ourselves. The myth of war made it seem noble and defining—it was historic, a fundamental human experience, something worth dying for. Better to go out in a blaze of glory during battle than to languish in anonymity and irrelevance down at the mall. But the reality of war dispelled such delusions as surely as it bleeds bodies dry. There's nothing glorious about been blown up in a dusty village by phantom fighters.

Back home our priorities have reversed. We once ditched our friends and families to set off overseas for months and years in search of adventure and meaning. Now we find meaning at home by drawing ourselves back toward those closest to us. We still feel the tug of war's allure, but we recognize the surrounding myth for what it is—a ruse that allows those who are older, more powerful, and more wealthy to send the young, eager, and idealistic to do their bidding. War pulled me into its orbit and I remained there for years. Some part of me wanted to experience the ugliness of human behavior while another part wanted to join the canon of those who have devoted their lives to documenting it. I stuck around longer than I should have, and it ground me down. I'll always carry my experiences with me, but war will remain in my past, where it belongs.

As midnight approaches, the two of us are alone in the living room. We reminisce awhile longer and joke about how far we've come since meeting at Kunjak.

"Yeah, now we're both unemployed journalists looking for work," TJ says. "Thanks a lot."

It's true, but as we sit together in his apartment with the sound of car horns and sirens drifting up from the streets below, it hardly seems to matter. The worst is surely behind us.

Fox News has been flickering in silence on the TV all night, and I ask TJ how he can possibly still watch such a right-wing network now that he knows what real journalism looks like. He grins.

"I was wondering how long it would take you to notice that."

He put it on just to provoke me. Good one. TJ takes pride in his rough edges and seems to revel in rubbing Columbia's lefty-liberal staff and students the wrong way. There are still many things we'll never agree upon, political and otherwise. For one, I still can't fathom how, back in Jacksonville, TJ lives with five dogs, including an enormous Great Dane that weighs more than I do. I cringe every time Mr. Luke nuzzles me.

"I can't believe you run around war zones and yet you're afraid of a harmless puppy," TJ says.

"I'm not scared of it," I say. "It's a big slobbering beast and it sheds all over everything. And it just tried to lick my ass. It's gross."

"Man, you're such a fucking pussy."

Eventually it's time to turn in. TJ offers to bunk side by side in his room—for old times' sake. Eyeing the dog, I opt for the living room.

TJ retreats to his bed and I stretch out on the couch. The night we met in Afghanistan four years ago, TJ and I hunkered down on camp cots in an open desert. The darkness was marked by constellations of stars, a heavy silence, and the prospect of death. Now there's the reflected light and ambient sound of New York City, the cadence and hum of life. And somehow, here we are, right in the middle of it.

ACKNOWLEDGMENTS

Finbarr

In the summer of 2012 I was sitting in a hotel lobby in Beirut, Lebanon, having a coffee with Ayperi Ecer, who was then vice president of Reuters pictures. I was about to take a year's sabbatical and was telling her about my evolving friendship with Sergeant Thomas James Brennan, a Marine I had photographed in Afghanistan in the two preceding years. After hearing about our collaboration, Ayperi, who has been a mentor since I began working as a photographer in 2005, said in her matter-of-fact way, "You guys should do a book."

A photo book? I asked her. No, she said, we should write something together that examined our experiences during and after war. That idea sat with me for the next ten months during my time as a Nieman Fellow at Harvard. I was there to study trauma psychology, but the fellowship offered so much more than an opportunity for academic research. It provided the intellectual and emotional space away from the rush of rolling deadlines to reflect on more than a decade spent working across the African continent and in Afghanistan. The diverse group of twenty-four fellows and their families formed a supportive community of like-minded journalists as we all explored the role of the media, our places within it, and the next stages of our lives and careers. For all I learned during my time at Harvard, I'm most grateful for the deep friendships and lasting collaborations that have continued to grow in the years since. For this life-altering opportunity I will always be thankful to Ann Marie Lipinski, curator of the Nieman Foundation for Journalism at Harvard. We were the first class she selected as curator and we will always value that distinction. Ann Marie's ability to manage an often demanding group is no small accomplishment, and we will continue to return to Cambridge from time to time, bringing with us fond memories and new demands. We're not so easy to be rid of.

I must also thank Stefanie Friedhoff, whose understanding of trauma and early support for my research gave me the confidence to move forward with the idea of writing a book. The Nieman nonfiction writing class taught by Paige Williams was not only instructive but also often raucous and funny and sometimes downright embarrassing—Paige knows what I'm talking about. Several of my fellows have housed me during the writing of the book, and my stopovers in Boston and New York were always welcome occasions to catch up with Jane Spencer, Alexandra Garcia, Chris Arnold, and Betsy O'Donovan, who also kindly offered input on early chapters. Jen McDonald undertook rigorous manuscript reviews that were fundamental to the book's final structure, tone, and content. Jen's critiques and reassurance helped me believe we might actually be writing something worthwhile. Jeneen Interlandi read so many versions of this book during the early stages and gave such valuable feedback and support over the years, especially when I snapped my Achilles tendon, that I've officially upgraded her from "colleague" to friend. She's earned it, mostly by eating all my food and drinking all my coffee on fellowship.

Bessel van der Kolk introduced me to the world of trauma psychology and he and his wife, Licia Sky, became valued friends. Gershon Ben Keren and Liz Berrien and the rest of the crew at Krav Maga Yashir provided a different kind of community and an outlet for training both body and mind in ways that offered regular bouts of adrenaline, and bruising. Leslie Dunton-Downer was possibly the best landlady ever during my time in Cambridge and rented me one of my all-time favorite apartments, where our late-night wine- and whiskey-soaked conversations influenced my early thinking on the book.

Bruce Shapiro, executive director of the Dart Center for Journalism & Trauma at Columbia University Graduate School of Journalism, has been a stalwart supporter of this book and a willing adviser, and I'm grateful for his invitation to be a 2014 Ochberg Fellow. Frank Ochberg's warmth and encouragement during that fellowship added momentum and depth to the writing.

At Reuters I was fortunate to work with outstanding journalists, photographers, and bosses. My years spent reporting on Congo's complexities were guided by Matthew Tostevin, David Clarke, Alistair Thomson, Katie Nguyen, and the legendary Kinshasa fixer and dubious driver Pierre Mambele. Radu Sigheti gave me a camera and turned me into a photographer while the support I received over the years from David Thomson, Tom Szlukovenyi, Monique Villa, Ayperi Ecer, and Shannon Ghannam gave me opportunities I had only dreamed of. Steve Crisp was the best manager a staff photographer could hope to have, for years giving me the responsibility and freedom to work in ways that allowed me to flourish. Reuters photographers Lucas Jackson (and his lovely wife Victoria Will), Goran Tomasevic, and Yannis Berhakis are an inspiring group of friends.

Like all journalists who work in foreign lands, I've relied heavily on the expertise, knowledge, and contacts of local fixers, translators, and journalists in countless countries. Without them my security would not have been assured, and my stories would not have been possible. I owe them all a deep debt of gratitude. They are too many to name here individually, but my Congo fixers Eric "Cowboy" Kapita, the late Pastor Marrion P'udongo, Aimee, and the aforementioned Pierre Mambele all deserve special recognition, as does the late Mamu, my adopted Congolese mother, who for years fed me the best grilled chicken and fried plantains I've ever tasted. Her palm oil likely still clogs my arteries to this day.

Michela Wrong helped me land my first Africa posting in Kinshasa, and colleagues from various quarters—David Lewis, Emma de Vise, Dino Mahtani, Arnaud Zajtman, and Marlene Rabaud—have kept me company in weird times, as did Matthew Green, Gianluigi Guercia, and Jerome Delay. Marco Longari has been a creative influence, mentor, and confidant over the years and I can't thank him enough for always listening and imparting his wisdom.

Marcus Bleasdale I met at a seedy hotel bar in Kinshasa in 2001, and he soon learned I had an expense account and a spare bed. We've been friends ever since. His hard work, generosity, and kindness are traits I've sought to emulate, even as we compete while traveling together to see who can ensure that the other's jeans return from the laundry with an ugly crease ironed front and center down the pant leg.

In Dakar my Senegalese friends, especially Adama Ndiaye and my basketball crew, made it a wonderful and ridiculous place to live for eight years. My AP counterpart Rebecca Blackwell became my surfing and drinking buddy as we shook off hangovers by ducking into the waves at Ngor Virage or Secret Spot between assignments. We sometimes traveled the region together covering breaking news, and it was always a better trip when we did, even on days when her pictures got better play. Jane Hahn arrived late to the Dakar party, but just in time to join the fun and to be handed the baton as Rebecca and I left West Africa.

Thanks to Uma Ramiah for tolerating and supporting me during difficult times, and for agreeing to share the good, the funny, and the sour parts of our relationship in this book. You pushed me to seek help when I needed it most and for that I will be forever grateful. Our continued friendship is a comfort.

Dr. Anthony Feinstein has been instrumental in helping me understand trauma and depression and how to manage them. His work on the psychological costs of covering conflict should be required reading for all members of the media, especially managers and corporate executives. His documentary film *Under Fire*, produced with director Martyn Burke, should also be required viewing. Thanks too to Dr. Brian Marien for agreeing to let me use material from our therapy sessions in the book.

My uncle Michael and aunt Trish have long been a grounding source of stability, and their willingness to host me for long stretches after assignments or while I'm figuring things out has always made me feel like I have a home where I can find warmth, a comfy bed, a hot meal, a strong pot of coffee, unexpected conversations, and instruction from Mike on how to do things properly. The same goes for my college basketball teammate JD Jackson, his wife, Saida, and their boys, Dorian and Liam, all of whom helped me decompress at their country home in France after numerous assignments to Afghanistan and elsewhere. My high school buddies Greg McDonnell, Damian Kettlewell, and David Williscroft know me as well as anyone, as does Murray Whyte, and the value of having old friends to rely on cannot be overstated. They have all gotten married and had children while I remained wedded to my cameras and my job. Thanks to each of them, and to Jill Borra, for always finding time to keep in touch, for visiting me in distant corners of the world, and for reminding me there are other ways to live, and love. Alison Bruce, who believed in me when I was just a bright-eyed student and whose humor has survived her own tragic loss, has been a true friend.

Idil Ibrahim has shown me the kind of fortitude and resilience people can have in the face of profound grief, and her strength and courage have taught me that it's always possible to keep moving forward while holding on to the past. I'm grateful for Idil's willingness to share in this book some of the time we spent together at an especially painful moment for her.

In Israel and Gaza my Reuters colleagues and AP photographer Oded Balilty all made me feel welcome in a troubled and hostile land. Oliver Weiken and Camilla Schick also helped keep me (more or less) sane, even if Oliver talked too loud and smoked too much. I'm not sure how I would have survived my time in Israel without Helen Woldu, who struggled as much as I did to make sense of the place. At least we were lost together. Your understanding and patience as I spent evenings and weekends writing is not something I will soon forget. And as difficult as that year was, I don't think I've ever laughed as hard as we did with JD that night at the birthday restaurant in Jaffa. Also, squirrels. Or, as Oliver would say, *Eichhörnchen*.

When I left Reuters in January 2015 in search of a new institutional home, Emma Sky gave me refuge as a World Fellow at Yale, where she is director of the university's global leadership program at the Jackson Institute for Global Affairs. The fellowship allowed me to write while studying post-9/11 war literature in a seminar taught by Adrian Bonenberger, whose experience as an author and Army veteran of the Afghan war kept the conversation lively long after classes ended. The work we read and the discussions Adrian and I have maintained since have informed this book. Emma's years spent as a top civilian adviser to U.S. forces in Iraq and later to NATO forces in Afghanistan mean she understands war, its perverse appeal, and the harsh realities and contradictions of life in conflict zones. Her insights, mischievous wit, and candor have made her a trusted friend and her feedback on early chapters steered the book forward.

Simon Chambers, my boxing trainer in Ireland while I was still working on the book proposal and then later as I wrote the manuscript, got me hooked on cycling, a sport that will no doubt keep me fit while draining my bank account for years to come. The parallels between writing a book and a long, hard ride on open roads are evident, and cycling has over the last year become an almost daily part of my creative routine. The mind circles the wheel, I was told by Santiago Lyon, the former vice president and director of photography of the Associated Press and a fellow cycling enthusiast.

Much of the book was written while I was a 2016 writer in residence at the Carey Institute for Global Good in Rensselaerville, New York. I extend my utmost thanks to Josh Friedman and Carol Ash, as well as Tom Jennings and Gareth Crawford, for allowing me to spend two months feasting on great food, cycling thousands of kilometers over local hills, and also finishing the manuscript between meals, fireside chats, and long rides.

I'm equally grateful to the MacDowell Colony, which also granted me a three-week writing (and riding) residency in the fall of 2016, where I worked on revisions and did my first semipublic reading of the book, gaining essential critical feedback in the final stages.

Thanks to Anastasia Taylor-Lind for always reminding me there's more to photography than taking pictures, and to my brother, Donal, and his wife, Lisa, for driving up from Washington to visit me on my various American sojourns. I'm even more grateful to Donal for procuring a bottle of whiskey when we ended up killing time together at Kandahar Airfield. Always good to run into a sibling in a war zone, but that's another story.

The story TJ and I share has its origins in the *New York Times*'s *Lens* blog, where my pictures of him in Afghanistan appeared in 2010. *Lens* coeditors James Estrin and David Gonzalez, as well as David Dunlap, have all been supportive, and their insights into the craft of photography are always welcome.

Chris (CJ) Chivers was kind enough to pass along our one-page synopsis outlining the original book idea to his agent, Stuart Krichevsky, who ended up investing two years helping us draft a thirty-thousand-word proposal. Without

Stuart's expertise, guidance, and patience, this book would not exist. Chris, a *New York Times* war correspondent and retired Marine, has also been a steady sounding board and moral compass for me and for many others, often inviting the war weary to his family home in Providence, where we engage in an informal kind of physical therapy by fishing, pulling potatoes, or splitting and stacking wood, then eating hearty meals by the fire. Words are spoken, but sometimes not. It's the performance of manual labor and the quiet presence of others that set things right.

Our editor, Wendy Wolf at Viking, has been a delight to work with from day one, when she and her team welcomed us into their offices with an enthusiasm and interest that haven't waned (at least not yet). She has pushed us to dig deeper and probe further than we could have on our own.

Thanks also to the team at Viking, including Georgia Bodnar, Ryan Boyle, Francesca Belanger, Tony Forde, and Jessica Miltenberger for the critical work (sometimes unseen) they all have done for our book.

I blame, and also thank, my parents for instilling in me a sense of adventure and curiosity that drove me forth to try to make sense of the world for myself. I'm still working on that.

Thanks, of course, are owed to my coauthor, TJ. I'm truly grateful he didn't "accidentally" shoot me in the foot during that first firefight. What a different book that would have been.

Last, but by no means least, my partner in crime, Louisa Baxter, has been my greatest supporter over the last two years, welcoming me into her wonderful family and always challenging me to be raw and honest in my writing. The thoughts and emotions I've spilled onto these pages are there because she gave me the courage and confidence to confront, process, and share them. This book would not have been what it is without her insight and her unwavering encouragement. She has made me see myself in new ways and steered me in the right direction when I didn't like what I saw. Louisa has not only made this a better book; she has made me a better person. Her presence is felt on every page and this book belongs as much to her as it does to me. Thank you, my Doctor Lady. Now let's get on with our lives.

TJ

I've been an asshole to lots of people. But I've treated my wife like shit. Mel, I love you and promise to be the better person that you deserve. Thank you for not giving up on me or us. You have always been and will always be my favorite part of our story. And my favorite butt to squeeze. I love you for loving me as the perverted, goofy, flawed, and quirky little kid that I am at heart. You inspire me to be a better man and father, and I am grateful for the countless times you've wiped my tears and each of the challenges we've overcome together. You are the passionate and dedicated nurse that every person in crisis deserves at their bedside—someone who understands what it is like to run toward chaos when most shy away. You're the backbone of our family—our Medium Goober and inspiration. Maddie is and always will be the single greatest gift you've shared with me. You complete me and always will—I love you whole bunches.

Goobs, thank you for being you—every goofy, nerdy, curious, animal-loving, artsy-fartsy, sarcastic, creative, and unique part of you that makes you the genuine, kind, and loving person who inspires me each day to never give up. I love you for letting me be your hero and for never complaining when I ask you to rub my head when I have my migraines. I hope you never stop planting seeds in the garden of your mind. I love you to the moon and back, kiddo. Thank you for saving me.

Mom and Dad, thank you for not killing me for everything I've put our family through and for raising me to be the person I am today. Mom, you've always pushed me to be the best version of myself I can be, and I still cherish our time watching *Oprah* before your night shifts in the ER. You were the loudest mom during hockey games and worked your ass off to give our family the best lives possible. Dad, I've watched life slowly rob you of your vision and, soon, your hearing. What it hasn't diminished is your determination to live life to the fullest and be the best person you can be for your friends and family. Thank you for being the role model every young man deserves.

The Yellow One, Taylor. You are strong and brilliant, exude passion, and love unconditionally. Kevin, I'm glad you've followed your calling in the kitchen. I couldn't ask for more supportive siblings.

Grandpa and Nedra, I will forever cherish the trips to Roche Brothers for bagels and doughnuts, the scalp massages, and sneaking me twenty-dollar bills. Thank you for always encouraging me to follow my own path. Grandpa, you were my inspiration to become a Marine and I will always be your little buddy.

Rob and Ann, thank you for supporting me and encouraging my work—a son-in-law who scribbles on the couch in front a crackling fireplace with music blaring, who then refers to it as "work." Heather and Travis, thank you for being such a positive influence in Maddie's life and for making it possible for me to attend journalism school across the country.

Becoming a Marine infantryman has been the most humbling and proudest moment of my life. Throughout my career, I interacted with thousands of men and women who shared our title, and each of them—inspirational leaders and toxic shit bags—taught me something. None inspire me more than the men of Able 3-4. Whether it was Huber stapling his nut sack, Moon burning part of our outhouse in our fire pit because he was cold, or me almost blowing Roche and myself up by popping a smoke grenade on top of a pressure plate—each of you taught me to cherish the little moments. Like when Brickman did his "party boy" lap dance for the Afghan police. I was lucky to lead each of you crazy fucks. I love you guys.

Frank and Dr. Webster, thank you for helping me overcome my demons. Thank you for encouraging my writing, not just as therapy. You continue to help me improve myself each and every day. Fin, thank you for helping me find my door. I am a better father, husband, and person because of you.

I find and lose note cards with reminders and ideas on them all the time. Mel is always piling them in small stacks. Papers with scribbled paragraphs or crossed-through sentences. "Do you need these?" she frequently asks. Yes. Mel has always been the one to help me gather my thoughts. I joke that she is my running memory. I hated her dry-erase boards and Post-its in the beginning. My desk is now littered with stacks of them. My nightstand has dozens inside. My truck's console has others. I'm a hoarder of thoughts. Mel has never seemed to mind and was the first person to support my writing. If it helps, she said, do it. She's the one who suggested I e-mail the letter I wrote to Fin to someone because I was nervous about my commas and basic grammar. "What do you have to lose?" she asked. That's when I e-mailed David W. Dunlap.

David and I had messaged on Facebook following Fin's piece about the day I was wounded, but nothing serious or frequent. I wrote David in December 2011, nearly two months after Frank first handed me a notebook during one of our sessions—*Will you review something I wrote for Fin? He writes for a living and I don't want to look like an idiot.* I expected David to insert a few commas, trim down run-on sentences—nothing substantial—after all, he was an editor at the *New York Times*. I was just a grunt. He was on deadline and Fin's story had run its course. David, thank you for believing in me and for being the mentor and friend that every budding writer and journalist deserves.

Working with David to write my story about Fin set me on a path that I could never have foreseen. Writing gave me the strength to look beyond my Marine Corps career. With Fin and David mentoring my writing, I soon pitched my first mental-health reflection to Jim Dao, the *At War* blog editor for the *NYT*. Our relationship grew with each piece I submitted to Jim; each time he offered me more feedback and encouragement. I was one of many veterans Jim mentored with *At War*. Jim's mentorship created a community of writers who now have careers in writing and journalism. Thank you, Jim, from our *At War* family. It is impossible to quantify the impact you had on each of us.

Whereas I wrote at my own pace with *At War*, things at the *Daily News* were different. My editors, Cyndi Brown and Timmi Toler, demanded the best from our team. Ten minutes ago. The two of you pushed me to challenge myself and pursue stories that mattered to our readers and sources. Chris Thomas, thank you for being our office Halfrican. Mike Todd, I look forward to more of our random late-night calls. Katie Hansen, I miss your infectious happiness. Anita Perrin, thank you for being our newsroom mom. Milkshakes from Cookout are on me.

It wasn't until I took vacation from the *Daily News* for the Dart Awards that I regretted my lack of enthusiasm toward any class that didn't involve journalism. D = diploma. For this reason I would like to thank the admissions committee at Columbia's Journalism School for overlooking my 2.3 GPA.

Meeting Bruce Shapiro at the awards reinforced that stories from war have a greater purpose—that they're more than just cathartic paragraphs upon a page, and that stories exploring trauma offer not only a window into a painful world but hope to others experiencing similar trauma. Bruce, you inspire a community of journalists to explore trauma across the globe, and I am very thankful to call you my friend. I look forward to many more hours and deep conversations among your many books.

My time at J-school began with Nick Lemann impersonating Hillary Clinton during our interviewing drills—he said he wanted to simulate the most difficult and scripted conversations possible. As the school year progressed, Mr. Luke became more and more popular. At graduation I was handed his diploma by Laura Muha, the Stabile class mom. Throughout graduate school I was surrounded by talented and passionate journalists—both professors and classmates. Thank you for creating an environment that encouraged me to become a better writer and journalist.

My time at the J-school was transformative. I found my love for features in Karen Stabiner's class and worked to refine it in John Bennet's magazine writing class. The first person I trusted with my plans after graduation was Jim Mintz, one of my investigative journalism professors. Week after week he helped me refine my idea—a nonprofit investigative journalism newsroom focused on the Departments of Defense and Veterans Affairs.

The War Horse launched in February 2016 and was funded by more than five hundred donors. We've since been supported by corporations, foundations, and people from around the globe. Journalism icons Robert Rosenthal and Daniel Ellsberg volunteered to join our advisory board. To the thousands of people who have helped me share the voices of veterans and civilians who feel compelled to discuss war and trauma, thank you.

Throughout all of this Mel and Maddie stood by my side. Fin reminded me I was on deadline. And I've made some incredible friends. I know I forgot a lot of you. I'll just blame my TBI.

SOURCES, RESOURCES, AND FURTHER READING

Events depicted in this book are reconstructed as accurately as memory—in all its fluidity—allows. We have bolstered our recollections by relying upon photographs, video and audio recordings, and online exchanges. Where needed, we have consulted others who were present to verify facts and details to re-create and portray scenes and events as truthfully as possible.

Because we are two narrators sometimes recounting the same events, there are occasional small discrepancies and big perspective shifts. Rather than bring these into line, we let these differences stand. We believe they add texture and tension to our story while speaking to the subjective nature of individual experience. They also acknowledge the fallibility of memory—that slippery foe we constantly battle but never overcome.

Conversations and dialogue are re-created and quoted directly from notes, video or audio recordings, transcripts of online conversations held over Skype or Facebook messenger, e-mails, and handwritten letters, our published articles, and journal entries. In rare instances quotes are from memory, but these are set in quotation marks only when the degree of certainty permits them to be precise. In situations where exact quotes cannot be remembered, wording is paraphrased without using quotation marks.

Names of individuals are the actual names of real individuals who have kindly given permission for their names to be used in the book.

We accept full responsibility for any errors contained within these pages. One advantage of having a coauthor, however, is that if an error should occur, then it's obviously the other guy's fault.

SOURCES OF EPIGRAPHS, STATISTICS, AND OTHER QUOTATIONS

Epigraph

vii **"It makes no difference"**: Cormac McCarthy, *Blood Meridian* (New York: Modern Library, 2020), 262.

Prologue: An Odd Alliance

1 **"We can imagine":** C. S. Lewis, *The Four Loves* (New York: Mariner Books, 1971), 65.

3 **"Every true war story":** Roy Scranton, "The Trauma Hero," *Los Angeles Review of Books*, January 25, 2015, https://lareviewofbooks.org/article/trauma-hero-wilfred -owen-redeployment-american-sniper.

4 **"Not only will America":** Frankie Boyle, www.youtube.com/watch?v=uZwuTI -V8SI.

5 **"We went to expose":** Elena Ferrante, *My Brilliant Friend* (New York: Europa Editions, 2012), 29.

Chapter 1: Misfits Go to War

17 **"Be polite, be professional":** General James "Mad Dog" Mattis, quoted in Thomas E. Ricks, *Fiasco: The American Military Adventure in Iraq* (New York: Penguin Press, 2006), 313. This was one of the rules Mattis gave his Marines to live by in Iraq.

Chapter 2: Outpost Kunjak

33 **"I wanted to live deep":** Henry David Thoreau, *Walden* (Create Space, 2017), 70.

35 **coalition troops killed since 2001:** "U.S. to Send 300 Marines to Afghanistan's Helmand Province," Reuters, January 8, 2017, www.reuters.com/article /us-afghanistan-marines-idUSKBN14S0G5.

35 **Obama launched his first major military push:** Operation Khanjak, "A Surge in Helmand," *Economist*, July 7, 2009, www.economist.com/node/13980912.

47 **its own distinct language:** Ben Brody, "U.S. Military Lingo: The (Almost) Definitive Guide," NPR.com, December 4, 2013, www.npr.org/sections/parallels /2013/12/04/248816232/u-s-military-lingo-the-almost-definitive-guide.

Chapter 3: Ambushed

50 **"I spit in a bamboo":** Johnny Cash, "Drive On," *American Recordings*, Sony, 1994.

54 **RPGs—originally designed:** Sidney B. Brevard and Howard Champion, *Weapons Effects*, U.S. Army Medical Department Center and School, citing U.S. Department of Defense personnel and military casualty statistics.

57 **the blast from such a warhead:** Mechanics of a blast injury: "Blast Injuries and the Brain," BrainLine Military, no date, www.brainlinemilitary.org/content /2010/12/blast-injuries-and-the-brain.html.

Chapter 4: Walking Wounded

62 **"The human brain has":** Michio Kaku, quoted in "Behold the Most Complicated Object in the Known Universe," *Leonard Lopate Show*, February 25, 2014, www .wnyc.org/story/michio-kaku-explores-human-brain. The quote appears at the 9:50 mark.

65 **For all the high-tech weaponry:** "The Invisible War on the Brain," Caroline Alexander, *National Geographic*, February 2015, www.nationalgeographic.com /healing-soldiers/blast-force.html.

65 **More than 357,048:** Defense and Veterans Brain Injury Center, "DoD Worldwide Numbers for TBI," http://dvbic.dcoe.mil/dod-worldwide-numbers-tbi. This is also the source of the annual statistics for rates of TBI in U.S. military.

65 **those with a TBI:** For TBI side effects and relation to PTSD, see Terri Tanielian et al., *Invisible Wounds of War: Psychological and Cognitive Injuries, Their Consequences, and Services to Assist Recovery* (Santa Monica, CA: Rand Corporation, 2008).

Chapter 5: The In-between

70 **"You get paid to travel":** Rory Peck, quoted in Paul L. Moorcraft and Philip M. Taylor, *Shooting the Messenger: The Politics of War Reporting* (London: Biteback, 2011), 250.

71 **"Living in such close quarters":** Finbarr O'Reilly, "Bonding with Subjects in Harm's Way," *Lens, New York Times*, November 4, 2010, http://lens.blogs.nytimes.com/2010/11/04/bonding-with-subjects-in-harms-way.

71 **The mission was a bust:** "Troop Morale Up in Iraq; Down in Afghanistan," Associated Press, March 6, 2008, www.nbcnews.com/id/23503220/ns/health-mental_health/#.WE5MJmQrInV.

72 **I leave the base the day after TJ:** Finbarr O'Reilly, "Embedded in Afghanistan," *Photographers' Blog*, Reuters, December 21, 2010, http://blogs.reuters.com/photographers-blog/2010/12/21/embedded-in-afghanistan/2.

73 **Every year in France:** "Liberte Versus Fraternite: A Dispatch from the French Dog-Poo Wars," *Independent*, December 5, 1997.

74 **"If love belongs to the poet":** Hanya Yanagihara, "Loneliness Belongs to the Photographer," *New Yorker*, July 10, 2016.

83 **cover behind a mud wall:** Finbarr O'Reilly, "Shooting in Line of Fire," *New Zealand Herald*, Saturday November 3, 2007, http://www.nzherald.co.nz/world/news/article.cfm?c_id=2&objectid=10473790.

86 **where postelection violence:** Center for Strategic & International Studies, "Background on the Post-Election Crisis in Kenya," August 6, 2009, www.csis.org/blogs/smart-global-health/background-post-election-crisis-kenya.

89 **"The list demonstrates":** Anthony Feinstein, *Journalists Under Fire: The Psychological Hazards of Covering War* (Baltimore: Johns Hopkins University Press, 2006), 73.

Chapter 6: Human Triggers

94 **"But there are *other* things which a man":** Fyodor Dostoyevsky, *Notes from Underground* (CreateSpace, 2012), 41.

95 **"You fuck up, they scream":** Ben Fountain, *Billy Lynn's Long Halftime Walk* (New York: Ecco, 2012), 3.

Chapter 7: Limbs Lost and Skull Tattoos

106 **"Love is a battlefield":** Pat Benatar, "Love Is a Battlefield," *Live from Earth*, Chrysalis Records, 1983.

106 **Canadian journalist, Dave Bowering:** Dave Bowering footage.

113 **Israeli military psychologist Ben Shalit:** Ben Shalit, *The Psychology of Conflict and Combat* (Santa Barbara, CA: Greenwood, 1998), 11.

113 **"Many combat veterans are denied":** Jonathan Shay, *Achilles in Vietnam: Combat Trauma and the Undoing of Character* (New York: Simon & Schuster, 1995) 42–43.

Chapter 9: Coming Home

130 **"For most problems, a Marine":** *Jarhead*, directed by Sam Mendes (2005).

130 **"10.a. During this deployment":** Department of Defense Post Deployment Health Assessment (Form 2796).

133 **The base and surrounding:** U.S. Marine Corps, "Marine Corps Base Camp Lejeune," no date, www.lejeune.marines.mil/About.aspx.

Chapter 10: Nosedive

143 **"I'm sure that I never":** Henry David Thoreau, *Walden*, 73.

150 **During the First World War:** Dan Snow, "DR Congo: Cursed by Its Natural Wealth," *BBC Magazine*, October 9, 2013, www.bbc.com/news/magazine-24396390.

150 **The nuclear bombs dropped:** Joe Lauria, "The Secret Race to Get Congo's Uranium Ore to Destroy Hiroshima," *Global Research*, August 8, 2016, www.globalresearch.ca/the-secret-race-to-get-congos-uranium-ore-to-destroy-hiroshima/5540073.

150 **"record the sufferings":** Alex Kershaw, *Blood and Champagne: The Life of Robert Capa*, (New York: Macmillan, 2002), 79.

Chapter 11: Forward into the Past

157 **"In battle, life would not":** Simon Armitage, *The Not Dead* (Keighley, UK: Pomona 2008).

163 **called prolonged exposure therapy:** For more information on prolonged exposure therapy, visit http://deploymentpsych.org/treatments/prolonged-exposure-therapy-ptsd-pe.

168 **"It has come to my attention":** Eric Jaffe, "Gen. Patton's 1943 Memo Accusing Mental Casualties of Cowardice," *Slate*, January 15, 2014, www.slate.com/blogs/the_vault/2014/01/15/george_s_patton_memo_accusing_mental_casualties_of_cowardice.html.

168 **The order, Jaffe writes:** Eric Jaffe, *A Curious Madness: An American Combat Psychiatrist, a Japanese War Crimes Suspect, and an Unsolved Mystery from World War II* (New York: Scribner, 2014), 143–44.

Chapter 12: The Voice

170 **"There's not a drug on earth":** Sarah Kane, *4.48 Psychosis* (London: Bloomsbury Methuen Drama, 2000), 220.

173 **Then there's the watchtower:** Bessel van der Koch, M.D., *The Body Keeps The Score: Brain, Mind, and Body in the Healing of Trauma* (New York: Viking, 2014), 62–64.

176 **"I wasn't sleeping at all"**: Bruce Arthur, "Flashback: Acron Eger's Shadow," *National Post*, December 24, 2010, http://news.nationalpost.com/sports/flashback -acron-egers-shadow.

178 **"Finbarr O'Reilly told my story"**: Thomas James Brennan, "From a Marine's Side of the Camera," *Lens, New York Times*, December 29, 2011, http://lens.blogs .nytimes.com/2011/12/29/from-the-marines-side-of-the-camera.

Chapter 13: Media Boot Camp

180 **"We tell ourselves stories"**: Joan Didion, "The White Album," *The White Album* (New York: Farrar, Straus and Giroux, 2001), 11.

181 **"When I have been traumatized"**: Robert D. Stolorow, *Trauma and Human Existence* (London: Routledge, 2007), 49.

184 **"PTSD is something"**: Thomas James Brennan, "Living with P.T.S.D. and Allowing Myself to Get Help," *At War, New York Times*, June 22, 2012, http://atwar .blogs.nytimes.com/2012/06/22/living-with-p-t-s-d-and-allowing-myself -to-get-help.

191 **"I found this outrageous"**: David Wood, *What Have We Done: The Moral Injury of Our Longest Wars* (New York: Little, Brown, 2016), 257.

194 **"Learning to draw"**: Betty Edwards, *Drawing on the Right Side of the Brain*, 4th ed. (New York: Penguin, 2012), xiv.

Chapter 14: Coming Undone

196 **"We look the same"**: Clark Elliott, Ph.D., *The Ghost in My Brain: How a Concussion Stole My Life and How the New Science of Brain Plasticity Helped Me Get It Back* (New York: Penguin Books, 2015), 71.

202 **"In the last eight years"**: Thomas James Brennan, "Ending a Life, and a Part of Yourself, for the First Time," *At War, New York Times*, December 14, 2012, http://atwar.blogs.nytimes.com/2012/12/14/ending-a-life-and-a-part-of -yourself-for-the-first-time.

Chapter 15: Home, Again

217 **"Whether recovery occurs"**: Jonathan Shay, *Odysseus in America: Combat Trauma and the Trials of Homecoming* (New York: Scribner, 2003), 4.

225 **"His words are more"**: Kevin Cullen, "TJ and Finbarr: A Friendship Made in the Desert," *Boston Globe*, April 12, 2013, www.bostonglobe.com/metro/2013/04/11 /and-finbarr-friendship-made-desert/1SQEdN3cnis4tI81iOCsNO/story.html.

Chapter 16: Echoes of Iraq

232 **"War exposes the capacity"**: Chris Hedges, *War Is a Force That Gives Us Meaning* (New York: PublicAffairs, 2002), 3.

233 **Six months after the bombings**: David Abel, "Boat Owner Seeks to Clarify Record on Tsarnaev Capture," *Boston Globe*, October 16, 2013, www.boston globe.com/metro/2013/10/15/six-months-later-man-who-found-dzhokhar -tsarnaev-his-boat-tries-move/fMSWzruQfE2EUNYXjXKOZP/story.html.

239 **During six weeks of fighting:** James A. Warren, "The Vicious Battle to Capture Fallujah in 2004 was a Close Fought Nightmare," *The Daily Beast*, July 16, 2016, www.thedailybeast.com/articles/2016/07/16/the-vicious-battle-to-capture-fallujah-in-2004-was-a-close-fought-nightmare.

239 **"As soon as I shot him":** Bradley Faircloth quoted on *BBC Newsnight*, BBC, November 24, 2004.

242 **In his book *On Killing*:** Lt. Col. David Grossman, *On Killing: The Psychological Cost of Learning to Kill in War and Society* (New York: Back Bay Books, 2009), 18–29.

243 **After his friend Patroklos:** Homer, *The Iliad* (New York: Penguin Classics, 1998); Homer, *The Odyssey* (New York: Penguin Classics, 1999), 363–90.

244 **Jonathan Shay devotes an entire chapter:** Jonathan Shay, *Achilles in Vietnam: Combat Trauma and the Undoing of Character* (New York: Simon & Schuster, 1995), 39–68.

245 **"an act of transgression":** Shira Maguen and Brett Litz, "Moral Injury in the Context of War," PTSD: National Center for PTSD, U.S. Department of Veterans Affairs, www.ptsd.va.gov/professional/co-occurring/moral_injury_at_war.asp.

246 **"To place someone in that":** David Wood, *What Have We Done: The Moral Injury of Our Longest Wars* (New York: Little, Brown, 2016), 190.

246 **"If human beings were shown":** Aldous Huxley, *Eyeless in Gaza* (New York: Vintage, 2004), 423.

Chapter 17: Marching Back Through Time

248 **"Think you're escaping":** James Joyce, *Ulysses* (Ware, Hertfordshire, UK: Wordsworth Editions, 2010), 341.

249 **"Inchon had the look":** David Halberstam, *The Coldest Winter: America and the Korean War* (New York: Hyperion Books, 2008), 295.

Chapter 18: Moving Forward, Sliding Back

257 **"We do not see things":** "Lillian was reminded of the talmudic words: 'We do not see things as they are, we see them as we are.'" Anaïs Nin, *Seduction of the Minotaur* (New York: Blue Sky Press, 2010), Kindle location 1987.

Chapter 19: No Easy Fix

263 **"I mean, it's affected":** Jim Otto in *League of Denial: The NFL's Concussion Crisis*, PBS, October 8, 2013, www.pbs.org/wgbh/frontline/film/league-of-denial.

269 **I vent my frustrations:** Thomas James Brennan, "Coping with Retirement," *At War*, New York Times, February 20, 2014, http://atwar.blogs.nytimes.com/2014/02/20/coping-with-retirement.

Chapter 20: Another War

272 **"When you're willing to die":** Emma Sky, author of *The Unraveling*, in conversation.

286 **"we're not here to capture":** Don DeLillo, *White Noise* (New York: Penguin Books, 1984), 12.

288 **not before Simone Camilli:** Associated Press, "AP Video Journalist Simone Camilli Killed in Gaza," August 13, 2014.

Chapter 21: Yellow Footprints

290 **"You are now aboard":** Lance Corporal Ed G., "Tradition of the Yellow Footprints," Recruit Parents, April 10, 2009, http://recruitparents.com/bootcamp/yellow.asp.

292 **In front of the Warrior Hope:** Thomas James Brennan, "Monument Unveiled as a Tribute to Families of the Wounded and Fallen," *Jacksonville Daily News*, March 8, 2013.

Chapter 22: No Wars and No Jobs, but Another Tasty Chicken

295 **"For the more haunted":** Mary Karr, *The Art of Memoir* (New York: HarperCollins, 2015), 12.

296 **"War journalists, like all":** Chris Hedges, quoted on the back jacket of Anthony Feinstein, *Journalists Under Fire, The Psychological Hazards of Covering War* (Baltimore: Johns Hopkins University Press, 2006).

298 **"an optimum inebriation":** A. A. Gill, *Pour Me: A Life* (London: Weidenfeld & Nicolson, 2015), 180.

300 **"start identifying a little":** Mary Karr, *The Art of Memoir* (New York: HarperColins, 2015), 31.

300 **"As long as you keep riding":** Sam Tanenhaus, "Noam Chomsky and the Bicycle Theory," *New York Times*, October 31, 2016, www.nytimes.com/2016/11/06/education/edlife/on-being-noam-chomsky.html.

301 **the piece is published:** Dave Phillips and Thomas James Brennan, "Unsettled at Home, Veterans Volunteer to Fight ISIS," *New York Times*, March 11, 2015, www.nytimes.com/2015/03/12/us/disenchanted-by-civilian-life-veterans-volunteer-to-fight-isis.html.

302 **"We know the hardships":** Thomas James Brennan, "The Curious Draw of the Battlefield," *At War, New York Times*, March 11, 2015, http://atwar.blogs.nytimes.com/2015/03/11/the-curious-draw-of-the-battlefield.

RESOURCES AND FURTHER READING

Alexander, Caroline. "The Invisible War on the Brain." *National Geographic*, February 2015.

Armitage, Simon. *The Not Dead*. Pomona Press, 2008.

Blassim, Hassan. *The Corpse Exhibition*. Penguin Books, 2014.

Capa, Robert. *Slightly Out of Focus*. Modern Library Paperback Edition, 2001.

Castner, Brian. *The Long Walk: A Story of War and the Life That Follows.* Anchor Books, 2013.

Clark, Elliot, PhD. *The Ghost in My Brain: How a Concussion Stole My Life and How the New Science of Brain Plasticity Helped Me Get It Back.* Penguin Books, 2015.

Epstein, Mark, MD. *The Trauma of Everyday Life.* Penguin Books, 2013.

Feinstein, Anthony. *Journalists Under Fire: The Psychological Hazards of Covering War.* Johns Hopkins University Press, 2006.

Finkel, David. *Thank You for Your Service.* Anchor Canada, 2014.

Fountain, Ben. *Billy Lynn's Long Halftime Walk.* Ecco, 2012.

Gellhorn, Martha. *The Face of War.* Atlantic Monthly, 1936.

Gonzalez, Laurence. *Surviving Survival: The Art and Science of Resilience.* Norton, 2012.

Green, Matthew. *Aftershock: The Untold Story of Surviving Peace.* Portobello Books, 2015.

Grossman, Lt. Col. David. *On Killing: The Psychological Cost of Learning to Kill in War and Society.* Back Bay Books, 2009.

Grossman, Lt. Col. David, with Loren W. Christensen. *On Combat: The Psychology and Physiology of Deadly Conflict in War and in Peace.* Warrior Science Publications, 2004.

Steven Gutkin. "My Life as an AP Bureau Chief in Israel,"*Goa Streets*, September 25, 2014, http://goastreets.com/life-ap-bureau-chief-israel.

Halberstam, David. *The Coldest Winter: America and the Korean War.* Hyperion Books, 2007.

Henderson, Artis. *Unremarried Widow.* Simon & Schuster, 2013.

Herman, Judith. *Trauma and Recovery: The Aftermath of Violence—from Domestic Abuse to Political Terror.* Basic Books, 1992.

Herr, Michael. *Dispatches.* Avon Books, 1978.

Hoffman, Cara. *Be Safe I Love You.* Simon & Schuster, 2014.

Hoge, Charles W. *Once a Warrior Always a Warrior: Navigating the Transition from Combat to Home Including Combat Stress, PTSD, and mTBI.* Lyons, 2010.

Homer. *The Iliad.* Penguin Classics, 1998.

Homer. *The Odyssey.* Penguin Classics, 1999.

Hood, Jean. *War Correspondent: Reporting Under Fire Since 1850.* Lyons, 2011.

Huffman, Alan. *Here I Am: The Story of Tim Hetherington, War Photographer.* Grove, 2013.

Kamber, Michael. *Photojournalists on War: The Untold Story from Iraq.* University of Texas Press, 2013.

Karr, Mary. *The Art of Memoir.* HarperCollins, 2015.

Klay, Phil. *Redeployment.* Penguin Books, 2014.

Kyle, Chris. *American Sniper.* Harper, 2012.

LeDoux, Joseph. *The Emotional Brain: The Mysterious Underpinnings of Emotional Life.* Simon & Schuster Paperbacks, 1996.

McCarthy, Cormac. *Blood Meridian.* Random House, 1985.

McCullin, Don. *Unreasonable Behavior.* Vintage, 1992.

Marinovich, Greg. *The Bang Bang Club: Snapshots from a Hidden War.* Arrow, 2001.

Marlantes, Karl. *Matterhorn.* Atlantic Monthly, 2010.

Marlantes, Karl. *What It Is Like to Go to War.* Atlantic Monthly, 2011.

Moorcraft, Paul L., and Philip M. Taylor. *Shooting the Messenger: The Politics of War Reporting.* Biteback, 2011.

Morris, David J. *The Evil Hours: A Biography of Post-traumatic Stress Disorder.* Houghton Mifflin Harcourt, 2015.

Morris, John G. *Get the Picture: A Personal History of Photojournalism.* Random House, 1998.

Ní Chonghaile, Clár. *Fractured.* Legend, 2016.

Percy, Jennifer. *Demon Camp: A Soldier's Exorcism.* Scribner, 2014.

Powers, Kevin. *The Yellow Birds.* Back Bay Books, 2012.

Roach, Mary. *Grunt: The Curious Science of Humans at War.* Oneworld, 2016.

Scranton, Roy. "The Trauma Hero: From Wilfred Owen to 'Redeployment' and 'American Sniper.'" *Los Angeles Review of Books*, January 25, 2015.

Shapiro, Francine, PhD, and Margot Silk Forrest. *EMDR: The Breakthrough "Eye Movement" Therapy for Overcoming Anxiety, Stress, and Trauma.* Basic Books, 1997 and 2004.

Shay, Jonathan, MD, PhD. *Achilles in Vietnam: Combat Trauma and the Undoing of Character.* Simon & Schuster, 1995.

Shay, Jonathan, MD, PhD. *Odysseus in America: Combat Trauma and the Trials of Homecoming.* Scribner, 2003.

Shephard, Ben. *A War of Nerves: Soldiers and Psychiatrists 1914–1994.* Pimlico, 2002.

Sherman, Nancy. *Afterwar: Healing the Moral Wounds of Our Soldiers.* Oxford University Press, 2015.

Smith, Rob. *Closets, Combat + Coming Out.* Blue Beacon, 2014.

Stolorow, Robert D. *Trauma and Human Existence.* Routledge, 2007.

Tick, Edward, PhD. *War and the Soul: Healing Our Nation's Veterans from Post-traumatic Stress Disorder.* Theosophical, 2005.

Trudeau, G. B. *The War Within: One More Step at a Time.* Doonesbury, 2006.

Van der Kolk, Bessel, MD. *The Body Keeps the Score: Brain, Mind, and Body in the Healing of Trauma.* Viking, 2014.

Vonnegut, Kurt. *Slaughterhouse Five.* Dial, 1969.

Williams, Kayla. *Love My Rifle More Than You: Young and Female in the U.S. Army.* W. W. Norton, 2006.

Wood, David. *What Have We Done: The Moral Injury of Our Longest Wars.* Little, Brown, 2016.

Zimmer, Carl. "Secrets of the Brain." *National Geographic*, February 2014.

INDEX